TOMATOES WERE CHEAPER

TOMATOES WERE CHEAPER

Tales from the Thirties

CHARLES A. JELLISON

 Syracuse University Press 1977

Copyright © 1977 by Syracuse University Press
Syracuse, New York

All Rights Reserved

First Edition

Charles A. Jellison is Professor of History at the University of New Hampshire, Durham, New Hampshire. He received his B.A. and M.A. degrees from Stanford University and his Ph.D. from the University of Virginia. Formerly a trade consultant in Hong Kong and mainland China, the author has been a visiting professor at the U.S. Naval War College and a Fulbright professor at the University of Witwatersrand, Johannesburg, South Africa. Professor Jellison is author of *Fessenden of Maine* and *Ethan Allen: Frontier Rebel.*

Library of Congress Cataloging in Publication Data

Jellison, Charles Albert.
   Tomatoes were cheaper.

   Bibliography: p.
   1. United States—History—1933-1945—Miscellanea.
I. Title.
E806.J35   973.917'08   76-54853
ISBN 0-8156-0130-1

Manufactured in the United States of America

Contents

Preface

FOR THOSE of you too young to remember, or perhaps too old, the title of this book is taken from a song hit of the early years of the Great Depression—"Now's the Time to Fall in Love." I can almost hear it now, as Eddie Cantor used to sing it in his peaked little voice on the Sunday night Chase and Sanborn hour. It was one of a number of what soon became known in the trade as "silver linings," the purpose of which (besides making money) was to fight off hard times by convincing the American people that things weren't really so bad as they seemed on the surface. "Life is Just a Bowl of Cherries," "On the Sunny Side of the Street," "Give Yourself a Pat on the Back," "Happy Days Are Here Again"—a seemingly endless parade of frothy little ditties, bubbling with good cheer and confidence, none of which, of course, had the slightest effect on the Depression. They did, however, make for great whistling, in case anyone happened to feel like it.

This book makes no claim to being a history of the 1930s—or an autopsy. Its purpose is simply to recapture something of the flavor of American life as it was during those years. To do this, I have wandered nostalgically through the shoals and narrows of that depression-ravaged decade, pausing at times to examine certain events that were, for one reason or another, of special concern to people back then in those not-so-distant days, when our hearts were young but often far from gay.

Here we see, in the pages that follow, a mixed parade of heroes and villains, of sages and fools, the great and the ungreat (mostly the latter), all caught up in the dreadful currents of one of our nation's most troubled decades: a corrupt judge who took the money and ran, but apparently not fast enough; a good-natured Southern farm boy who rose from the appalling poverty of the cotton fields to mind-boggling fame and fortune on the strength of his blazing fast ball and a fair-to-middling curve (I once heard him say, not long before his death: "My wife Pat, she keeps tryin' to get ole Diz to go on a diet. 'Dizzy,' she says, 'you're fatter than a hog. You eat all the time.' 'Well, honey,' I says, 'the reason for that is I didn't eat nuthin' at all till I was eighteen, and I ain't got caught up yet' "); a gang of Midwest bandits who set out to make Dillinger "look like a piker," and succeeded, for a while; and, a plucky little twelve-year-old boy who, like the nation itself, lost his way—but not his faith or courage.

From such characters and events as these we catch a fuller glimpse and sometimes different perspective of those disturbed times, and are reminded that there was more to the '30s than bank failures and bread lines. Life went on. People were born and buried; they stole and cheated, made love, went to the movies, and played cribbage by the kitchen stove. It was not the worst of times, at least not for most of us. And yet, always a presence, never far from center stage, was the spectre of the Great Depression, coloring our every act and attitude, and constantly assaulting what Emerson once called "the quality of our days." Few Americans felt its full fury (after all, 75 percent of us or more never lost our job, or our money in a bank failure, or even saw a bread line), but in at least one important respect we were all deeply affected by it: psychologists tell us that individually and as a people we suffered a severe security trauma, but a friend of mine and fellow survivor put it better, I think, when he said that the Depression "made our acid drip." And small wonder—that huge, devouring beast with the eye that never slept, forever dogging our steps and casting its ominous shadow over everything we were and hoped to be. Those were indeed anxious times back then, filled to the brim with worry and frustration. It is understandable perhaps that, hag-ridden as we were by apprehension, we sometimes, like the characters of this book, behaved in strange and unseemly ways.

The following chapters are as true as I could make them—down to the fussiest fact and fragment of conversation. Nothing has been manufactured or fictionalized. The information contained in them was taken from a variety of source materials that will be referred to elsewhere in this book. Not the least of these were dozens, possibly hundreds, of taped interviews and informal conversations with people who, like myself, lived through the 1930s and remember their tone and tempo, if not always their finer detail. To all those individuals, famous or otherwise, who shared their recollections with me, and the many others who in one way or another helped in the preparation of this book, I am indeed grateful, but to none more so than the late Frankie Frisch, the greatest Gashouser of them all and raconteur without peer, and my old friend Bob Stone, recently retired from the University of New Hampshire Library, whose memory of the old days, like Tennyson's "Brook," goes on forever. I would also like to single out for special thanks my Durham neighbors Gardner Hinckley and Don Murray, and former Ambassador and Mrs. Artemus Weatherbee of Kennebunk, Maine, all of whom read the manuscript and offered helpful suggestions and overall encouragement.

And then, of course, there was my wife Phyllis, who, I am happy to say, did not type the manuscript or read proof. For these and certain other reasons accrued during our quarter-century of life together, it is to her that this book is lovingly dedicated. Would that it were *War and Peace.*

Durham, New Hampshire   Charles A. Jellison
Autumn 1976

TOMATOES WERE CHEAPER

Coming Apart

BY THE BEGINNING of the 1930s there were nearly 123 million Americans, none of whom could buy a drink without breaking the law. In Washington, President Hoover was finishing up his first year in office. Mickey Mouse was going on two. Contract bridge, recently imported from Europe, was all the rage. So were radios and electric refrigerators—but not dial telephones, which were looked upon with considerable disfavor by those few Americans, all of them city folk, who had actually used one. After a trial period of two weeks, the United States Senate voted overwhelmingly to have them removed at once. "An abomination!" growled the venerable Senator Carter Glass. "I object to being transformed into one of the employees of the telephone company without compensation." And yet, there were a few among his colleagues, mainly of the younger set, who made so bold as to predict that within fifteen or twenty years the dial phone would be as much a part of American life as the automobile.

In those days people read "Boob McNutt," *The Literary Digest*, and *Farewell to Arms*, went to the movies at the rate of over 50 million a week to see the likes of Tom Mix and Norma Shearer (who had suddenly learned to talk), and listened to Frank Crumit sing "Adbullah Bulbul Amir" on fancy new radio sets with horns, which took up half the living room. They also fretted a lot about the current slump in the economy and wondered, naturally enough, how long it would last.

The Depression had come down like the wolf upon the fold and then backed off for a time, as if to survey the damage of its initial lunge. Following the Wall Street crash of the autumn before, the stock market rallied somewhat during the early months of 1930, thereby giving rise to a wave of optimism among the nation's business and political leaders—or so at least they claimed. After a careful study of the terrain, President Hoover announced in March that "conditions are not so bad, after all." There was, he believed, good reason to suppose that the worst was over. A few weeks later the *Washington Post* reported: "Economists who have taken a calm view of the situation have believed for some time that the corner has been turned and that conditions are steadily improving."

So, the country had suffered a temporary setback on its way to what President Hoover, not so long before, had predicted would be "the final triumph over poverty." But recovery was now obviously on the way, and the best thing the American people could do to speed it along would be to take their money out of hiding and start spending. These were days of great bargains for the American consumer, and he could help both himself and his country by taking advantage of them.

Consider automobiles as a case in point: never before, the *Wall Street Journal* informed its readers, had automobiles been a better buy. For instance, only $965 for a new, straight-eight De Soto. Now, at first blush that might seem like a rather hefty price, but when figured by the pound, it was ridiculously low. In fact, the average cost of the nation's eight leading autos (including the De Soto) was only 27.1¢ a pound—more than 7¢ below what it had been in 1925. This meant that per pound a new car cost about the same as beefsteak or pork. "Indeed," declared the *Journal*, "one pound of rayon used in your wife's dress is almost six times the price of your automobile per pound." It was hard to understand why it was that in times of such attractive prices, auto sales were down 38 percent from the year before.

During the summer and early autumn of 1930 it was noted by some skeptics that business conditions, rosy predictions notwithstanding, seemed to be getting worse rather than better. The stock market had resumed its downward course, and by late October had dipped a full thirty points below where it had been a year before, during the weeks immediately following the crash. Furthermore, sales were down all over. Savings accounts were inching up, and so was unemployment. In November, A.F. of L. president William Green estimated the number of unemployed at more than four and a half million. "A gross exaggeration; closer to half that," replied the government, although it did concede that unemployment was definitely on the rise.

No matter. To those in a position to know about such things, it was clear that these minor fluctuations were merely "normal signs of readjustment." They were certainly nothing to worry about. Naturally, it had been hoped that recovery would be a bit more rapid, but one must be patient in matters of this sort. "The readjustments made necessary by the abnormal conditions of the past few years are proceeding toward fruition," commented a spokesman for one of the nation's largest investment houses, "and solid foundations for a resumption of business activity are being laid." Exactly! "The processes of adjustment are moving," agreed a prominent Wall Street banker. "They do not move according to a time schedule, and no one knows when they will be completed, . . . but all indications are that spring will see improvement."

Thus, it was finally proclaimed by those in the temple that 1930 would be counted a time of readjustment, painful to some, no doubt, but a necessary precondition for recovery, which was bound to appear during the coming year. Only it didn't. As in the days of Jeremiah—and so often since—the prophets had prophesied falsely. How falsely, neither they, not the priests who bore rule by their means, nor the people who loved to have it so, would have dared imagine.

1931 began with Secretary of the Treasury Andrew Mellon's firm assurance that: "During the coming year the country will make steady progress." It ended with President Hoover's admission that "The march of progress has been retarded." Sandwiched somewhere in between was former President Calvin Coolidge's shrewd observation that "When more and more people are thrown out of work, unemployment results."

It was a good year for young Ethel Merman, who stole the show in *George White's Scandals* with her brassy rendition of "Life is Just a Bowl of Cherries." It was also a good year for Philadelphia A's pitcher, Robert Moses "Lefty" Grove, who ended the season with a 31-4 mark. This set a new won-lost record for major league baseball, but there was little rejoicing because of it in the

A's clubhouse, where Grove was not a great favorite with his team-mates, nor they with him. "He was a surly bastard," one of them would recall years later. "It's not true though, like they say, that he never spoke to any of us. Fact is, he spoke to all of us. One a day."

For L. A. Gimbel, 35, World War veteran, Yale '19, promi-nent Manhattan stockbroker and former vice president of Gimbel's Department Store, it was not such a good year. In fact, it was over before it began. At dusk on New Year's Eve he took off his top-coat and hat, placed them neatly on a chair, and jumped from the sixteenth floor of the Yale Club onto a roof nine stories below. "Mr. Gimbel had been depressed of late," explained a family spokesman.

On January 2, F. A. Gosnell of the United States Census Bureau returned to Washington after an extensive visit to the ma-jor cities of the East and Midwest, during which he helped set up machinery for the soon-to-begin census of the unemployed. As a result of his observations he ordered that street-corner apple ven-dors be counted as "employed persons." Mr. Gosnell had seen enough to convince him that "many people selling unemployed apples are making a good living."

On the afternoon of the same day, a crowd of from 300 to 500 farmers assembled on the main street of the little town of England, Arkansas, twenty-two miles southeast of Little Rock. They were starving. Not so long before, they had been prosperous, living the good life off the best land in the state. But the drought of the previous summer had been brutal. For forty-two days the temperature had stood at a hundred or above, and all the while not enough rain for a man to wash his socks in. As the sun beat down upon the parched land, crops and livestock withered and died. So did the local bank, sweeping away the life's savings of these stricken people. For months now they had been surviving on turnip greens, roots, and nuts from the woods, but they had finally reached the limit of their endurance.

At about four o'clock they began converging upon the office of the local Red Cross. Many of the women were hysterical. Some were burdened down with infants wrapped in rags and too listless to cry. About half of the men were armed with rifles or shotguns. A few carried pitchforks. "We don't want no trouble," they shouted, "but we ain't gonna stand by and see our families starve." An argument arose among them. Some were in favor of storming the grocery stores and helping themselves. Others were for visiting the Red Cross office first. An attorney came out to talk with them. "We don't want somethin for nuthin," they told him. "Just give us work and we won't come back. We'll work for fifty cents a day." But, of course, there was no work. There was food, though, and the men meant to have some of it.

The Red Cross agent put a hurried call through to Little Rock and got authority to issue each family $2.75 worth of emergency supplies from the local stores. By 9:30 that evening everyone had been fed, except one man who was judged too well dressed to qualify. Once the distribution had begun, it had proceeded rapidly until near the end when the yellow requisition forms ran out and several people were forced to wait while more were brought in from Little Rock. "There must be orderly distribution upon proper requisition," the Red Cross worker explained. From his office the attorney watched and wondered; $2.75 worth of food wasn't much. He wouldn't be surprised if they were back before long. "The merchants hereabouts had better move their goods or mount machine guns on their stores."

Meanwhile in Boston, Cardinal O'Connell decried the widespread unrest among the people and urged all good Christians to stop wallowing in discontent. "The times are so agitated that one hardly knows what to do," complained His Eminence. "This is a terrible condition for any civilized country. What is the cause? What is in back of it? Lack of faith. That is the cause of this universal disease. Men have forgotten God and are absorbed by some petty trifle of today."

And a transient trifle at that. In New York City an unknown benefactor calling himself "Mr. Glad" appeared one day with a truck in Times Square and for more than six hours distributed gloves and nickels among the needy. More than that, he brought them a message of cheer and reassurance: The Depression was over, because "the jinx of 13 has gone," his printed flyer explained. "There was a panic in 1903 = 13, and 1912 = 13, and 1921 = 13, and 1930 = 13. By this system of reckoning there won't be another until 2029 = 13, and that is ninety-nine years away. Good luck to you in 1931, which adds up to 14." According to Mr. Glad, he had already handed out more than 50,000 copies of his message since beginning his charitable work some months before, and he had yet to see one of them thrown in the gutter.

Back in Arkansas, some children were bitten by a mad dog. Local officials said the town and county treasuries had been exhausted. There was no money to buy serum. "Are you going to let those children die?" asked a Red Cross worker. "Well, I just don't know what we can do about it. We don't have any money left."

From the northern parishes of nearby Louisiana came persistent but unconfirmed reports of cannibalism.

And so it went during the early days of January of 1931—a fitting introduction to a year when America, cruelly put upon by depression, disease, and natural disaster, would come perilously close to national ruin. In Washington, President Hoover worked sixteen to eighteen hours a day, every day, trying desperately to stem the tide. What had happened was not his fault. It was no more Hoover's Depression than it was Frank Lloyd Wright's or Clara Bow's. In fact, he had warned of its coming and urged that preventive measures be taken. The trouble was that people hadn't listened, at least not enough of them—or the right ones. And when the crash came and there was wrath and frustration to unload, it was heaped upon the man in the White House who, people thought, was running the show, but who, in reality, was every bit as bewildered as his countrymen, and just as helpless.

Several of the President's critics charged him with being "extremely disinclined to act," but this was unfair. He was not disinclined at all; he simply didn't know what to do. He recognized well enough that the essential prerequisite for recovery was the restoration of the nation's confidence in the fundamental soundness of its economy. But with banks closing at the rate of fifty a week, and unemployment soaring, and the price of Kansas wheat dipping to its lowest level in over a century, it was no easy chore to make the people believe—no matter how often they were told—that prosperity was just around the corner. What corner? Where?

The President's personality didn't help matters. Although warm and outgoing to those close to him, to others he seemed aloof and insensitive, a man who didn't really understand people as human beings, or, if he did, didn't care about them. "I have no Wilsonian qualities," he once remarked. "I can't seem to reach out to the people." His appearance was also against him. "What can you expect," Americans asked one another, "from a man who looks like a pig?" A couple of years later when a more handsome and radiant President assured the American people that they had nothing to fear but fear itself, they chose to believe him. When

Hoover said the same thing, people merely shook their heads in disbelief or disgust.

They blamed him for everything, including the drought that continued to broil scattered sections of the country, especially the Northwest, and the plague of grasshoppers that descended upon the Middle States in July of that year. To make sure that no stone was left unthrown, the Democratic National Committee opened a special "public information" office in the Press Building in Washington. Designed to serve as a sort of national clearing house for vilifying the President, and provided with apparently unlimited funds, the new office (commonly called Michelson Mills after its chief hatchet man, Charles Michelson) did its job well. While taking care not to deal too harshly with the Republican Party or even the Republican delegation in Congress (some of whom might be persuaded to desert the unpopular President and swing their support to the Democrats in 1932), the Michelson group missed few opportunities to heap abuse upon Hoover himself in an unprecedented attempt to denigrate him in the eyes of the American people. Remarked the venerable Socialist John Spargo, certainly no great admirer of the President or his policies: "This is the most shamefully scurrilous machine for discrediting a public man that this or any other nation has known in my time."

There was plenty of help from others who were ready, even anxious, to believe the worst about President Hoover and his Administration, and pass it on for what it was worth. And sometimes it was worth a great deal—say $12,000, which is what the *New York World* paid an employee of the Interior Department for an exposé of shady government land deals with private companies. Billed as "another Teapot Dome Scandal," the story was run in a series of exclusive articles in the *World* after much advance publicity. Apparently, however, it didn't occur to the paper's editor, Walter Lippmann, to have the story verified. When it turned out to be a barefaced lie, the *World* was good enough to print a retraction (after being threatened with a libel suit by the Secretary of the Interior), but who reads retractions? Shortly thereafter the *World* went out of business, "a victim," it explained to its readers, "of the financial vicissitudes of our day." Just like Herbert Hoover.

The grasshoppers appeared first in Utah and Montana, great hordes of them coming out of the ground as if on some prearranged signal and swarming together for their ruinous assault upon the land. Moving eastward along a broad front that stretched from

Colorado to the Canadian border, they traveled at better than fifty miles a day. By mid-July they had reached the Dakotas, where their ranks were swollen by billions of new recruits. Generally they would first be seen as a small black cloud on the distant horizon. Then, as the cloud grew closer and bigger, the awful ominous drone began to be heard. Soon the day would begin to darken and before long the sun would be blotted out and the entire world would become a raging, relentless torrent of frenzied black flecks, whose shrill chorus was almost more than the human ear could abide. In their wake not a leaf, not a stalk, nor a blade of grass was left standing. Total, voracious destruction. Endless reaches of the nation's finest farm land denuded, as if by some giant reaper.

The hoppers were neat, thorough, and unstoppable. In a desperate attempt to save at least part of his crop, a Dakota farmer hoisted a huge cloth sheeting to keep out the intruders. It was devoured in a matter of seconds. Elsewhere electrified wire-mesh fences were erected, but the hoppers went under and over and through. In Pierre, South Dakota, a farmer who had heard that turkeys would feed on the insects, turned out his flock. The birds came back with their feathers chewed off.

Moving in impressive battle array across the Missouri River, the hoppers continued their orgy of devastation into Iowa and Minnesota, and then suddenly disappeared once again into the earth. By then, nearly sixty thousand square miles had been stripped bare, and thousands of families, many of whom had experienced the agonies of the great drought the year before and had somehow managed to survive, were totally wiped out. In one Nebraska field of 1600 acres the vegetation left behind was not enough to feed a single animal.

Not far to the south in Oklahoma there was a different kind of trouble. The price of crude oil had plunged to twenty-two cents a barrel and the state's crusty old governor, William "Cocklebur Bill" Murray, was not pleased. Denouncing the refiners as a bunch of "low-life, blood-sucking varmints," the Governor invoked a half-forgotten Oklahoma law passed during the early days of statehood that prohibited oil production whenever the price dropped below a dollar a barrel. Since "Cocklebur Bill" liked to think of himself as a fair man, even when dealing with the likes of Harry "Teapot Dome" Sinclair, who was "stealing food from the mouths of our schoolchildren," he gave the refineries fair warning: within two weeks oil would be selling at the wellhead for at least a dollar a barrel, or nothing. When questioned by newsmen the governor declared: "The price of oil must go up to one dollar. Now don't ask me any more damned questions."

Within a few days after Governor Murray's announcement, the price began to climb. But not enough. And so, after adding a couple of days' grace to the deadline date, the governor made good his promise by ordering out the National Guard to shut down the oil fields and keep them shut. "We're here on orders of the Governor," went the usual introduction. "Sergeant, take six men and close these wells."

By capping more than three thousand wells, Governor Murray outraged not only the refiners, but many of the drillers as well, and a lot of other folks who, in one way or another, depended upon oil for their livelihood. The governor tried to explain that it was his duty to prevent the state's most precious natural resource from being squandered for a few pennies a barrel, but people complained that he had no right to interfere with the free flow of legitimate private enterprise. There was some talk of stopping him with a federal court injunction, to which "Cocklebur Bill" responded: "Federal injunction? Just let 'em try that old Federal court injunction stuff on me. It'll be like a jackrabbit trying to tree a wildcat." In the end the governor fell far short of his dollar-a-barrel goal. He did manage, though, to push the price up to fifty cents, which was more than twice what it had been. And that, in the melancholy year of 1931, was no mean feat.

Meanwhile another Oklahoman, cowboy-turned-humorist Will Rogers, was saying that "the American people will be the first in history to ride to the poorhouse in their own automobiles." Not exactly. As the economy continued to crumble, millions of Americans somehow managed to remain on wheels, but millions of others could no longer afford to. In New York's Nassau County alone, over fifty thousand families were unable to buy their 1931 license plates. A generation later a Rhode Islander would recall having to take the family car off the road:

> I was a sophomore in high school then, and probably had as good an idea as most kids my age of what was going on, but I don't think I really understood just how tight things were with us until one Saturday afternoon I came home and found my Dad decommissioning the old Essex, which was just like one of the family to us. I helped him take out the battery and drain the crankcase and radiator and take out the

plugs. Then we put a little oil in the cylinders and jacked her up on blocks and took off the wheels. Dad was not much of a mechanic and neither was I, but we knew what to do well enough. Everybody did. By then, putting the car on blocks had already become an American ritual —sort of a public admission that the pinch was on. It was a very solemn affair. I remember saying to my Dad that we ought to have the priest over to say something in Latin, but Dad didn't think that was very funny. You don't joke about anything as serious as jacking up the car.

As if things weren't already bad enough, 1931 turned out to be one of the worst years on record for polio—only then it was called infantile paralysis. In New York State alone there were over six thousand cases, nearly 90 percent of them among children under five. The center of the epidemic was Brooklyn, where 4000 cases were reported throughout the summer and early autumn. During this period New York City was in a condition of partial quarantine. Outsiders were warned to stay clear of the city, and New Yorkers themselves were considered unwelcome guests by their out-of-town relatives and friends. Many children's summer camps refused to allow visitors from the New York area. Commuters returning home from the city were urged to shower, change their clothes, and gargle before going near their children. Schools remained closed throughout the city until late September, when with the coming of cooler weather the epidemic began to ebb. Doctors did their best but got nowhere in their attempts to treat the victims, while each day medical researchers progressed further down the wrong road in their search for the cause of the terrible crippler.

For parents with small children it was a time of awful anxiety, when a cry from the crib at night might mean nothing—or everything—and a common headache could be the beginning of a lifetime of tragedy. "I remember it all so clearly," said Mrs. S many years later:

We had just come back from a week's vacation at the Lake. Bob was unusually quiet and went to his room to lie down. An hour or so later he called to me and said he had a bad headache and asked for a drink of water. I felt his forehead and could tell he was running a temperature. When I handed him the water, the glass slipped through his fingers. He couldn't close his hand. It was then I knew, but I couldn't believe it. It had all happened so fast.

By October fresh haddock and tinker mackerel were selling at the pier in Portsmouth, New Hampshire, for 4¢ a pound and lobster for 15¢. It hardly paid the fishermen to go out, but what else was there to do? Hundreds of the unemployed and underemployed dug clams along the flats of New England and sold them door to door for 25¢ a peck. In grocery stores prices continued to plummet. At the First National iceberg lettuce sold for 10¢ a head, top sirloin steak for 35¢ a pound, and prime rib roast for 29¢. In several New England newspapers the A&P ran an autumn advertisement showing that food bargains were getting better all the time:

	Price, 1930	Today's Price	Saving
A&P Family Flour (24½ lb. bag)	75¢	59¢	16¢
Borden's Evaporated Milk (3 tall cans)	27¢	20¢	7¢
Del Monte Pineapple, crushed or shredded, (#2 can)	25¢	20¢	5¢
Del Monte Fruit Salad	37¢	29¢	8¢
Baker's Cocoa (½ lb.)	19¢	15¢	4¢
Sultana Red Salmon (#2 can)	35¢	29¢	6¢

. . . and so on down the list of several representative items to show the customer that an assortment of groceries that had cost $7.89 only a year before could now be had for $6.48—a drop in price of $1.41, or 18 percent.

Other prices continued their downward plunge. Bull Durham Roll Your Own Tobacco dropped from 8¢ to 5¢. Hamburgers, hot dogs, and banana splits could be bought for as little as a nickel at Grant's lunch counters on weekends. A matinee movie at the local

Bijou cost a dime on weekdays. Men's suits (coat, vest, and two pairs of pants) went for $15.50, boys' blue serge knickers for as little as $3.00, sneakers for 39¢, and women's fur-trimmed tweed suits for $7.95. Broadcloth slips cost 15¢.

One of the few things in the entire country to defy deflation was imported liquor, most of which came down from our wet neighbor to the north. Johnny Walker Black Label hovered around $4.75 a fifth, while the price of Canadian beer remained fairly constant at $9.00 a case. Among the gentry, including the more than a million American families with maids, the demand for these foreign imports was brisk—all that the traffic could bear, and then some. Most people, though, if they drank at all, had to settle for domestic concoctions such as relatively nontoxic "Grade C" gin, which sold for around 75¢ a pint, or "needle beer," which, depending upon its alcoholic content, generally went for anywhere between a dime and 20¢ a glass. None of this was legal, of course. Theoretically, the nation was still bone dry, but in actuality the "noble experiment" was no longer noble (if it ever had been) or an experiment. It had become an ugly travesty that mocked the nation's laws and corrupted its morals. In Trenton, New Jersey, a United States judge, recently transferred from relatively dry Montana, asked a federal prohibition agent:

"How many saloons would you say there are in this State? Would you say 300 or 400?"

"Well, Your Honor, it's been estimated by the press that here in Trenton there are 3000 of them."

"What! In Trenton alone? Then there would probably be at least 10,000 in the State, wouldn't there? And if each one of them sold only twenty drinks a day—they couldn't stay in business on less—that would mean 200,000 violations a day, and in a year that would make 75,000,000 violations. My, my!" Had the judge applied the same sort of reckoning to Manhattan, where an estimated 40,000 speakeasies were said to be operating more or less openly, he would have come up with a figure considerably in excess of a quarter of a billion.

In mid-October the American Bar Association decided that it had had enough, and urged that Prohibition be repealed. Other groups, including the American Legion and most labor unions, did the same. So did the American Medical Association, "with certain reservations." The National Grange, with its 800,000 members, thought otherwise, however: "It stands to reason that if the American people spend a large percentage of their earnings for beer, they would have just that much less to spend for food, clothing, and shelter." Also they would drink less milk. According to Grange statistics, since the beginning of Prohibition less than a dozen years before, per capita milk consumption in American had risen from 745 to 997 pounds per year. President Hoover agreed and produced his own statistics to prove that the repeal of Prohibition would also be harmful to the country's soft-drink industry.

But by far the most outspoken in their devotion to dryness were the nation's clergy, of whom none was more vehement or eloquent than the aging but still fiery evangelist Billy Sunday, who proclaimed that "the return of the saloon would mean the overthrow of civilization in our land:

> It was because I didn't want our boys to die drunkards that I fought and fight. I'm going to live long enough to see America so dry that you'll have to prime a man before he can spit. And I'll fight the saloon from Hawaii to Hoboken, and I'll kick it as long as I've got a foot, and I'll hit it as long as I have a fist, I'll butt it as long as I have a head, and I'll bite it as long as I have a tooth. And when I'm old, and footless, and fistless, and toothless, I'll gum it until I go home to glory and it goes home to perdition.

While all this was going on, the nation's economy was giving every sign of coming apart at the seams. During the latter half of 1931 industrial production, already badly slackened, fell off an additional 18 percent; factory payrolls dropped another 20 percent; and construction contracts decreased by a full third. Banks continued to founder (522 in October alone), while businesses, large and small, failed by the thousands. By December unemployment had risen to nearly seven million, half again as high as in the previous January, and for millions of other Americans still lucky enough to be working, wages had been severely slashed, often to a bare subsistence level—or below.

Although the unskilled workers suffered most, no class or group was unaffected. Steamfitters, carpenters, assembly-line workers, engineers, accountants, dentists, business executives, and college professors with Phi Beta Kappa keys dangling from their vests shared the common despair and humiliation of not being able to provide themselves and their families with a decent living. Failing to meet their mortgage payments or rent, countless families were turned out of their homes to find shelter elsewhere as best they could, and in the only nation in the so-called civilized world not to have some form of unemployment compensation, a million Americans stood dumbly in lines a quarter-mile long, waiting for their bowl of soup or plate of beans. And worse: "I have been seeing things with my own eyes," reported the writer Sherwood Anderson:

> men who are heads of families creeping through the streets of American cities, eating from garbage cans; men turned out of houses and sleeping week after week on park benches, on the ground in parks, in the mud under bridges. . . . Our streets are filled with beggars, with men new to the art of begging.

Among those who still had a roof over their heads, the coming of cold weather caused many an anxious thought to be given the winter's fuel supply. Even by switching (as most people did) to the formerly despised soft coal, which at $7 a ton was $2 cheaper than anthracite, a family living in the northern latitudes could hardly hope to keep warm during the winter for much less than $70, and this was more money than many people were making in a month—or a year. In Brookline, Massachusetts, a twelve-year-old boy happened across his father crying in the empty coal bin:

> We had owned a small bakery that had failed a few months before. A little later we lost most of our savings at a local bank that went under. We still had our house, and we were eating, which was more than could be said for some of our friends. But that was about all, and I guess the thought that he wouldn't be able to buy enough coal to get us through the winter was just too much for my father to take, coming as it did on top of everything else. Things would get worse for us later on, and for a couple of years we were in really bad shape, but to me the low point of the depression will always be the sight of my father that day, crying in the coal bin.

At the same time in various parts of the country, dozens of coal mines were closed down or operating at reduced production because of lack of demand. Hard or soft, coal was just not selling well that year.

In his annual message to Congress in early December, President Hoover expressed alarm over the growing budget deficit and urged the imposition of higher taxes. As for the plight of the people: "I am opposed to any direct or indirect Government dole." What was needed to lick the Depression ("and the time is ripe for forward action to expedite our recovery") was more good old-fashioned self-help, and the President was confident that the people of this great country were up to it.

"Self-help, indeed," snapped an irate Democrat a few days later on the floor of Congress. "President Hoover has given an outright dole to the railroads. He would give a dole to the building and loan associations. He would come to the aid of banks with frozen assets. . . . To these interests he would give billions, but to starving American women and children he wouldn't give one red cent."

"The issue is clear-cut," replied a Republican. "The Democratic Party in the House would commit the Government to the dole."

"Yes," agreed another. "The Democratic Party has abandoned the principles of Thomas Jefferson for the principles of Karl Marx."

"Well," stated a Democrat, "you Republicans can get up here and . . . talk about the Democrats not being solid and all that kind of stuff but what the people want to know is where is the prosperity around the corner you've been talking about?"

"A dole? I'm not in favor of a dole," declared a leading Southern Democrat. "But I'm not willing to see men, women, and children starve. . . . You Republicans are ready to give a dole to the predatory interests, to the lords of industry, to the international bankers. But when in the midst of this terrible panic we attempt legislation to help feed hungry millions, you accuse us of standing for the dole."

Republican Representative LaGuardia of New York:

Under normal conditions this party sniping and repartee would be amusing, but this is no time for politics and political speeches. Let's stop all this and get down to work. . . . I can go down to the market here and buy a parrot for $2. And in one day I can teach it to say: "Dole, Dole, Dole." But that parrot would never understand an economic problem. By the sinister use of "Dole" to stigmatize necessary relief,

> we're not going to solve this problem. . . . You can't ignore it by talking politics. You can't becloud the issue by nagging the President. . . . The situation is very, very serious and the issue is not the success of the Republic Party or the Democratic Party. It is the very preservation of the Union.

Actually, however, things were not nearly so bad as Congressman LaGuardia and many other alarmists seemed to believe. So at least concluded a feature writer for *American Magazine*, who after much research had pieced together a very reassuring article on the typical American family for 1931. "Out there where great continental railways and airways and motor highways meet," the article began, "out there at the crossroads of the continent, I found that family which is most typical of these United States."

The search had by no means been a helter-skelter one, but rather an exercise in simple logic. Since, according to the census of the year before, the nation's population center had shifted to Greene County in southwest Indiana, and since 56 percent of all Americans lived in cities, it made sense that the typical family would be living in Indianapolis, the nearest major city to Greene County. Once that much had been established, the rest was time-consuming but fairly simple. The Indianapolis telephone directory revealed that among the twelve most common (and therefore typical) names listed, Smith led the pack with 597, while White was last with 174. Between these two extremes (obviously not typical or they wouldn't be extremes) were 2594 Millers, Johnsons, Wilsons, Browns, Thompsons, etc.—of which the most typical was judged to be Brown.

Specifically, the nation's typical family turned out to be that of Merrill J. Brown, 44, five-foot-eight, with grey eyes, a hearty handshake, and a friendly smile. Mr. Brown, along with his pretty, dark-haired wife and their two children, a boy and a girl (which was typical), lived in a two-story, eight-room house on Carrollton Avenue, "a friendly street . . . , one of yards and trees and detached dwellings:

> And theirs is a friendly home, this home which they own . . . , attractive, well-furnished, and equipped with conveniences that millions of us enjoy today—bath, steam heat, electric sweeper, washer, and ironer, automatic refrigerator, telephone, and radio. They have a garage of course.

Like most typical American families the Browns enjoyed being together. When Mr. Brown was not busy working as sales manager at a nearby pharmaceutical company, the entire family went on picnics or played tennis or golf at the Avalon Country Club, of which they had been members for several years. During the summer months they enjoyed vacationing in northern Michigan or Canada. "This is the kind of family that has so multiplied on this continent that it makes up the ballast and keel of our nation," concluded the writer in his article, which he entitled: "Is This YOUR Family Too?"

> I do not claim that anything about them is extraordinary. They do not claim to be superior. They are an interesting family, fine examples. And I want to emphasize now that I think of them, not merely as a typical family of America, but as THE typical family of America: that family which represents all of us and most clearly typifies in every respect the twenty-nine million families comprising our population.

On the day before Christmas in Philadelphia a nineteen-year-old boy, unhappy over not being able to buy presents for his little brothers, decided that at least they would have a Christmas tree, and set out to steal one from a downtown lot. Surprised in the act by a policeman, he started to run and was shot dead. That same afternoon a local constable broke into an apartment in Sullivan County, New York, barely in time to save its occupants, an elderly married couple, from starving to death. On the following day, Christmas, over ten thousand people lined up for a free chicken dinner with all the trimmings at the 25th Street Pier in lower Manhattan. Meanwhile, at various points throughout the city the Municipal Public Welfare Department distributed free purchase tickets for over thirty thousand food packages, each containing a five-pound ham and a quarter-peck of potatoes. These were, as the City Fathers pointed out, "gestures of great generosity and compassion." But of course they weren't much help to the ninety-five New Yorkers who had already starved to death since the beginning of the year.

As 1931 drew to a close, the city councilmen of Rochester, New York, found themselves faced with a problem of sorts. Recently they had learned that the city's new bridge over the Genesee River, to be opened early the following year, had become the sub-

ject of a giant underground lottery. For 50¢ a ticket people from
as far away as Buffalo and Utica were snapping up chances for the
grand prize of $10,000, payable to the number corresponding
most closely to the exact month, day, hour, and minute of the
first suicide off the bridge. Low numbers were considered desir-
able. "The only thing I can see to do," declared the city coroner,
"is that when somebody jumps, we just won't report what time it
happened." The Council agreed.

On New Year's Eve the usual crowd was on hand in Times
Square—several thousands milling about cheek to jowl, some of
them sneaking an occasional drink from forbidden bottles of
homebrew hidden inside their overcoats, while others picked their
neighbors' pockets, with precious little to show for their effort. Inside in the ballroom of the Hotel Astor a gathering of 2500 enjoyed dancing and "spritely fun" at $6 a head (down from $7.50
the year before). "I noticed that many of them appeared less well-
dressed this year than in the past," reported a society columnist.
"There was definitely less ermine and mink." Shortly before midnight a little rubber dirigible named "Prosperity" was christened
with soda pop and launched from the center of the ballroom floor.
The balloon, which ascended slowly to the great chandeliered ceiling amidst much cheering and prophecies of better days to come,
was said to be an exact model in miniature of the recently completed USS *Akron*, the world's largest dirigible. Scarcely more
than a year later during a storm off the coast of New Jersey, the
Akron exploded and sank into the ocean with all hands lost.

Judge Crater, Where Are You?

EARLY AUGUST, 1930. New York City was like a giant furnace. No one could remember a worse heat wave. For several days running, the temperature soared into the nineties, while the sun bore down brutally from a near-cloudless sky. The air was searing and still. On the streets and in the stifling tenements of Harlem and the Bronx, people collapsed and sometimes died. Throughout the city, stores and offices closed down or remained open only until noon, and in Brooklyn a judge was forced to recess his court because of what was officially termed "an overheated jury."

At 7:30 on Wednesday evening, August 6, a distinguished-looking man of about forty approached the Arrow Theatre Ticket Agency, on Broadway not far from Times Square. He was a tall, well-built, swarthy person of rather handsome features, who carried himself proudly and walked with the purposeful stride of one who seemed to know exactly where he was going and how best to get there. Obviously a person of some consequence, he was impeccably dressed in a light brown suit with green stripes, a colored shirt, a bow tie, pointed shoes, pearl-gray spats, and a Panama hat. Aside from the fact that he wore no vest (an important point perhaps), he appeared to have made no concession to the heat, or for that matter to have been at all affected by it. His clothes were neatly pressed and fresh-looking, and his face showed no trace of perspiration or discomfort.

What was most distinctive about his clothing, however, was his high choker-type collar, a device long since abandoned by all other Americans except Herbert Hoover. Unlike Hoover, who had no neck at all and tried to hide the fact behind a choker, the man entering the ticket agency had a neck that was uncommonly long and thin (size 14), and he must have reasoned that a choker would fill it out a bit. In this he was probably right, although it must be added that the choker also tended to accentuate how surprisingly small his head was in comparison with the rest of his body—a deficiency about which he was known to be very sensitive and which he did his best to obscure by parting his hair in the middle and wearing his hat (size 6-5/8) at a rakish angle.

The operator of the ticket agency immediately recognized the man as Judge Joseph Crater, recently appointed justice of the New York Supreme Court. The judge, an inveterate theatre-goer, was a regular customer, and a welcome one, for although not a handsome tipper, he was a friendly sort who always found time to exchange pleasantries. On this occasion he had come to purchase a ticket for that same evening to *Dancing Partner*, a frivolous little comedy that had opened just recently at the Belasco Theatre on West 44th Street. Naturally he was disappointed to learn that the play was a complete sell-out—but the ticket agent would see what he could do. Most likely there would be cancellations because of the heat. If the agent could find a ticket, he would leave it at the theatre box office in Crater's name. The judge was most appreciative, and as the ticket agent would later state, "departed in what seemed to me like a happy mood."

From the Arrow Ticket Agency Crater proceeded, probably on foot, to Billy Haas's restaurant at 332 West 45th Street in the old tenderloin district. Haas's place catered to actors, theatre buffs, and assorted hangers-on. It was a great favorite with the judge, who enjoyed show people and was often seen in their company. He entered the restaurant shortly after eight o'clock, and was immediately spotted by a friend, theatre attorney William Klein, who invited the judge to join him and his showgirl companion at their table. Crater was in good humor, Klein later recalled. He showed no anxiety and seemed very natural. The three of them enjoyed a leisurely meal while they talked about the new plays in town. The judge may or may not have spoken of his plans to see *Dancing Partner* later that evening. Klein couldn't remember. He did recall, though, that at one point Crater mentioned something about leaving the city soon in order to spend some time with his wife at their summer cottage in Maine. At 9:15, fifteen minutes after curtain time, Judge Crater and his friends left the restaurant. They chatted for a moment or two on the sidewalk while the judge hailed a cab, and then parted company. The showgirl remembered waving good-bye to the judge as he rode off in a tan taxi in the direction of 9th Avenue. He was never seen or heard of again.

For Joe Crater life had always been something very special. He had worked hard to get where he was, but he hadn't minded. In fact, it had been fun all the way. He was bright, big, and healthy, and he liked to meet and beat the world on its own terms. Born near Easton, Pennsylvania, in January of 1889, he was the fourth and youngest son of straight-laced German-American parents, who put him to work at an early age, on weekends and after school, in the family's flourishing produce business. The work was physically hard, but that was all right. "I was one of the strongest kids in school," he once boasted. "That's how I got these broad shoulders of mine—tossing around crates of vegetables." And there was no denying that his shoulders were indeed unusually broad and squarecut, which was in a way too bad because they made his head appear even smaller than it was.

At eighteen Crater entered Lafayette College in Easton, where he became an outstanding student and an avid fraternity man. His house was Sigma Chi, and he so dearly loved it that be-fore graduating he had its Greek letters tattooed on his right fore-arm. His attachment to the fraternity, its songs and secret symbols, would remain an important part of his life. Often in later years when moved, as he frequently was, to express great feelings of love and tenderness for his wife, he would take her hand in his and sing her "The Sweetheart of Sigma Chi."

After graduating with honors from Lafayette, he moved on to Columbia Law School, where he impressed his professors as "keen-minded and conscientious." When the time came to take his bar examination in 1913, he passed with little difficulty. In the meantime he had met Stella, the first and probably only woman he ever really loved. Born and reared in a small, upstate town, she was pretty, Presbyterian, and save for an early exhibition of femin-ism (which she later regretted), very proper. From their first date she and Joe got along well together, and before a month had passed, she was wearing his Sigma Chi pin. The courtship was hard-

ly a whirlwind affair, however. The way Stella later explained it,
Joe had wanted to get married right away, but she had insisted
that they wait until he could get started in his own practice. Of
course, the fact that somewhere or other Stella already had a husband may also have had something to do with the delay. At any
rate, on March 16, 1917, four years after their first date and seven
days after Joe Crater, acting as her lawyer, had obtained Stella's
divorce for her, the two were married in a small Methodist parson-
age on the West Side. He was twenty-eight, and she was thirty.

Professional success was not long in coming to Joe Crater. He
had the training and the ability to do the job, and he worked hard.
His briefs were always prepared with great thoroughness and skill,
and his courtroom appearances, while not brilliant, were very
businesslike. Dressed in cutaway and striped formal trousers, he
presented his points quietly but forcefully—and more often than
not won his case. Before long he was recognized by those who
made it their business to know about such things, as one of the
"comers" among the city's young lawyers. In June of 1920 he
received a big boost when he was chosen secretary to New York
Supreme Court Justice Robert F. Wagner, a very big man in the
Democratic machinery of the state. Crater immediately set out
to make himself indispensable to the judge, and obviously succeeded. Bright, likable, accommodating, and always available, he
soon became Wagner's confidential assistant, a position of considerable trust and importance. "I doubt that the Judge would
pick out a hat without first asking my advice," he once boasted to
Stella.

By the time Wagner left for the United States Senate in 1927,
Joe Crater was a man of some standing in his own right. His law
practice had become very lucrative, and his reputation as a gifted
attorney stood high among his colleagues and the public alike.
Occasionally there was a whisper of wonderment or even disap-
proval over the large number of celebrated gangsters who hired
his services, but this was probably more envy than anything else.
"Somebody has to defend them," he explained to Stella. "That
doesn't mean I approve of them." Meanwhile he had set out upon
a simultaneous career as a teacher of law at City College, Fordham, and New York University. Here again he was a great success,
"a natural teacher" it was said, who was much admired by both
students and colleagues. There were times when he toyed with the
notion of abandoning his practice entirely and taking up teaching

fulltime, for this was what he enjoyed most. Still, he admitted, he would probably miss the excitement of the courtroom. Besides, his teaching salary was impossible. "I want to provide you with the better things of life," he told Stella. And for a while he did.

In 1919, two years after his marriage, Crater joined the Cayuga Democratic Club in the 19th Assembly District on the Upper West Side, where he and Stella had taken an apartment on West 122nd Street. The Cayuga Club was one of the many neighborhood cogs in the sprawling Tammany machine that controled New York City, and often the rest of the state as well, and it was here that Joe Crater began his swift climb up the political ladder. From the first he was a devoted party regular who did what he was told, from running errands for the ward bosses to making speeches at women's luncheons. As usual, he performed flawlessly, and within a few years had taken over the presidency of the club. By the late 1920s he was frequently seen in the company of Jimmy Walker and Al Smith. It was clear that Tammany was grooming him to go somewhere—perhaps all the way. And why not? As far as anyone could tell, he was the man who had everything.

Meanwhile, his standard of living had kept pace with his rising professional and political importance. He now expected Stella to set a formal table, with linen napkins and silver candlesticks, even for their dinners alone. Always a fastidious man, he became even more so, especially about his appearance. Clothes took on an increasing importance for him, until they became something of an obsession. A frequenter of the finest tailors and haberdashers, he purchased the best obtainable—and he purchased often. At the time of his disappearance he had thirty tailored suits and dozens of custom-made shirts. Once, in an offhand way, he suggested to Stella that she pay more attention to her clothes. She did. In October of 1927 they hired a cook and a chauffeur, and moved into an elegant Fifth Avenue apartment in the Washington Square area just north of Greenwich Village. "Can we afford all this?" Stella asked when she discovered that it cost $14,000 a year plus maintenance. "Don't you worry about that, Stell," Joe replied. "You leave that end of things to me."

As became a person of his standing, Joe Crater entertained a lot, and, as might be expected, he entertained well. The parties that he and Stella gave were large and lavish, and were attended by some of the biggest people in the city. On these occasions Joe, who rarely drank or smoked, was in his glory—or appeared to be.

Moving jovially among his guests, with a glass of orange juice in his hand and a ready smile that seemed to light up the room (a credit to his dentist, who had fashioned him a handsome set of dentures) he was more apt than not to be the center of attention. A hearty, big, strapping fellow whose booming laughter could periodically be heard above the din, he seemed the most natural and friendly of men. People took to him and agreed that he was bound to go places. Sooner or later someone at the party would ask him to play the piano, and Joe was always happy to oblige. As a musician he was no virtuoso, but he dearly loved to play, and with the help of sheet music he was good enough to get through most of the popular tunes of the day. Sometimes Stella would join him on the mandolin. Their favorites were the slow numbers, like "That Old Gang of Mine" and "I'm Dancing with Tears in my Eyes."

As time went by, Stella came to figure less and less in Joe's life. It seemed to her that with each passing month he spent more time away from home. Exactly what it was that kept him so busy she couldn't say. Joe was not much given to confiding in her about matters that didn't concern her, and Stella didn't like to probe. On those occasions when they were together they were completely happy, or so at least it seemed to Stella. A game of bridge with friends, the opening of a new play, dinner at their favorite little restaurant in the Village, or just an evening at home by the fire— Joe made them all seem very special. Every so often they would take in a Giants game at the Polo Grounds or go to the races at Belmont or Aqueduct. If they bet at all they did so very modestly, for Joe Crater was not a gambling man, which helps account for the fact that when the market crashed in 1929, he was left virtually untouched.

There were the good times, the times with Joe. But as the years passed, they became increasingly infrequent, and Stella, the small-town girl from upstate, was left more and more to herself. There were no children to occupy her time and attention, and no cooking or housework, for the hired help took care of all that. At home in her lavish Fifth Avenue apartment there was only her large, orange cat, Chickie, to keep her company. "I was quite a lonely woman during this period," she later recalled. "But how could I put myself ahead of such dedication? I kept myself in the background, content with his striving and his happiness." It was enough for her to know that Joe loved her, and of this there was never any doubt in her mind. In fact, he phoned her several times a day to tell her so. He also sent her bouquets of long-stemmed roses with sweet messages enclosed. And if rumors sometimes reached her that her husband was being seen frequently in the company of other women, Stella chose not to hear them.

In early 1929 events began to unfold that may well have had a lot to do with Crater's subsequent disappearance. They started in February when the Libby Hotel (sometimes known as "the Jewish Ritz"), a massive, twelve-story brick building on Delancey Street on the Lower East Side, went into bankruptcy. Attorney Crater was named receiver of the property. His job: take possession of all available funds, collect all debts, dispose of the property for as much as he could get for it, and divide the total assets among the various claimants. In other words, a seemingly routine bankruptcy case.

But what started out as just another run-of-the-mill receivership, soon developed some rather bizarre twists. In late June, Crater reported that the Libby had been purchased on bid for $75,000 by the American Mortgage Loan Company. In early August the city of New York announced its plans for a street-widening project and took over the Libby property in a public condemnation proceeding. In return the American Mortgage Loan Company was awarded a compensation settlement of $2,850,000—thirty-eight times what it had paid for the property only six weeks before.

Understandably, eyebrows were raised. Plundering the public treasury in fraudulent condemnation proceedings was a favorite sport of Tammany, dating back to the old days of Boss Tweed, and the Libby deal had all the old familiar signs and odors. Soon angry charges were being bandied about, especially by the press and the political opposition—so much so that the City Fathers felt compelled to announce that payment in the Libby transaction would be withheld until the entire proceeding had been subjected to a thorough investigation.

As sometimes happens in such matters, the investigation would be a long time coming. Meanwhile, life went on as usual for Joe Crater. Why shouldn't it? There were no grounds for suspecting him of any wrongdoing. He had merely acted as receiver and had discharged his responsibilities as best he could by selling the property to the highest bidder. Still, it was no secret that as a Tammany stalwart of some consequence he was in a position to know about many things that happened or were about to happen at City Hall, and perhaps even influence them a bit. Years later,

when questioned about the Libby affair, Mayor LaGuardia snorted:
"Page Judge Crater. There was *so much graft* in the condemnation
procedure on that project."

In the early spring of the following year, 1930, a vacancy occurred on the State Supreme Court, and Joseph Force Crater, just
turned forty-one, was chosen to fill it by Governor Franklin Roosevelt. It has always been thought that Crater owed his appointment
to the intercession of his former boss, Senator Wagner. The Senator vigorously denied this, but at the same time admitted that he
was pleased with the choice and considered it a very good one.
Others must have thought so too, for his colleagues in the New
York Bar Association had strongly recommended Crater for the
position. So had several Democratic luminaries at City Hall, including, it was reported, Mayor Walker himself. In the elegant
Crater apartment on Fifth Avenue, Stella learned of the appointment from the newspapers. "You might at least have mentioned
something about it to me," she protested. "Oh, Stell," he said. "I
don't want you worrying your head about politics."

His appointment to the bench was a source of great satisfaction to Joe Crater. For years he had dreamed of a judgeship, and
now he would have the honor of sitting on the highest court in the
state. True, his appointment would be good only until the following autumn when an election would have to be held to fill the regular fourteen-year term. But the advantage of his incumbency, together with the backing of Tammany, should be enough to win
him an easy victory at election time. All things considered, Judge
Crater had good reason to be pleased. He had attained a high and
honorable position—a fitting recognition of his past achievements,
as well as, perhaps, a promise of even greater things to come. And
if he had any misgivings about surrendering his $75,000-a-year pri-
vate practice in exchange for a fixed salary of less than one-third
that amount, he gave no indication of it.

By all accounts, Crater did an excellent job during the spring
term of the court, and by the end of the session there was no
longer any doubt, if indeed there ever had been, that he had the
makings of an outstanding judge. In late June, not long after adjournment, he boarded the Bar Harbor Express and joined Stella
at Belgrade Lakes, Maine, where they had purchased a summer
cottage several years before. Stella later recalled that he seemed
very tired, but gratified by his performance on the bench and in

generally good spirits. In the days that followed, time passed pleasantly for the judge. Two miles removed from the nearest telephone, and a million from New York, he and Stella swam and boated and lounged in the summer sun. His weariness soon left him, and he appeared completely relaxed and at peace with the world.

One morning, a week or so after his arrival, Stella noticed a sudden change in Joe. He seemed troubled. He had gone out onto the dock to read the newspaper just in from New York, but when Stella joined him a few minutes later, she found the paper lying beside him and the judge sitting strangely still, gazing off across the lake. Something was obviously wrong, but he wouldn't say what. "I don't want to talk about it, Stella," he said and got up and walked back to the cottage. Later that day Stella came across the following item in the paper:

District Attorney Thomas C. T. Crain announced today that he would soon subpoena witnesses in the investigation into charges that Magistrate George F. Ewald paid Tammany Leader Martin J. Healy the sum of $10,000 for his appointment to the bench.

Disturbing news indeed! Stella may not have known much about Joe's business, but the names of Healy and Ewald were certainly familiar enough to her. Both men were long-time political cronies of her husband. In fact, back in May of 1927 at a victory dinner in the Bronx celebrating Ewald's appointment to the bench, Joe Crater had been the principal speaker. Soon after, at Ewald's induction at the Washington Heights Court House, he had acted as master of ceremonies. As for Healy, not only was he the Democratic boss of the Nineteenth Assembly District, in which Crater had risen to political prominence, but he was also known to be Joe's personal friend.

Two days later a telegram arrived for the judge. He read it in Stella's presence, folded it and put it in his pocket. "Nothing," he explained. "Just a professor friend at NYU telling me to relax and have a good time." Not long after that, he surprised Stella by suggesting that they take an automobile trip to Canada. This was unlike the judge. He had never cared for motoring long distances. On this occasion, though, he seemed to enjoy himself. After a leisurely trip up, by way of Jackman, and a brief stopover in Quebec

City, they headed home again. Just outside the city in a small sub-
urban town, Joe had the chauffeur pull up in front of the local
bank. "I want to change some money," he said. Stella waited for
him in the car. It seemed to her that he was gone for quite a while.

A week or so after returning to the lake from Quebec, the
judge received another telegram, and informed Stella that he
would have to leave right away for Atlantic City. "A political
meeting about the Healy matter," he explained. "Nothing serious."
On the weekend of July 26-27 he was seen in Atlantic City in the
company of two of his political associates and four women. Nothing is known of what took place there, save that Crater and his
friends attended a road production of the new stage play, *Dancing
Partner*, the very same show for which the judge would purchase
a ticket less than two weeks later on the evening of his disappearance.

Midway through the following week he dropped around to
the New York office of Senator Wagner, presumably to wish him
bon voyage on the eve of his vacation trip to Europe. "We did not
talk politics," Wagner reported. "Our chat was quite good-humored
and informal. Politics was not mentioned." However, several members of Wagner's staff noticed that when Crater left he seemed
"distracted." Later, after the judge had disappeared, it was conjec-
tured that Wagner had taken this occasion to notify Crater that in
view of his known association with the Libby Hotel affair and now
the Ewald-Healy allegations, Tammany couldn't risk supporting
his candidacy for the full-term judgeship in the upcoming election.
On Friday, August 1, the Craters' chauffeur, Fred Kahler, came
down from Maine with the limousine and drove the judge back
to the lake, where he arrived early the following morning. Stella
was still in bed. "Did anything happen?" she asked. "Yes," he announced. "Fred and I just beat the Bar Harbor Express up from
New York."

That afternoon Joe and Stella went motorboating about the
Lake. That evening they bowled with friends in the village. Joe
seemed in high spirits, but several times during the evening he was
absent from the others for long periods. Later, on the walk back
to the cottage, he told Stella that he would have to return to New
York in the morning. "I've got to straighten out a few people,"
he said. "It shouldn't take long." Next day, Sunday, he had Fred
drive him to the little station in the village where he boarded the
train for the city. Before leaving he gave Stella her usual kiss and

promised he would be back in plenty of time for her birthday on the following Saturday. She would never see him again.

Crater arrived at Grand Central early Sunday evening and apparently went directly to the Fifth Avenue apartment, where he spent the night. On the following morning when the maid arrived to clean, she found him getting ready to go out. Before leaving, he asked that she come again on Thursday, and added that after that she wouldn't be needed until the 25th of the month, when court was scheduled to reconvene. Late that afternoon he kept an appointment with a doctor friend in the Village to see about a finger that he had recently jammed in a car door. At 10:00 the following morning he was seen entering his chambers in the new county court house on Foley Street. About an hour later he left. That evening he had dinner with his doctor friend, and stayed on at his place until 11:00 or so. Early in the afternoon of the same day, an attractive, richly dressed woman who called herself Lorraine Fay and spoke with a slight accent, consulted with a midtown lawyer about initiating a $100,000 breach of promise suit against Judge Crater. The lawyer had not seen her before, nor would he again. She never returned, and subsequent investigations by the police and private detectives failed to discover who she was, or what, if anything, happened to her.

On Wednesday, the day of his disappearance, Judge Crater arrived at his chambers about mid-morning and remained there for nearly three hours. During that time he was visited for a few minutes by an old friend, Simon Rifkind, who had succeeded Crater as Wagner's confidential secretary. Rifkind later recalled that during his visit the judge had kept himself occupied, pulling papers out of his file and sorting them into piles on his desk. Soon after Rifkind had left, Joseph Mara and Frederick Johnson, Crater's attendant and secretary, entered the inner chamber briefly to consult with the judge. They found him putting the piles of papers into several cardboard portfolios and two large briefcases.

Late in the morning the judge sent Mara to cash two personal checks, one for $3000 on his account at the Chase, and the other for $2150 at the Empire Trust. Both were made out to cash. Shortly before noon Mara returned with the money in two manila envelopes. Without bothering to open them, Crater put the envelopes into the inside pocket of his suit coat. Later, when questioned by the police, Mara would deny having cashed the checks or even having any knowledge of them, a story he stubbornly stuck to until finally confronted with the canceled checks bearing his endorsement. "I guess I was confused about that," he explained.

Soon after Mara's return, he and his boss took a taxi to the judge's apartment, carrying the briefcases and portfolios of papers with them. According to Mara, the judge seemed "very blue and moody" during the taxi ride. When they reached the apartment, the two men put the briefcases and portfolios on a chair in the sitting room. "You may go now," Crater told him. "I'm going up to Westchester for a swim." Whether he did or not is anybody's guess. Despite a careful coverage of all of Westchester County, the police were never able to turn up any evidence that the judge was actually there on the afternoon of his disappearance. On the other hand, they were unable to place him anywhere else. Significantly or otherwise, by accident or design, Crater's whereabouts have remained completely unaccounted for from the time he dismissed Mara early on the afternoon of Wednesday, August 6, until he entered the Arrow Ticket Agency that evening at 7:30, just prior to his dinner at Billy Haas's and his subsequent ride into oblivion.

Back at the lake the sun shone brightly for Stella's birthday on Saturday. Shortly after noon Ira Bean, the local storekeeper, drove up in his truck from the village and unloaded a new, bright red canoe that Joe had ordered a few weeks earlier as a present for his wife. Friends came to dinner that evening. But no Joe. This was unlike him. He had often been late in coming home, but he had always sent word. She gave some thought to trying to reach him by phone, but decided against it. She didn't want him to think she was interfering in his affairs.

The weekend passed, and Monday came on rainy and cold, laying a thick haze over the lake. Inside the Crater cottage, Stella, alone except for her orange cat Chickie, was worried. She had begun to imagine the worst. Perhaps Joe had suffered a stroke in the apartment and was lying there helpless. At about noon she had Fred drive her to the village, where she phoned the apartment.

There was no answer. She then phoned Joe's friend, Simon Rifkind, who was surprised to learn that Joe had not returned to the
lake. He didn't doubt for a moment that Joe was all right, but just
to be on the safe side he would make a few inquiries. In the meantime it would be best to keep the matter as quiet as possible. With
the judge about to stand for election, it would be unwise to run
the risk of any unwanted publicity.

After four days of no word from Rifkind, Stella, now badly
wrought-up, sent Fred to the city with instructions to check the
apartment and a number of other places where her husband might
be. Six days later the chauffeur was back at the lake to report that
he had been unable to find any trace of the judge. He would have
kept on looking, but the judge's friends advised him against "hanging around." It might stir up suspicion among the newspaper
people.

For the next five days Stella did nothing but wait. No longer
able to eat or sleep, she seemed to have lost both the power and
will to make a decision. And then, on the 27th, she was suddenly
jolted out of her stupor by a message that there was a long-
distance phone call for her in the village. Could it be Joe? By the
time she reached the phone she had all but convinced herself that
it was, and the sound of another voice on the line came as a terrible
disappointment. It was one of her husband's court colleagues, calling to inquire why Joe hadn't shown up for the opening of the
session two days earlier. For Stella this was staggering news. Joe
Crater would never have missed the opening of court unless something awful had happened to him. Two days later, in a state of
near nervous collapse, she arrived in New York and began searching about frantically for some trace of her husband. She found
nothing.

Meanwhile, "at the request of certain friends of the Judge,"
Detective Leo Lowenthal of the Metropolitan Police had begun an
unofficial and wholly unauthorized investigation of the case. This
was a highly irregular procedure for which Lowenthal would subsequently be called to account (and cleared) by his superiors, but
it was nonetheless understandable enough. After all, Tammany
was not without friends in the police department, and Lowenthal
happened to be one of the best of them. In fact, his loyalty to the
Democratic machine was so highly regarded that he was privileged
to serve as Senator Wagner's personal bodyguard whenever the
senator was in town. Just the man to be trusted with the political-

ly delicate assignment of finding a missing Tammany judge in election season. On August 31 he visited Stella in the apartment and
informed her of his progress, which admittedly had not been very
encouraging. About all he had been able to learn for certain was
that the judge was not in any of the metropolitan hospitals—or
morgues.

With Stella's help, Lowenthal gave the Fifth Avenue apartment a thorough going-over. Only one of the judge's thirty suits
was missing. All of his traveling bags were in place. In fact, everything appeared as it should have been—except: there in plain view
on the judge's dresser were his monogrammed watch, pen, business-
card case, and other personal effects that he ordinarily carried
with him. Stella thought this rather strange. So did Detective
Lowenthal, and he noted it down in his little book. Later, just
before leaving, he advised Stella to return to Maine. "Senator
Wagner is on his way back from Europe," he said. "I don't think
anything should be done until he get here. After all, I'm sure the
judge is all right, and we don't want to hurt his chances for election, do we."

In the late afternoon of September 3 the *New York World*
broke the news of the missing judge on its front page. On the following day, as Senator Wagner came steaming into New York harbor on the SS Bremen ("Judge Crater's disappearance has no political significance," he assured newsmen at the dock), Simon Rifkind
officially reported the matter to the Missing Persons Bureau of the
New York Police Department. Immediately thereafter the bureau
opened its long and costly investigation of what would prove to be
the most baffling vanishing act of modern times. The fact that
nearly a month had passed since the judge had last been seen
would not make its job any easier.

Using information that Detective Lowenthal had come up
with during his earlier investigation, the police proceeded to prepare a reward circular bearing a recent photograph of the judge,
together with a detailed physical description and a complete list of
the clothing he was thought to have been wearing at the time of
his disappearance. In all, more than ten thousand copies of the circular were printed and distributed throughout the United States

and several foreign countries, to be posted in well-frequented places such as post offices, banks, theatres, train stations, and vacation lodges. In addition, copies were widely scattered among law enforcement agencies, including the FBI, and, of course, the newspapers. To anyone alert enough, or lucky enough, to spot the man on the poster, or to anyone who could tell where to find him, the city of New York promised to pay the sum of $5000.

Later, as an indication of its deep concern for Judge Crater's welfare, the *New York World* upped the reward to $7500. In fact, through it all the press, especially the New York papers, showed an intense interest in the vanished judge. Naturally. With its many tantalizing ingredients, including hints of illicit sex and political scandal, the Crater disappearance made for great copy, and the press played the story for all it was worth—and then some. Supposedly responsible reporters and editors engaged in the shabbiest sort of sensationalism. Rumor was paraded as fact; innuendo abounded; and when the big story threatened to turn cold for lack of new developments, enterprising men with typewriters and cameras managed to find ways to heat it up again. Nothing was too trivial, or too private. "What about those other women, Mrs. Crater? How many did he have?" Stella would never forgive them, and yet—grudgingly—she had to admit that, for all their sins and insensitivity, it was the newspapers, much more than the police circulars, that made Judge Crater the most widely known man in America, and for months, even years thereafter, kept the search for him alive.

In their investigation of the Crater case the New York City police proved to be painstaking and, on the whole, efficient. That their work was more plodding than imaginative was hardly their fault, for they had precious little evidence to go by. Furthermore, imagination can be dangerous for a working cop, particularly when applied to a situation touching upon interests close to City Hall. This is not to say that the investigation was deliberately hamstrung by Tammany, but rather that had the case been politically less sensitive, it might have been handled by the police with a bit more aplomb.

As it was, they played the whole thing strictly by the book. Hundreds of leads were doggedly checked out. Metropolitan detectives traveled to places as far away as Florida to follow up reports (thirty-seven in the first week alone) that the judge had been sighted—all at considerable expense to the city's taxpayers. At Bel-

grade Lakes, Stella was questioned time and again, particularly
about her relationship with her husband. Had they quarreled?
They had not. Had she heard rumors about other women? Perhaps.
If she had, she certainly hadn't paid any attention to them because
she knew they weren't true. With the help of the Maine police, the
area around the cottage was thoroughly searched. The lake was
dragged twice. Nothing. And then on September 12, Stella received
a ransom note demanding $20,000 for Joe's return: "Otherwise
you will not see your darling husband again." After attempting
unsuccessfully to trace the note, the police turned it over to New
York District Attorney Thomas Crain, who pronounced it a hoax
and let it go at that. Most likely he was right. At least, the "kidnaper" was never heard from again. But then, neither was Joe
Crater.

Back in the city the police soon managed to come up with
several scattered bits of information, the significance of which
they could only guess at. Among other things, they found out that
the theatre ticket Crater had ordered from the Arrow Ticket
Agency less than two hours before his disappearance had been
picked up by somebody later that evening at the Belasco Theatre
box office. They also learned that the judge had $12,000 on de-
posit at the Empire Trust Company, a balance of $1500 with his
brokerage firm, and a debt due of $9500 on his Fifth Avenue
apartment. While at the bank the police discovered that for some
time the judge had been renting a safe deposit box there. For what
purpose no one could say. Stella had no idea. Neither did the police, for when they opened it, they found it empty. Then too,
there was the not-too-surprising revelation that for a half-dozen
years or more Crater had been maintaining an attractive divorcee
in a midtown apartment, and that he also was on friendly terms
with several chorus girls. One of these was June Brice, whose sudden disappearance early in the investigation introduced a further
element of mystery into the case.

Of special interest to the police was the discovery that earlier
in the year, at about the time of his appointment to the Supreme
Court Bench, Crater had withdrawn $7500 from his bank accounts
and sold $15,779 worth of securities. His broker recalled that
Crater had asked for his money in thousand-dollar bills. The fact
that the total amount was suspiciously close to the $22,500
annual salary that Crater would be receiving on his new job,

couldn't help but underscore the possibility that Crater, like his friend Ewald perhaps, had purchased his judgeship. Remarked one of the investigators assigned to the case: "It looks to me as though Crater may have been abiding by the old ward-heelers' rule of thumb—a year's salary for any political plum granted." If this were true, then Judge Crater would have had good reason to be worried. With the principals in the Ewald-Healy allegations both known to have been closely associated with him, his own appointment was bound to be given a hard look sooner or later. In fact, there were already indications in Albany that as a result of the Ewald affair, the State Assembly would soon appoint a high-level committee to conduct a sweeping investigation of the New York court system from top to bottom.

All told, the police were able, despite their late start, to fill in a goodly number of blanks—but not enough to permit them to progress very far toward solving the case. There were simply too many questions that remained unanswered. Among the more perplexing and perhaps significant:

(1)   Who was the mystery woman, Lorraine Fay—she of the proposed breach of promise suit? What had become of her? Was there in fact any such person, or had she been invented by a person or persons unknown to deliberately false-scent the police?

(2)   What of the judge's showgirl friend, June Brice? Why had she disappeared? And where?

(3)   What about the missing theatre ticket? Was it the judge who had picked it up? If not, who? And why hadn't that "who" come forward and identified himself? Surely he must have been aware that the police were looking for him. Also, why should Crater, who had attended the same play in Atlantic City less than two weeks before, want to see it again—especially on such an uncomfortably hot evening?

(4)   For what purpose did Crater have his assistant, Joe Mara, withdraw such large sums of money for him on the very day of his disappearance? A payoff perhaps? If so, to whom? Lorraine Fay? June Brice? A fellow politician? Furthermore, why had Mara denied having made the withdrawals?

(5)   What had happened to the briefcases and portfolios that

Crater and Mara took from the judge's chambers? More important, what was the nature of the papers they contained? A careful inspection of the judge's files gave no clues. Certainly no official documents were missing.

(6)   Was it nothing more than coincidence that Judge Crater had disappeared on the opening day of the Ewald-Healy hearings, to which he was almost certain to be subpoenaed as a witness? And why on that particular day did Crater, a man of rather fixed habits in matters of this sort, neglect to take his personal effects along with him?

And so on, and so on, including of course what might have been the biggest question of all: What, if any, was the connection between Judge Crater's disappearance and the year-old Libby Hotel transaction, which, it was generally understood, was at long last about to come up for investigation before a public board of inquiry?

Of all the missing pieces and dead ends, none was more taunting to the police than the mystery of the phantom taxicab. Neither of Crater's dinner companions that night at Billy Haas's restaurant could recall anything about the cab that the judge had ridden away in, except that it was tan, a not uncommon color among the city's huge fleet of taxis. For weeks the police worked their way methodically through mountains of trip sheets, but, even allowing wide margin for entry error, they found no record of the fare. Hundreds of drivers were questioned, reminded of the reward money, and then questioned again. Copies of the Missing Persons circular were run in the taxi trade publications. But the results were always the same: Of the thousands of cabbies in the city of New York, not one could remember the fare in question, or anything that even came close. At least, no one was willing to say so—not even for $7500.

On September 15, 1930, about six weeks after the judge's disappearance and nearly two weeks after it was reported to the police, the Crater case came before the New York County Grand Jury. From that time until January 9 of the following year—a period of almost four months—the Jury held forty-five sessions, during which it heard 300 witnesses give 2000 typewritten pages of testimony, none of which shed much light on the case. When the hearings finally ended, the judge's disappearance was as much of a mystery as ever, if not more so. Declared the jury in its statement of findings:

> The evidence is insufficient to warrant any expressions of opinion as to whether Crater is alive or dead, or as to whether he has absented himself voluntarily, or is a sufferer from disease in the nature of amnesia, or the victim of a crime.

"Hell!" snorted a member of the police commissioner's staff when news of the verdict reached him. "Crater's disappearance was premeditated."

Meanwhile Stella had stayed on in Maine. Since the early autumn she had been living in seclusion at the Eastland Hotel in Portland, trying to avoid reporters and maintain her sanity. When summoned to appear before the grand jury, she refused. She was too ill, she declared. Besides, she couldn't bear the thought of having to listen to slurs against her husband, especially those having to do with other women. Not until the middle of January, a week or so after the hearings had ended, did she return to the city. And then, on the twenty-first of the month, while rummaging through the apartment she made a startling discovery that further compounded the mystery. In the top drawer of her bedroom dresser were four large manila envelopes, all addressed to her in her husband's handwriting. Contained in the first three were: $6690 cash in bills of large denomination; a few securities; four insurance policies, totalling $30,000, made out to Stella; the judge's five-year-old will naming his wife as his sole heir; and three checks for $500, $12, and $9, all made payable to Joseph Crater and signed and endorsed by Crater himself. One of them was dated August 30, 1930, nearly three weeks after the judge's disappearance.

Of greater interest to the police was the fourth envelope, marked CONFIDENTIAL, which contained a long memo to Stella listing the names of twenty or so persons and organizations that Crater claimed owed him money in the aggregate of more than $20,000. Although the handwriting was undeniably Crater's, it appeared labored and erratic. Sprawled over three pages of legal foolscap and written in pencil, the words were often ill-formed and sometimes barely legible. At the bottom of the final page the judge had scrawled: "Am very weary. Love, Joe," followed by an underlined postscript: *"This is all confidential."*

Most of the names on the list, all of which were immediately checked out by the police, seemed innocent enough. ("I loaned Alexander Konta $5000. His note enclosed. It is to be paid on September 10.") One, however, did not:

> There will be a very large sum due me for services when city pays the 2 and ¾ millions in condemnation. Martin Lippman will attend to it—keep in touch with him.

Now here was an interesting nugget. It was no secret that Lippman was the principal attorney for the American Mortgage Loan Company, the buyer of the bankrupt Libby property. Question: since Crater's fee as receiver in the Libby case had already been paid from the assets of the liquidated property, why should he have any additional money due him on that transaction from Martin Lippman, or anyone else? When questioned by the police, Lippman was mystified. Judge Crater had obviously been confused. Neither Lippman nor the American Mortgage Loan Company owed him a cent.

Another puzzler posed by Stella's discovery of the envelopes was: how had they managed to get where they were? On three separate occasions the Crater apartment had been thoroughly searched, twice by the police and once by members of the grand jury. All three search teams were willing to swear that they had gone through the dresser with great care and found nothing of consequence. One detective specifically recalled searching through the very drawer in which the envelopes were subsequently found:

> I remember it particularly well because the drawer was covered in front with a bureau scarf and contained some women's clothing and a palm fan. It was hot when we were there, so, for a joke, I took out the fan and tossed it over to my partner so he could cool off. There were no envelopes there then.

In view of all this, it seemed clear that somebody had placed the envelopes in the drawer sometime between the final search in late September and Stella's return to the apartment in mid-January. Whoever it was must have let himself in with a key, for there were no indications that the lock had been tampered with or the door jimmied. At the earliest it could not have been done less than six weeks after the judge's disappearance; so that ruled him out. Or did it? And if not the judge, then who? More questions without answers.

From 1930 to 1960 the city of New York spent over a quarter of a million dollars trying to find Judge Crater. Police and private investigators in other parts of the country, and in several foreign nations, spent perhaps twice that amount, while newspapers and insurance companies chipped in another $50,000. Even though he was officially declared dead in June of 1939, reports of his whereabouts continued to be received with some frequency until well into the 1960s. All told he was seen thousands of times: tending bar in Tangiers, operating a bingo game in Morocco, and panhandling in Newton, Illinois. He was a dance instructor at a California resort, a river-boat gambler, a pimp, and an insane asylum inmate. Tips came in from all over the world. Mediums and clairvoyants had a field day. A "radiation perception expert" living in Jonesboro, Arkansas, was able to discover the judge in San Francisco without even leaving his front porch. All but the zaniest of these reports were checked and sometimes rechecked. A sheepherder in northeast Oregon, who happened to be a dead ringer for Crater, was picked up by the police seven times. "For a while he spent half his time proving he wasn't the runaway judge," commented one of his tormentors. "Finally we decided not to bother the poor fellow anymore." Although in the end none of the leads amounted to anything, a few of them provided some interesting twists along the way. Consider, for instance, the case of Lucky Blackiet.

Late in the summer of 1936, Blackiet, a grizzled old prospector with a gnarled beard and disposition to match, appeared out of the California desert and informed the Los Angeles police that he had recently seen Judge Crater in a remote part of the Cuyamace Mountains. "He is a prospector now like me." The police were impressed and sent two of their detectives to accompany Blackiet back to the mountains. With them went a dozen reporters, photographers, and newsreel cameramen. Once they reached the desert, however, Lucky refused to go on until he had been paid fifty dol-

lars. The newsmen passed the hat for twenty-five, and Lucky settled for that, although not very graciously. For the next five days
they wandered about the desert and up and down mountains, with
the 300-pound Lucky leading the way on his sagging mule. In tiny
settlements along the route they talked with natives who more or
less confirmed Lucky's story. One of them, a storekeeper at Banner, exclaimed upon being shown Crater's picture: "My God,
that's the man! He came into the store May 1st and bought some
salami!"

In time, Lucky's band of followers became tired and irritable
and showed signs of losing faith in their guide. The crisis came
when a group of them detached themselves from the main party
and went off to search for the judge on their own, without consulting Lucky. This was too much. When he learned of what had
happened, Lucky quit on the spot. "To hell with the lot of ya," he
roared, and rode off, leaving them all to fend for themselves. When
the expedition finally got back to Los Angeles, emptyhanded and
hopping mad, the police decided to run a check on Blackiet. They
discovered that two years earlier he had led a similar operation into the same area. About the only difference was that on that occasion it was not Judge Crater that Blackiet had spotted, but Pretty
Boy Floyd.

Even more bizarre than the Blackiet expedition was the fas-
cinating performance of the Dutch clairvoyant, Gerard Croiset. In
February of 1955, a quarter-century after Crater's disappearance,
Croiset was approached by a young American writer and amateur
sleuth, Murray Bloom, who had heard of the Dutchman's remarkable record in helping European police solve cases similar to the
Crater mystery. Without announcing the purpose of his mission,
Bloom arranged for an interview with Croiset at the Institute of
Parapsychology at the University of Utrecht. There in the presence
of three witnesses, including the Institute's director, Croiset was
given a picture of Judge Crater and asked to tell what he could
about him. After placing the picture face down on a table in front
of him, and drifting off into what the director later described as a
"light trance," Croiset demonstrated his remarkable powers: "This
man is not alive," he declared in a half-drone. "I see him sitting on
a chair raised above the floor . . . two men sitting below him, one
on each side. He has to do with criminals but not as a lawyer . . .
ah, a judge. He was murdered long ago . . . , maybe twenty-four,
twenty-five years ago." The man in the picture had been kidnaped,

Croiset explained, "no, enticed away, tricked." On the back of the picture, Croiset then sketched a rough map of New York City on which he placed an X, showing where the subject was buried.

Bloom hurried back to New York and presented his information to the police. They were admittedly interested, especially in Croiset's X, which seemed to indicate an area just over the city line in Yonkers, where, it was known, one of Crater's political cronies had been living at the time of the judge's disappearance. This was one lead, however, that the police had no intention of following up. The revelations of a clairvoyant, 3000 miles and twenty-five years removed from the event, were considered "too unsubstantial" to warrant digging up a taxpayer's yard. Besides, if the dig failed to produce anything, the police would look pretty silly.

Bloom persevered, however. Four years later he managed to get the Yonkers property dug up—not by the police, but by LIFE magazine, which finally succumbed to Bloom's argument that if nothing else the project would yield a good picture story. It didn't. The resulting article, featuring piles of dirt and rubbish photographed from various angles, proved to be one of the dullest in LIFE's thirty-six-year history. And of course there was no trace of the judge. Clairvoyant Croiset was most apologetic. He offered to go into a trance and draw another map, but LIFE and Bloom both declined, with thanks.

The mystery of what happened to Judge Crater remains unsolved and probably always will. For some time after his disappearance the police were convinced that the judge, faced with the prospect of some great unpleasantness, had simply stepped out of one life and into another, assuming a new identity in accordance with a carefully devised plan. So did the public at large, among whom the expression "pull a Crater" gained wide currency during the 1930s and can occasionally still be found, with variations, scribbled on latrine walls. Certainly much of the evidence in the case, as well as many of the gaps, pointed to a calculated run-out by the judge.

On the other hand, those who knew him well stoutly maintained that Joe Crater would never have chosen this way. It was completely out of character. "If he was in trouble, he would have fought, not run," insisted Stella. Furthermore, it appears that at least as far as his public life was concerned, the judge's problems were not nearly so bad as many people imagined. Within a few months after his disappearance, prolonged public inquiries into the Ewald-Healy bench-buying allegations and the Libby Hotel transaction ended without damage to Crater's reputation. In fact, in the final report of the commission charged with investigating the Libby bankruptcy, the judge was explicitly cleared of any wrongdoing. As for problems in his private life, who can say? There may well have been some very serious ones, perhaps even of blackmail proportions. Still, could they conceivably have been so unmanageable as to cause Crater to voluntarily forsake a life of such great accomplishment and promise?

As time passed without the discovery of a single solid clue as to the judge's whereabouts, the police began to alter their thinking about his disappearance. With each year it became more difficult to explain why he had not been found. With his undersized head (which had received widespread publicity) he was not exactly inconspicuous. Besides, it was hard to believe that Joe Crater's temperament would permit him to remain in obscurity for very long. Sooner or later his outgoing ways would be bound to betray him— that is, if he were still alive. And maybe he wasn't. Although the police had never ruled out the possibility and had dutifully checked out all unidentified corpses, from the beginning they had tended to discount the idea that Crater's disappearance had been involuntary. By the end of the decade, however, the failure to produce a live Crater had prompted them to think more seriously about the likelihood of a dead one.

And why not? Wasn't it possible that in their eagerness to prove the obvious they had misread the signs? Suppose, for instance, that the judge had left his personal effects behind on the dresser simply because it happened to be very hot that day and he wore no vest in which to carry his watch and card case, etc. And suppose that the belatedly discovered envelopes had been placed in the bureau drawer by Stella herself. Perhaps Crater had left them with her in Maine, and Stella, fearing that they might in some way compromise her husband, had deliberately withheld them until after the grand jury had adjourned and then taken this convenient way to produce them—as produce them she must, sooner or later, in order to settle the estate. Of course, all this was just conjecture, but was it any less believable, say, than that the envelopes had been placed in the apartment by the judge himself, six weeks or more after his disappearance? The point is that all of the evidence used to bolster the police's original pet theory that the judge was alive and well somewhere, could, if viewed in a different light, lead to a more ugly conclusion: namely, that Crater had come to a violent end at the time of, or soon after, his disappearance. Suicide and accidental death seemed pretty unlikely, mainly because of the absence of any witnesses—or a corpse. That left murder. The motive? For a man of Judge Crater's many parts, it could have been anything from the apprehensions of a crooked politician to the fury of a wronged husband.

Through the years many interesting, and often very persuasive, theories concerning Judge Crater's death by murder have been concocted by the police and others. Only twice, however, has the crime been completely "solved." It happened first in July of 1939 when Stella threatened to bring suit against the companies that had underwritten her husband's life insurance. Claiming that Judge Crater had met with an unnatural death and that his widow was therefore entitled to double indemnity, Stella's attorney, Emil K. Ellis, presented the following case, pieced together from his own intensive investigation: On the night of his disappearance, Crater visited the showgirl June Brice to offer her $6,000 to get out of town and stop blackmailing him. On hand at the girl's apartment were two of her strong-arm boy friends, who tried to bully Crater into upping the payoff to $50,000. When he refused, a scuffle followed and Crater was killed. Later that same night his body was taken by car to an underworld crematory in New Jersey and disposed of.

A reasonable enough story, to be sure, and perhaps even a true one, but, as the insurance companies were quick to point out, based entirely on hearsay. What was needed was the testimony of an eyewitness, like the missing June Brice. This was, of course, out of the question. Or was it? A few months later, Ellis, working on his own, managed to accomplish what the New York Police Department had failed to do in nearly ten years of trying: namely, find June Brice. With a lot of perseverance and a little luck he was able to trace the ex-showgirl to a mental institution in Brooklyn. She was hopelessly insane. "Poor thing," commented a chorus-line friend who had seen her on the night before she vanished, "she was so terribly frightened. She was afraid she was going to be murdered because of a dreadful secret she knew."

The second and only other "solution" to the murder came many years later. Like the first, it was solely hearsay, but so elaborate was it in its detail, and so seemingly sure of itself, that for some Craterologists it carried a convincing ring. Furthermore, the very fact that it was far removed from those more conventional theories long cherished by the police and others, seemed, oddly enough, to give it added credibility. According to an ex-convict who had struck up a prison friendship with convicted murderer Harry Stein, Stein told him this story not long before being executed at Sing Sing in the summer of 1955:

Early in 1929 a New York City businessman, Joseph Lesser, was indicted on forgery charges involving $190,000 worth of real estate mortgages. Joe Crater, not yet a judge but nonetheless influential with the courts and known to be a first-rate fixer, was offered $5000 by Lesser's friends to arrange for a "guaranteed acquittal." Crater accepted the money, but then failed to get Lesser off. He also failed to return the $5000—all of which rubbed Lesser's friends the wrong way. Determined to set things straight, they laid plans to get their money back (plus a little something extra) by kidnaping Crater and holding him for ransom. Manhattan hoodlum Harry Stein was put in charge of the operation.

Things moved slowly, and it wasn't until after more than a year had passed and Crater had been elevated to the bench, that Stein made his move. At about 8:00 P.M., August 6, 1930, after learning from one of Crater's showgirl friends that the judge would be having dinner that night at Billy Haas's, Stein pulled up in a borrowed taxicab to within a few feet of the restaurant and waited. Crouched on the floor in back were two imported thugs from Philadelphia. About an hour later the judge came out, said goodbye to his friends, and stepped into the cab. With a gun pointed at his head he was taken directly to an alley off 11th Avenue, where he was shifted into the rear of a panel truck that would take him to a prearranged hideout in Philadelphia.

After being held for two days in an upstairs flat in Philadelphia, Crater was moved to Clifton, New Jersey. By this time Stein and his friends had begun to lose some of their enthusiasm for the project. According to Stein, Crater himself was largely responsible for this. At every opportunity he would drum away at them about what an important man he was, etc., and how they had made a great mistake by presuming to play with the big boys. They were out of their league, in over their heads, etc., etc.

What bothered the kidnapers most was Crater's refusal to take them seriously. He kept laughing at them. For no reason at all. He kept laughing and calling them "poor saps." This was very unsettling, so much so that after a few days of it, Stein and his friends lost their nerve and decided to cut loose from the judge while they could still cover their tracks. Thus, the ransom plan was abandoned, and at about two o'clock on the afternoon of August 13, a week after his final taxi ride, Crater was shot twice in the back of the head. His body was taken to an abandoned paper mill outside of Clifton, where it was dumped into a large vat of hydrochloric acid. Sometime later, the mass of pulp that had once been New York Supreme Court Justice Joseph Force Crater was transported to a lonely spot a few miles away and poured into the Passaic River.

So ran what some newsmen chose to call the "death-bed confession" of Harry Stein. When the story broke in the *American Weekly* on September 23, 1956, it created a considerable stir among amateur Craterologists, some of whom, apparently be-dazzled by its fine detail, pounced on it and swallowed it whole. The police were less impressed, however. True, the judge could conceivably have ended up as pulp in the Passaic River, but there wasn't a shred of solid evidence to prove that he actually did. The Stein story was hearsay of the flimsiest sort—a convicted felon's report of what was supposedly told him by another convicted felon. For the police this was not good enough, especially since it was known that the story had been bought and paid for by the press. They preferred to believe, as they always had, that, volun-tary or otherwise, Crater's disappearance was in some way linked with his womanizing or, more likely, with a deep involvement in some sort of political corruption.

Beyond this point there has never been any generally shared official view as to what actually happened. The favorite theory is that Crater was done in by hired killers for reasons having to do with the Libby Hotel transaction. Possibly he had grown greedy and in seeking a bigger share of the take had pushed the wrong people too far. Or perhaps he had begun to show signs of losing his nerve in the face of the upcoming investigation into the Libby affair, and had thereby become a source of concern to certain of his business associates. It must be remembered that the Libby deal involved nearly three million dollars, and that at the time of Crater's disappearance payment was still dangling, pending the official inquiry. Over such a sum as this a person could get himself killed for any number of reasons, or for no reason at all.

Indeed, this might explain the sudden, unhappy demise of Vivian Gordon, the beautiful "flaming-haired madam of Manhattan," who was known to have many close friends among the gentry of the New York underworld. A passer-by discovered her garroted corpse in Van Cortlandt Park early one February morning in 1931, her crepe dress pulled up over her head, and an eight-foot length of clothesline noosed around her neck. On the following day she was to have appeared before the Libby investigating commission, where, it had been rumored, she intended to even a score with someone. Later the police found her diary. According to the newspapers it was "RED HOT." Among the names most frequently mentioned—Joe Crater.

The fate of Judge Crater has long since ceased to be the national guessing game it once was, and at New York City's Missing Persons Bureau the Crater case (file #13595), although still officially open, receives little attention these days. Here and there throughout the country a dwindling number of amateur sleuths continue to ponder the mystery and swap their newest theories by mail, but they don't pretend to be any closer to the answer than the New York police were four decades ago.

For years Stella kept the faith, stubbornly insisting that Joe was still alive. One day he would return to her with a logical explanation of what had happened, and she would believe him. Finally, though, the time arrived when even she was forced to admit that her husband was probably dead, murdered "because of a sinister something connected with politics." Still, she could never be sure, and until her death in 1969 at the age of 82 she went alone each year on the anniversary of the judge's disappearance to their favorite café in the Village. There she would sit in their regular booth and order a cocktail, with which she would toast her missing mate: "To you, Joe," she would whisper softly. "Good luck, wherever you are."

Long Trail A'Winding

My bonus lies over the ocean;
My bonus lies over the sea.
They gave all that dough to them Frenchmen,
But won't give my bonus to me.

BY EARLY 1932 there were nearly 700,000 jobless in Chicago and almost half again as many in New York City. In Cleveland 50 percent of the work force was idle, in Akron 60 percent, in Toledo 80 percent. In Donora, Pennsylvania, only 277 out of 13,900 still had jobs.

In Portland, Oregon, Walter W. Waters, husband and father of two, walked the streets alone at night. Thinking. Like almost everyone he knew, he was out of work and penniless, without really understanding why. Unlike the others, though, he had a plan. It was this plan that he thought about during his lonely night walks through the streets of downtown Portland.

Waters was thirty-four. He was a fine-looking man of medium size, with wavy hair and a slight swagger to his walk that gave him an air of self-assurance, if not arrogance. There was a special vitality about him that helped set him off from others, and because that vitality sometimes erupted into sudden displays of temper, those who knew him well nicknamed him "Hot." Men liked him and listened when he spoke.

He had been born in Oregon just before the turn of the century, and reared in nearby Idaho. In 1916, when he was barely eighteen, he joined the National Guard and served under Pershing along the Mexican border. Later he went to France where he saw plenty of front-line action. When he came home for discharge in 1919, he was a sergeant. He was also slightly shellshocked, and during the next two years spent several months in various hospitals "for which," he later pointed out, "the Government was not asked to pay a cent."

After the war, Waters couldn't seem to get started. He tried and failed at many jobs: auto mechanic, salesman, farmhand, and bakery helper. Some said he was shiftless. Perhaps he was. Certainly he moved about a great deal during those years, mainly in the Pacific Northwest. And then, one day in his late twenties, he surprised his friends by getting married and settling down to a steady job as a cannery worker in Portland. He did well. Within a couple of years he had been promoted to assistant superintendent, and had saved over a thousand dollars. But in December of 1930 the cannery closed down, and "Hot" Waters suddenly found himself a member of what writers and politicians were already beginning to call "the great army of the unemployed."

For a year he and his wife and two small daughters managed to get by on their savings. After that, they pawned or sold everything of value. By the spring of 1932 their furniture and most of their personal belongings were gone, and eviction was imminent. In debt, afraid, and often hungry, they somehow made do on the 75¢ a day they received from local relief. But with thousands of other families unemployed in the Portland area, and the number growing daily, public relief agencies and private charities were showing signs of drying up in the near future. What then?

The plan that had taken root in Waters' mind was simple enough. Back in 1924, Congress had decided that America's World War veterans were deserving of something more than they had received, and had voted an across-the-board bonus to the nation's 3½ million former doughboys. Issued in the form of paid-up insurance annuities, the bonus was originally scheduled to come due in 1945, but the ravages of the Depression caused Congress early in 1931 to authorize immediate borrowing on the policies, up to 50 percent of their face value. Not surprisingly, Hoover vetoed the bill, which he labeled "financially irresponsible" and "special class legislation." However, it passed easily over his veto, and the funds were at once made available to all who chose to apply. About two-thirds of the veterans so chose, and when after a few months the money had been spent, a clamor arose for the other 50 percent.

Perhaps sensing political advantage, Democratic Congressman Wright Patman of Texas proceeded to introduce a bill to that effect. Hoover was furious: "I am absolutely opposed to any such legislation," he declared. "I do not believe it can become law. . . . The first duty of every citizen is to build up and sustain the credit of the Government. Such an action would irretrievably undermine it." There was no question that the President would again use his veto if necessary, and this time it seemed likely it would be upheld.

This was roughly the situation when Waters' nocturnal musings began to come into focus. Why wouldn't it be a good idea, he wondered, for the veterans themselves to do something really out of the ordinary to help the Patman Bill along? Specifically, why not get a group of them together and march on Washington in order to dramatize their support for the measure? Waters remembered having read somewhere that during the depression of 1893 a number of unemployed men had converged on the Capital in an attempt to get government-sponsored jobs. Their effort hadn't turned out very well. But that was forty years ago. Times had changed. Besides, those earlier people had made mistakes that could be learned from. For one thing, there hadn't been enough of them.

In mid-March of 1932, Waters presented his plan in a speech before the Portland chapter of the National Veterans Association. In it he pointed out that in the Portland area alone there were nearly two thousand unemployed veterans—surely enough to provide a respectable nucleus for a march on Washington. Have such an outfit set out from Portland, and it would be bound to attract attention and encourage groups from other places to join in. Eventually Washington would be overrun by thousands of veterans. Once there, they could act as a giant lobby in support of the Patman Bill. Their presence would certainly be felt by Congress. Even President Hoover would have to take notice. This was the first speech Waters had ever given. He had written it out carefully and committed it to memory, word for word. When the time came to deliver it, however, he was so frozen with fright that he could hardly make himself heard. He didn't have to be told that he had made a fool of himself.

All right. He would try again. He rewrote his speech, practiced it in front of a mirror, and presented it before another veterans' group, and then a third and a fourth, gaining confidence and momentum with each outing. The banks and railroads and big insurance companies, he told his audiences, had received lavish amounts of government money that they didn't even have any claim to. Why? Because they had powerful lobbies working for them in Washington. Well, maybe the time had come for the veterans to do some lobbying of their own, not for any special favors like the big-money boys, but only for what was theirs by rights. The best way to do this would be to march on Washington and present their case in person before the powers-that-be.

Within a few weeks Waters' plan had caught on among a fair cross section of veterans in the Portland area. Finally, on a pleasant day in early May, three hundred or so of them, flags, banners, and spirits aloft, paraded down the main street of the city to the Union Pacific freight yards, where after presenting their leaders with proof of their military service and swearing to uphold the Constitution, they stretched out in the noonday sun to wait. A motley lot indeed: tall men and short; a few fat, but mainly thin. Some wore faded army pants or overalls and service caps; others appeared almost elegant by comparison in Panama hats and neckties. Most of them had knapsacks or suitcases, while a few others carried shopping bags. Some had bedrolls. The great majority of them were in their thirties or early forties, although there were more pushing fifty than might have been expected. This much they had in common, however: they were all veterans of the Great War (or claimed to be) and they were all out of work. They were also about to start off on a 3,000-mile trek with an aggregate cash-on-hand of $35, or about 10¢ a man. In downtown Portland the betting was seven to five they wouldn't make it beyond the city limits.

They almost didn't. At 11:45 that night, after a twelve-hour wait in the yards, the little army bestirred itself, doused its fires, and prepared to board the midnight freight to Chicago. A few minutes after 12:00 the train's giant headlight could be seen bearing down on them from a distance. The veterans picked up their belongings, waved goodbye to loved ones and well-wishers, and then watched as the freight roared by at fifty miles an hour. By and by, an important-looking man with a lantern came to tell them that the Union Pacific had no intention of transporting free-loaders, and warned them to leave the yards or face arrest for trespassing. A few complied, happy perhaps for an excuse to abandon the project and go home. But the rest refused to budge. At 6:00 the next evening, following a threat by the veterans to disrupt traffic in the yards, the company relented and allowed them to take over several just-emptied cattle cars. Three days later, hot, tired, and rancid, the veterans arrived at Pocatello, Idaho.

The 700-mile trip from Portland had been a horror. Food had been the least of their problems, since word of their coming had preceded them and handouts were plentiful at stops along the way. But conditions in the cars had been appalling. Too much congestion, together with the fetid smell of damp, dung-littered straw, had been bad enough, but to make matters worse some of the men, because they couldn't or wouldn't wait to go outside, had used the corners of the cars for toilets. Others, sickened by the stench or by cheap bootleg liquor, had vomited over the floor and themselves. Upon arriving in Pocatello, the men poured out of the yards in search of food, hot baths, and a little fun. Some took to panhandling. A few others were arrested for drunkenness, lewdness, and petty theft.

Waters was disgusted. They had come less than a quarter of the way to Washington, and already the bonus marchers had degenerated into a dirty, ill-behaved mob. Where was the discipline? Before setting out from Portland the men had elected a large staff of officers (including Waters himself, who had declined to serve), but it soon became apparent that anything resembling effective leadership was missing. At Pocatello, Waters called the men together, gave them a stern talking-to, and then threatened to leave for home: "If we can't go as decent citizens," he declared, "then I don't want to go at all. This way we'll only wind up in some western jail." The men agreed and elected him supreme commander of the bonus army.

Waters accepted, but only on his own terms, which were: "I am the boss, and whatever I say goes. When you don't want me as your leader any longer, you can vote me out, but until then I expect to have my orders obeyed." Again the men agreed, some of them perhaps because they didn't believe he meant what he said. But he did. The new commander's first act was to set up a corps of military police composed of the burliest men he could find. His next move was to order the veterans to find brooms and buckets and clean out their cars. And then, while the momentum was still with him, came what would become known as "Holy" Waters' three commandments: "As long as I am your commander there will be no liquor, no panhandling, and no radical talk."

After that, things went more smoothly. At Cheyenne 5000 people turned out to greet the bonus marchers and provide them with hot food, after which the veterans staged a thank-you parade through town and then continued eastward in fourteen box cars made available to them by the Northern Pacific. At stops along the way they found that local American Legion and Veterans of Foreign Wars posts had set up soup kitchens in anticipation of their coming. Civic groups supplied them with plenty of hot coffee, and housewives brought fresh pies and donuts. At rural sidings farmers pulled up in Model T's and horse-drawn buggies, loaded with eggs and butter and cans of milk.

Three days out of Cheyenne they arrived amidst cheering crowds at Council Bluffs, Iowa, where they paused to shower and shave at the Salvation Army Rescue Mission and the YMCA before setting out again, this time on the friendly Wabash line. The farther east they traveled, the better and easier things seemed to get. But then in East St. Louis, Illinois, only 700 miles away from their destination, they hit a snag when the Baltimore and Ohio announced that under no conditions would the bonus marchers be permitted to ride B&O freights. The veterans saw things differently, however:

> We're gonna ride the B&O.
> The Good Lord Jesus told us so.

As thousands of spectators looked on, Waters and his men refused to budge from the B&O yards. The company countered with threats and petty harassment, while the governor sent in six National Guard units to keep the veterans from getting out of line. For three days both sides stood firm and glowered at one another as tensions and the likelihood of violence mounted. Finally, on the fourth day, the City Fathers ended the impasse by offering to transport the veterans across the state in private vehicles. Thus, the little army from Oregon was soon moving eastward again across the prairie country of southern Illinois in fifteen automobiles and seven trucks:

> We're on our way from Oregon
> To get some dough from Washington.

The confrontation at East St. Louis brought the bonus marchers to national notice. For the first time the wire services,

their attention focused mainly these days on the Lindbergh kidnaping and Amelia Earhart's solo flight across the Atlantic, gave
coverage to what would develop into one of the great human-
interest stories of the Depression decade—the quixotic attempt of
a ragbag army of unemployed veterans to pressure the United
States Government into paying them the rest of their bonus, thir-
teen years ahead of time. Several of the big eastern papers carried
a front-page picture, showing a hundred or so scruffy-looking men
in the East St. Louis yards, crowded together under a large banner:

BONUS MARCH
ON TO WASHINGTON

All this, of course, was made to order for the bonus marchers.
Publicity was what they needed most if their idea were to catch on,
and the sooner the better. Within a few days, dozens of other veterans groups had set out from widely scattered parts of the country to converge on Washington.

Getting the rest of the way was easy for Waters and his men.
Taking their cue from East St. Louis, authorities in Indiana, Ohio,
the West Virginia panhandle, and Pennsylvania piled the bonus
marchers into trucks (provided for the most part by the National
Guard) and hustled them across-state before they could cause any
trouble or embarrassment. "Look," said Pennsylvania's Governor
Pinchot to an aide after providing the veterans with a hearty meal
of mulligan stew: "I want those men out of the State in five hours."

On Saturday evening, May 28, seventeen days after setting
out from Portland, the main body of bonus marchers arrived at
Cumberland, Maryland. Here, a hundred miles from Washington as
the crow flies, they were fed and bedded down at a local roller
rink by order of Governor Ritchie, who then sent off a telegram
to General Glassford, chief of the District of Columbia Police:

> They will leave tomorrow—Sunday morning—at seven o'clock, and
> should reach the District line at Wisconsin Avenue sometime between
> one and two o'clock tomorrow afternoon. They number about 300.
> Good luck and best wishes.

By this time 1200 veterans from nearby states had already arrived in Washington, and Glassford was not particularly anxious to have more:

> Request no transportation facilities under your control be utilized to transport veterans toward District of Columbia unless you provide transportation to receive them at District line 48 hours after their arrival here and veterans themselves agree not to stay longer.

"I know of nothing I can do to discourage their visit to Washington," the governor replied, and in the early afternoon of the following day his trucks dumped Waters and his men at the District line. There they were officially welcomed to Washington by General Glassford, who notified them that they must leave within forty-eight hours. But none of the men took him seriously, least of all Waters. They hadn't come 3000 miles to be rousted after two days—or twenty-two. They had come for their bonus, and they intended to stick around until they got it.

On the evening of the following day the Portland veterans, joined by hundreds of other recently arrived bonus marchers, made their formal debut in the nation's capital as participants in the traditional Memorial Day parade. The weather was balmy, and the parade, which was held at nightfall down Constitution Avenue, attracted a large crowd. At the head of the column came the regulars from Ft. Myers across the river, handsomely astride their cavalry mounts or sitting stiffly upright on artillery caissons with their arms folded across their chests. After the regulars came several units of the National Guard, and then a half-dozen or so cadet corps, followed by several American Legion and Veterans of Foreign Wars contingents, looking very grand. Dozens of bands blared out "The Stars and Stripes Forever," "The Washington Post March," and "The Thunderer." People cheered.

And then, toward the end of the long column, marching in close formation behind a large American flag, came the bonus marchers. Gaunt, slouching, no-longer-young men, the spring now gone from their step, many of them threadbare (but all clean-shaven), some with medals on their chests, some missing limbs or eyes—here were "the boys," the Yankee Doodle Dandies for whom, fifteen years before, nothing had been too good. At first sight of them the crowd cheered and applauded, but as they drew nearer the mood of the spectators changed and they became strangely silent. From his vantage point near the front of the crowd, veteran reporter Floyd Gibbons, he of the white eye patch and the rapid-fire spiel, saw it all and winced. "My God," he exclaimed, "how the mighty have fallen!"

During the following week, better than five thousand more veterans arrived in Washington. Fruit pickers from Florida, coal miners from Pennsylvania, mountaineers from Tennessee, clerks from New York City, and factory workers from Ohio and Michigan—balding men, down-at-the-heels men, with rotting teeth and signs strapped to their backs, like: "Suppose the Kaiser had won!!" and "Remember 1917-18." They came by train and truck and rickety old automobiles. Two arrived by plane and a few by foot. Several brought their wives and children with them.

Many, probably most, had come for the bonus. For some, however, the bonus was only an excuse. Driven by loneliness or despair, they had come in search of the camaraderie and group security of the old days when, despite the war (or perhaps because of it) life had seemed happier and easier to cope with. Others, not many, had come to stir up trouble and thereby hasten the day when the great American proletariat would rise up and smite their oppressors. Whatever else may have prompted the marchers, nearly all had felt the urge to get away from home (if they still had one), where they had grown ashamed of hanging around the house while their womenfolk took in washing, and relatives dropped by on Sunday after church with handouts. Now these tormented frayed men were a common sight on the streets of the capital. Floyd Gibbons saw them as "ghosts of a forgotten past." Someone else called them the Bonus Expeditionary Force, and the name stuck.

From the very outset it was apparent that Washingtonians had mixed feelings about their uninvited guests. It was hard not to feel sorry for them. Here were several thousand down-on-their-luck fellow Americans, and war veterans at that, whom the awful conditions of the times had reduced to little more than beggars. They were deserving of something better. On Capitol Hill politicians of both parties said as much, and the people of Washington agreed.

At the same time it was no secret that their presence in the city was resented, both by officialdom and a sizable cross section of the people at large. At best they would be a nuisance and an embarrassment, and probably a considerable expense as well at a time when money in Washington, as elsewhere, was extremely hard to come by. In addition, they could also create problems of disease and hooliganism and (to be frank) unsightliness, that could have all kinds of unpleasant results. And, of course, the possibility of violence against the government could not be ruled out. This was not considered very likely to happen, but just to be on the safe side, in early June contingents of the Capitol and White House police began holding daily riot drills, and rumor had it that thousands of sandbags were being brought into the city by night and stacked in the basements of public buildings on Pennsylvania and Constitution Avenues. On his occasional rides through the city, President Hoover saw bonus marchers everywhere he looked, and was not pleased. "Their continued presence here will have a depressing effect on Wall Street," he declared.

And what business did these people have in Washington anyway? No one could deny their need, but no one could deny either that they had already been given far more than their share of special favors from the government. In fact, throughout the entire history of the Republic no other group had even come close to getting such generous (some would say lavish) treatment from Washington as the veterans of the Great War. By the time the Bonus Expeditionary Force invaded the capital in the late spring of 1932, World War veterans and their families had received some seven billion dollars from the Federal Government—roughly $2000 per man. Indeed, during the past ten fiscal years the government had paid out in veterans' benefits more than half the total national income. Small wonder that many Americans had begun to cry RACKET and were openly denouncing the veterans and their friends in Congress for plundering the public treasury.

But even if this hadn't been so, even if the veterans had been as shamefully neglected as many of them seemed to think, did this give them the right to do what they were doing? What was involved here was a barefaced attempt to bully the United States Government, and to many people in Washington and elsewhere this seemed downright un-American. The press was particularly outspoken on the subject. With few exceptions, the most notable being the Hearst chain, the nation's newspapers and magazines had little good to say about the bonus marchers and what they were up to. "A disgrace to the name of veteran," complained the *Sacramento Bee*. "A malicious raid," grumbled the *Boston Herald*. "This Country has not yet sunk to the level of mob rule," the Springfield (Ill.) *Union* declared angrily. "Outrageous!" "Unthinkable!" As the Omaha *World-Herald* saw it: "If this sort of thing is permitted to go unchecked, then free government is dead."

And yet, was it really fair to place the blame entirely on the bonus marchers? Wasn't it a fact, asked the *Washington Post*, that these desperate and bewildered men were little more than pawns being callously manipulated by others? Although it was obvious that there was virtually no hope whatever of the veterans' getting the rest of their bonus, scheming politicians of both parties, with an eye to the autumn elections, had deliberately egged them on. And, of course, the results were more or less what one might have expected. "After all," as one editorial commented, "if you dangle a ready sum of money before any class of men, you give them the incentive to organize to obtain it." Especially if they're down and out.

Pawns or not, welcome or not, the legions of the BEF kept pouring into Washington during early June. "It is too bad," remarked Democratic Speaker of the House John Garner. "There isn't a chance for the bonus. If the bill passes, it will be vetoed. It can't get a two-thirds vote to pass over a veto. I never heard of a more useless trip than this being made to Washington." But still they came. By the middle of the month, when the Republican Convention met in Chicago to nominate Hoover for a second term, the BEF had grown to 15,000, with more on the way.

The problem of what to do about this indigent army was left almost entirely up to General Pelham Glassford of the District police. There could hardly have been a better man for the job. Personally Glassford was opposed to payment of the bonus, and although he didn't say so at the time, the entire idea of the bonus march was repugnant to him. However, as a former army man himself he had a special sympathy for the veterans that would temper his dealings with them. He was not a soft man, but he was fair and honest, and his forthright treatment of the bonus marchers did much to win their confidence and respect— even affection. Presented with a difficult and potentially explosive situation, he responded with such uncommon patience, good humor, and finesse, that, if left to his own devices, he might well have succeeded in averting the tragedy that was to follow.

In many ways Pelham Glassford was a remarkable man, and was so recognized by all who knew him well. His first love was painting. As a boy he had gone to art school, but being the son of a regular army officer, he eventually entered West Point, class of

1904, where his classmates called him "Happy." In France in
1918, while serving as the youngest line general in the American
Expeditionary Force, he was wounded and decorated for gallantry.
Afterwards, he returned to complete his military career in the un-
exciting, undernourished peacetime army. During those dull garri-
son years of the 1920s, Glassford often allowed his annual leave to
accumulate until he had several weeks due him, and then, shedding
his uniform, he would set out alone on his motorcycle for parts
unknown. Once he crossed the entire country, pausing here and
there to work at odd jobs, including brief stints as an electrician,
a circus barker, and legman for the *San Francisco Examiner.* And
all the while he painted. Rather well too.

As soon as he had completed his thirty years' service, he retired from the army and headed for the Arizona desert to paint.
Within a year or so, however, he was offered the job of police
superintendent for the District of Columbia, and, at the urging of
his friends, took it, despite his own misgivings. "What do I know
about police work," he protested, "except that I've been arrested
twice: once for driving through a red light and once for speeding
on my motorcycle." Still the idea of a new career, especially this
career, had a certain appeal for him. "There should be lots of fun
and excitement," he told his wife. In Washington he and his family
moved into a huge old house in Georgetown. On the top floor
Glassford set up his art studio. Directly below was his son's carpen-
ter shop. Part of the first floor was taken up by a museum of family memorabilia. Visitors found the place "very interesting."
Friends called it "The Borneo Embassy."

At the time of the bonus invasion Glassford was new on the
job. He was in his late forties. Unusually tall (he stood over 6' 3"),
he was an erect, trim man of striking appearance, the sort of person that passers-by turn to stare at on the street. His voice and
manner were subdued, but there was an air of authority about
him that left no doubt that he was accustomed to commanding
others, and himself. Before beginning his new job he swore off
drinking, because as a police officer it would be unfitting for him
to engage in an illegal practice. "Besides," he said, "I never cared
much for the stuff anyway."

When the bonus marchers started streaming into Washington
in the late spring of 1932, the District Board of Commissioners did
what practiced politicians anywhere would have done in the face
of such an unpromising situation—they passed the buck. And

Superintendent Glassford got it. This was a police matter, Glassford was told, and it was up to him to handle it. Although he didn't entirely agree, Glassford accepted full responsibility and proceeded to deal with the veterans as best he could. At times, when the situation threatened to get out of hand, he sought firm orders from the commissioners, but none were forthcoming. In fact, not until nearly two months had passed did the commissioners officially intervene—and then with disastrous results. They were seldom slow to offer Glassford advice and criticism, however:

"Why not turn them over to the Salvation Army?"

"Fifteen thousand men?"

"Or maybe some other charitable organization. Have you tried the YMCA?"

Glassford's patience was remarkably long, but it was not infinite. "Look," he finally told the commissioners at the end of an especially trying session with them, "I have listened to a thousand different suggestions on this subject. So far the responsibility has rested entirely on me. I am taking no suggestions from anyone. You are my superior officers. I am ready to obey your written orders, but not your suggestions. Is that clear?"

Glassford's handling of the bonus crisis was simple, pragmatic, and compassionate. First he sent telegrams to the governors of the forty-eight states and to leaders of the local American Legion and VFW posts, asking them to discourage veterans in their area from joining the BEF. For the most part the Legion and the VFW cooperated. The governors did not. At the same time he did what he could to speed up Congressional consideration of the bonus bill, reasoning (incorrectly, as it turned out) that, pass or fail, once the bill had been acted on, the veterans would leave. His efforts took him on several occasions to the Capitol, where he was not without friends, and eventually to the White House to ask the aid of the Administration in hastening action on the bill.

"You are embarrassing the President," he was told by Hoover's secretary. "You shouldn't have told the press why you were here."

"What should I have told them?"

"Well, you could have told them you were here for something else—say, on personal business."

"When I tell them anything I will tell them the truth."

Meanwhile, as part of his strategy (and his nature) Glassford did what he could to make the veterans' stay in Washington as comfortable as possible. Soon forgotten was the forty-eight-hour ultimatum he had delivered to Waters and the other early arrivals. That was obviously no way to deal with hungry, frustrated men. "Fellow veterans and comrades, I shall do everything I can to help you," he told a group of them at an informal meeting in late May. "I can't tell you how much in sympathy I am with you and all others who are unemployed." Still, he wished for their own sake and everyone else's that they hadn't come, and he offered a day's rations and free transportation out of the District to anyone who would agree to leave and not come back. There were no takers. "Of course," the general concluded, "the time may come when I'll have no choice but to move you on. But until then let's be friends."

With the permission of the Federal Government and the District Commissioners, Glassford found billets for many of the early arrivals in several abandoned public buildings, located mainly off lower Pennsylvania Avenue not far from the Capitol. Most of these buildings dated back to the days of President Grant or before and were scheduled for demolition in the near future. Although structurally sound, they were little more than hollow shells, long since cut off from water and electricity and stripped of everything of any value or utility. Plaster hung in shreds from the walls and ceilings, and those windows that had not been boarded up were fringed with jagged pieces of shattered glass. In some of the buildings large sections of the exterior walls were missing.

Into these crumbling relics several hundred veterans swarmed during the final days of May, 1932, and when there was no room left inside, hundreds of others gathered debris from the ruins and erected makeshift shelters on the grounds nearby. None of this was very elegant, but contrasted to most of the other twenty-three billets that would ultimately spring up in and about the city, conditions here were almost lavish. It was in one of these abandoned buildings on lower Pennsylvania Avenue that the final trouble would erupt in late July.

Across the Anacostia River from the city proper lay a broad, level stretch of poorly drained land called Anacostia Flats, after an Indian tribe that used to frequent the place in the old days. The property of the District Park Commission, which hoped one day to fill in the area and make it into a children's playground, this crescent-shaped spread of mud and potholes was about as unsightly and generally uninviting a spot as could be found anywhere in the

District. Fronting on the oil-slicked river and reaching back less than a quarter mile to a poplar-rimmed bluff, the Flats covered at the most ten acres, all brown, barren, and alive with mosquitoes. At night the river fog descended upon the place like a damp shroud.

Here the BEF set up its main camp, and onto this soggy wasteland the bonus marchers flocked by the thousands until, toward the end of June, the area could hold no more and was declared closed to all newcomers. At that time there were probably close to 10,000 veterans at Anacostia, or about half the total strength of the BEF at its mightiest*. In addition there were 800 women and children. This meant that the population density at Anacostia, which came to be called Camp Marks after a local benefactor, was in excess of 1000 per acre—more than three times the maximum level prescribed by the United States Army for its military garrisons.

Whatever else might be said of it (and a lot was, mostly bad), Camp Marks was a marvel of improvisation. Its architecture and decor were determined mainly by the nature of the building materials available. Right next to the Flats was a large public dump, and although this tended to cause a serious rat problem for the new community, it also provided an almost limitless supply of such handy items as egg crates, automobile fenders, garbage cans, bedsprings, burlap bags, etc.—all of which the men put to good use. It was a common sight to see huts and lean-to's, some of them not much bigger than chicken coops, with roofs of corrugated iron or peeling plywood, supported by a stove pipe or axle or the rusty remains of a discarded baby carriage. The rear of one shack near the river was propped up by a child's folding blackboard on which someone had scrawled: "Stay till they pay!"

Here and there amidst the shanties could be seen a scattering of pup tents, perhaps as many as five hundred, that General Glassford had procured on loan from the army. In addition, he had somehow managed to get enough lumber to construct two large barracks-type buildings, in which the various administrative offices

---

*Since records are incomplete, the actual size of the BEF can only be guessed at. Waters claimed that at its peak strength it reached nearly 23,000. He also estimated that the total number of veterans who at one time or another attached themselves to the BEF was somewhere between 60,000 and 80,000. Glassford's figures were considerably lower. He doubted, for instance, that there were ever more than 17,000 bonus marchers in the capital at any given time. A peak figure of 20,000 seems about right, however.

of the BEF came to be housed, along with a modest medical center that the general kept stocked with iodine, aspirin, salt pills, and a few bandages left over from the Great War. Nearby was a large Salvation Army tent, supplied with around two hundred books and magazines, and a few makeshift writing tables with pencils and paper. Out front a hand-printed sign read: "Jesus Saves." A few feet away in front of one of the pup tents another sign said: "So does Hoover."

Although finding a place for the nearly 20,000 bonus marchers was hard enough, keeping them fed was even more so. Here again Glassford did his best, by persuading the regular army and the National Guard to lend mobile mess kitchens to the various camps. For the first two weeks the army also provided short rations for most of the veterans at the rate of two 3¢ meals a day per man. After that, however, the problem of finding food and the other necessities for survival would have to be taken care of by the veterans themselves, with the help of friends and sympathizers.

Several of the camps staged fund-raising affairs, often with considerable success. A baseball game between the BEF and Glassford's police did well when the hat was passed, and an all-BEF boxing exhibition netted nearly $3000, enough to provide each of the bonus marchers with one good meal or two skimpy ones. Donations from organizations, such as the Salvation Army and the YMCA also helped, but mainly it was the thousands of individual donors in various parts of the country and all walks of life who kept the veterans eating. An unemployed plumber in Richmond sent a couple of boxes of spaghetti. Someone in San Francisco mailed in a ten-dollar bill. A retired manufacturer in upstate New York had 1500 pounds of beef flown in. At an especially critical moment in early July, when the veterans' cupboard was all but bare, a group of well-wishers in New Jersey sent down three trucks loaded with a ton of meat, 1100 pounds of coffee, 2700 loaves of bread, and 18 tons of potatoes. And from the Shrine of the Little Flower in Royal Oak, Michigan, came a cash contribution of $5000 from the radio priest, Father Charles Coughlin, along with a friendly bit of advice: "Keep the radicals out."

Despite all this, however, food remained the vets' biggest problem. Throughout those long weeks in Washington there was seldom enough of it, and what there was tended to be coarse, unappetizing, and redundant. The most common (it would be wrong to say favorite) dish was mulligan stew, which offered the advantages of being simple to prepare and adaptable to whatever ingredients happened to be available. "Water and anything that can be boiled in it," was the way one veteran described it. Beans were also much in evidence, as were coffee, bread, and, of course, potatoes, which in those days sold for as little as 75¢ a barrel.

Periodically the camps were inspected by the District's chief health officer who, after completing his rounds, would shake his head in disbelief. "The worst health conditions in the history of the District," he declared publicly on June 9 (when the worst was yet to come), and urged that the camps be evacuated at once. The District Commissioners so directed Superintendent Glassford, but then churlishly changed their minds when Glassford refused to comply without written orders.

"You understand," warned one of the commissioners, "that if you continue this way, the President may order you summarily removed."

"Under the circumstances such an action would be of great value to me," Glassford replied.

Of all the BEF billets the worst by far was Camp Marks at Anacostia, where sanitary conditions were described by a health official as "primitive in the extreme." Slit trenches, which doubled as latrines and garbage pits, were often too close to the feeding areas, and sometimes the dirt (or lime, when available) that was used to cover the refuse in the trenches was so carelessly spread that particles of swill and human excrement protruded, to the delight of Anacostia's rat population and the festering hordes of flies that plagued the area. With inadequate storage facilities and inexperienced mess attendants, food sometimes became putrid or contaminated long before it reached the veterans' stomachs. Cooking utensils were hard to keep free of grease because of a chronic shortage of soap and hot water. Cockroaches and other types of vermin were everywhere.

The worst part of the problem was the men themselves. Even among those who cared about such things (and many didn't), personal cleanliness was often neglected. At first the men bathed and did their laundry in the Anacostia River, which at that point was little more than an open sewer, but this practice was soon abandoned when several hundred of them broke out with boils and rashes. In time Glassford was able to have two fire hoses run into the camp from a distant hydrant, and from these, extensions were flared out in all directions to provide water for washtubs and makeshift showers—one for every 700 men. This meant that if a man were willing to wait long enough for his turn at the faucet, he might manage to wash himself and his socks once every week or ten days. Most of the men were crawling with lice. They were also underfed, undersheltered, and overcrowded—in short, excellent prospects for any disease or infection that happened along.

By the end of June, Washington's health officials were publicly prophesying disaster. "Powderkeg," "critical situation," "another Chickamauga in the making," came the reports from inspectors sent out to the various camps. "Rats, lice, flies, and filth! It will be a miracle, A MIRACLE, if there's no epidemic," warned one official after visiting Anacostia. But miracles can happen—and in this instance did—for, despite the long odds against it, the bonus marchers had a surprisingly fine health record. In fact, far from being ravaged by epidemic, they escaped virtually untouched by serious sickness of any kind. Of course, dysentery and other intestinal disorders were fairly common, as were trench mouth, clap, colds, and skin infections, often caused by scratching lice or mosquito bites. But those ancient scourges of camp life, typhoid and typhus, failed to put in an appearance, probably because most of the men still retained some immunity from their army inoculations of fifteen years earlier. Nor was there a single case of influenza (the horror of 1918) or diptheria reported from any of the camps. In other words, Waters was right when he kept insisting that in spite of all hardships and inadequacies, the BEF had no real health problems. But so were those who said that the camps constituted a major health hazard and ought to be destroyed.

Everyday life in the BEF billets was not much different from what it was in those hundreds of other shanty towns that had sprung up in and about most American cities during the early years of the Depression. On the whole, the bonus marchers probably represented a somewhat higher type of tenant, and in some respects, such as age and ethnic origin (the BEF was heavily Anglo-Saxon), were more homogeneous. Certainly there was a greater spirit of cohesion and purpose among them, because of the dazzling two-billion-dollar prize they fancied they saw dangling before them. Still, like their counterparts in Houston and San Francisco and Wilkes-Barre, they were lonely, discouraged, frightened men who puttered, played cards, smoked, slept, complained, scratched, and swapped worn-out stories while waiting for their next meal, whenever that might be. And beyond that, more of the same.

Sometimes, on sunny days, they played ball, wrestled, and frol-
icked like the young pups they had been fifteen years before. But
not for long, for their wind was shorter nowadays and their stomachs emptier.

At Anacostia the scene was more varied than at the other,
smaller billets. But the tone of life was no different. As elsewhere,
boredom and apprehension hung like a pall over the place. Spirits
seldom soared. Yet, there was no indication of surrender. Talking
and acting for all the world as if they really meant to "Stay Till
1945" if they had to, the men of Camp Marks, and the scattering
of wives and children among them, hung on and made do. "We're
not budging," read a sign in front of one of the shacks. "The
Kaiser tried for eighteen months and couldn't do it."

Here on a day in late June a veteran from Baltimore, wearing
pants made out of an oilcloth advertisement for hot dogs, could
be seen patching the roof of his shanty, not far from the Salvation
Army tent. Next door, someone was using a rock to straighten
nails he had found in the dump. A few feet beyond, a half-dozen
men in BVD tops sat hunched around a gramophone listening to
"Cohen on the Telephone," while not far away, Mrs. Clarence
Belt, lately of Philadelphia, watched over her nine children and
wondered about her tenth, due that October. By the edge of the
dump another woman swept out the cab of the derelict Oldsmobile
sedan where she lived with her husband and three young children.
Directly behind in a small pen at the foot of the bluff was the
camp's mascot, a pig named "Andy Mellon" after President
Hoover's multimillionaire secretary of the treasury, who, after
having paid a personal income tax of $650,000 the year before,
had come out foursquare against the bonus. Next to that, on a
barren little strip of ground, stood a dozen or more white crosses
marked with RIPs and the names of unfriendly congressmen and,
of course, Hoover and Mellon, the archvillains of the bonus drama:

> Oh, Mellon pulled the whistle, boys,
> And Hoover rang the bell.
> Wall Street gave the signal,
> And the Country went to hell.

Close to the center of the camp was a rude wooden platform
that had been pieced together out of scrap lumber. Here, at practically any time of day, every day, the camp orators shouted out

their complaints and panaceas, sometimes at audiences of no more than half a dozen:

> Now, here's a plant that can turn out everything that every man, woman, and child in this country needs, from potatoes to washing machines, and it's broken down because it can't give the fellow who does the work enough money to buy what he needs with. Give us the money and we'll buy their bread and their corn and beans and their electric ice boxes and their washing machines and their radios. We ain't holding out because we don't want them things. We can't get a job to make enough money to buy them—that's all.

Every once in a while an outside speaker would show up, usually a congressman or some other politician. For such special appearances a good-sized crowd was generally on hand to be flattered, cajoled, exhorted, and reassured that "you buddies have a lot of good friends on your side."

"You'll get your bonus if I have anything to say about it." (Wild cheering!)

"I'm the only Congressman from Connecticut to support the bonus." (More cheering.)

In another part of the camp, Joe Angelo lay buried in a wooden box four feet underground. A tube ran down into his coffin to provide him with air and soup and to permit the curious to peek down and talk with him for a penny apiece. Eventually the police broke up the act, and Joe surfaced—but too late: his partner had disappeared with the take. Nearby, a friendly fellow from one of the New Jersey outfits, posing as a dentist and using stolen instruments, repaired and extracted his buddies' teeth free of charge. Before long, he too would disappear, taking with him five hundred dollars' worth of gold fillings. Down near the river someone with a harmonica kept struggling with "Back Home Again in Indiana."

In charge of this strange menagerie that called itself the BEF was Walter "Hot" Waters, who soon after arriving in Washington had taken to carrying a swagger stick and wearing knee-length leather boots with his army breeches. There are several versions of how he got to be boss. Some have it that he was duly elected by the men. Others say he was appointed by the heads of the various state units, and still others claim that, supported by goons from his Oregon contingent, he simply assumed command. No matter. He was the nearest thing to a boss the bonus marchers had, and most of the men seemed to be willing to accept him as such. "He had a way about him," one of his lieutenants later recalled.

He was a likable fellow, sort of boyish-looking, but you could tell he meant business. He seemed to have a lot of confidence and pride in himself, when the rest of us were having a hard time keeping our spirits up. I remember how neat he always looked. He kept himself shaved and his clothes were clean and even had a press in them. And he wore a pair of knee-boots that shined like a nigger's ass. We used to wonder how it was that in all that mud and shit he always looked like he just stepped out of a bandbox. There was talk he was getting money from Mussolini.

As commandant of the BEF, Waters proved to be something of a martinet: "I'll do what I want whether you like it or not, and those that don't can get the hell out. I'm going to be hard-boiled." With his corps of hand-picked military police standing ready, and his bodyguard, ex-prizefighter Mickey Dolan, seldom more than ten feet from his side, he kept a tight rein on the men, at Anacostia and elsewhere. Once, acting on a report from one of his intelligence agents (he had more than three hundred of them), he visited a newly arrived Chicago contingent at one of the downtown encampments and made its leaders take down a sign that read: "We Demand Our Bonus!" "You don't make demands on the United States Government," Waters declared.

Sometimes he was known to resort to kangaroo courts in dealing with troublemakers, such as drunkards and brawlers, who posed a threat to camp discipline or were giving the BEF a bad name on the outside. A few stripes across the bare back with a leather belt was the ordinary punishment for first and second offenses, and for any further mischief, expulsion. For lesser infractions, such as staying out after taps or too much whoring around, a word of caution or perhaps a little unofficial roughing-up by Waters' MPs usually sufficed. None of this was legal, of course, but it worked. "I've never seen a more orderly band of men," remarked Glassford, who was good at looking the other way and letting Waters handle his people pretty much as he saw fit.

From the first, Glassford and Waters got along well together. Waters called Glassford "my friendly enemy"; Glassford called Waters "an outstanding leader of men." Whenever possible in his dealings with the bonus marchers, the police superintendent worked through and with Waters and helped him in any way he could. He even agreed to serve as BEF treasurer, not a very demanding job, given the state of the BEF's finances, and to oversee purchasing and supply. At Waters' request Glassford also assigned some of his own men to assist in the impossible attempt to register and keep track of the tens of thousands of men, women, and children who attached themselves, permanently or in passing, to the BEF during its two months in Washington:

> Arrived this morning [read a typical entry in the daily register] the O'Brien family with six children, all redheaded and mean as hell.

And another, not so typical:

> Born today [June 29] a baby boy. 7 lbs. 2 oz. to Mrs. Ruby Pippenbrink of Jacksonville. The first bonus baby.

Or:

> To Commander Waters, my husband John is in your army somewhere. Please send him home immediately, for he is needed here and has no business traipsing around the country. If you don't send him home I'll report you to President Hoover.

Some of the men resented Glassford's intrusions into BEF affairs. After all, he was not only an outsider, but a cop as well and therefore the object of considerable suspicion. But most of the veterans seemed to appreciate his assistance, and none more so than Waters himself who needed all the help he could get. The job he had to do was a staggering one. It would have been hard enough just keeping his rag-tail army fed, bedded down, and out of trouble. But there was also the matter of getting the bonus, which was what they had come to Washington for in the first place. On the whole, Waters did remarkably well, given the meager resources he had to work with. That he failed in the end was no fault of his.

His task was not made any easier by the Communists, who were forever doing their best to cause trouble. Their leader was John Pace, an ex-serviceman from Detroit, who had joined the

Party soon after his contracting business had gone bankrupt in 1931. According to Pace's testimony before a Congressional committee several years later, Moscow had immediately taken an active interest in the bonus march, and had scolded Earl Browder, the Party's American boss, for not having thought of the idea himself. Quick to make amends, Browder sent out a call to local cells throughout the country, and eventually a couple hundred or so of the faithful, a goodly number of them nonveterans, flocked to Washington:

> I was ordered by my Red superiors to provoke riots [Pace reported]. I was told to use every trick to bring about bloodshed in the hopes that President Hoover would be forced to call out the army. The communists didn't care how many veterans were killed. I was told that Moscow had ordered riots and bloodshed in the hopes that this might set off the revolution.

They were not made to feel very welcome by the BEF. In fact, the first few Communist arrivals were so badly treated by Waters' men that Glassford became concerned for their safety. For this reason, and because he wanted to keep a close watch on them, he provided the Red contingents with their own billeting area at 13th and B Streets, Southwest. But this was not what the Communists had in mind. Soon, singly and in small groups, they began infiltrating the various camps, where they harangued, distributed incendiary literature, and did whatever else they could to hasten the day of the classless society.

But the men of the BEF were simply not fit material for revolution. For the most part they were old-line Americans from the nation's farms and towns and smaller cities, where traditional American values were deeply rooted and Communist activity and influence virtually nonexistent. Remarked Waters: "To them Karl Marx is one of the Marx brothers—the know-it-all one with the moustache." Pushing middle age, set in their ways, and proudly patriotic, these men were not interested in trying new systems. What they wanted was to see the old one start working again, and, despite their despondency, most of them had no doubt that one day it would. "You'd be pretty hard put to find a Red around here," said one of the veterans. And then he laughed, exposing teeth that had rotted away to the stubs. "We may not look it, but we're really a bunch of capitalists. If you don't believe me, just dangle a dollar bill in front of any one of us."

As for actual, real-life Communists, most of the men had never seen one before, but they knew that they were dirty, un-American, and not to be trusted. Therefore, whenever they found one, they proceeded to beat him up and drive him out of camp. Occasionally Waters himself would catch one trying to stir up trouble and bring him to trial before the BEF staff. The result: fifteen lashes and expulsion. When Pace complained to Glassford, the superintendent lectured Waters on the subject, but not very forcefully. "I left the Red situation practically in the hands of the vets," Glassford later commented. "They handled it well too."

The Communists were not easily discouraged, however. Having been ousted from the camps, they circulated about the city in groups of twenty or so, pausing here and there to give out literature and denounce the capitalist system to anyone who happened within range. Wherever they stopped they planted the American flag, and beside it a white banner that showed a workingman, a sailor, and a legless Negro soldier, arm in arm. In keeping with their main purpose, about fifty of them, led by Pace himself, began picketing the White House, with the hope of provoking violent reaction from the police.

Of course, all this made for good reading in the reports sent to Moscow. But in actual fact the Communists, for all their orneriness accomplished nothing of importance—except possibly an improvement in conditions for the rest of the bonus marchers. Looking back on it at a later time, Glassford thought that the presence of Communist agitators on the streets made Washingtonians more appreciative of the essentially conservative nature of the BEF and consequently more generous in their donations to it. Especially the merchants. Or, as one of Waters' aides put it: "The Communists meant meat in our stew. Without them we could of damn well starved."

In the early afternoon of Tuesday, June 14, Congressman Edward Eslick of Tennessee, a friend of the BEF, stood beside his desk on the floor of the House of Representatives, arguing for passage of the bonus bill: "Mr. Chairman," he said, "I want to divert from the sordid. We hear nothing but dollars here. I want to go from the sordid side——." He coughed, slumped to the floor, and was carried unconscious from the chamber by his colleagues.

Ten minutes later he was dead. "The Lord giveth and the Lord taketh away." On the following day the House passed the bonus bill by a vote of 211-176, and then authorized $2,300,000,000 in fiat money to pay for it. There was great rejoicing that night at Anacostia and the other camps. But not at the White House. "Just like Germany in 1922," declared the President when he heard the news.

It was the bonus marchers' first and only real victory, and they had worked hard to help bring it about. Perhaps too hard. Beginning with their arrival in late May they had swarmed by the hundreds over Capitol Hill, where they were commonly seen loitering about the corridors or on the steps outside, waiting to button-hole passing congressmen. At first all of this was done in a totally haphazard way, but in time the effort came to be more or less coordinated, so that special delegations were chosen by the BEF leadership to concentrate on congressmen from their own states or regions. Major attention was given those members of Congress known to be opposed to the bonus—called "Hooverats" by the men. Waters himself made several trips to the Hill, where he was cordially received and listened to. His efforts to see Hoover were repeatedly rebuffed, however. "The President is too busy," announced Mr. Hoover's secretary on each occasion.

By all accounts the men selected for the lobbying were well behaved. On orders from Waters through his 182 group commanders, they were careful to show courtesy and respect at all times, and to avoid any sign of pressure or controversy. They also kept themselves clean shaven and as neatly dressed as possible. Still, the very fact that there were so many of them always hanging around was an embarrassment for most congressmen, and a decided irritant for some. Even those members most friendly to the bonus marchers, including Representative Patman himself, often wished they would ease off a bit. Others, like the redoubtable Senator Borah of Idaho, found the whole thing outrageous, and angrily denounced "those veterans seeking by their bodily presence and numbers, amounting to force, to compel Congress to pass this legislation." But members who reacted this strongly probably already had their minds set on voting against the bill anyway. On the whole the veterans probably did their cause more good than harm by their persistent presence on the Hill. They were almost certainly responsible for persuading the Lower House to dislodge the Patman Bill from the Ways and Means Committee, where it had been shelved since early May, and their efforts may even have provided the narrow margin of victory in the House vote of June 15th.

All in vain, however. On Friday evening, June 17, only two days after its passage by the House, the Patman Bill reached a vote in the Senate, where to the surprise of practically no one it was resoundingly defeated. "Why, this bill could very well push us right off the gold standard," warned one senator, who probably spoke the mind of most of his colleagues. "Gold standard, be damned," snapped one of the bill's supporters. "These men are hungry and out of jobs. They did their work and earned their pittance. Must they wait for a generation for the money we owe them?"

Outside, nearly 8000 veterans milled about, waiting for news of the vote. Many had been there since early in the day, standing, leaning, sitting, sprawled out on the lawn—smoking, joking, complaining, and bumming cigarettes from passers-by. Most of them were not deluded. They knew there was little hope that the Senate would pass their bonus, and yet, there was always a chance, wasn't there, no matter how slight, and these days who could expect much better? In the late afternoon a field kitchen from one of the nearby camps arrived in back of the Capitol, dished out hot soup while it lasted, and then retreated back up Pennsylvania Avenue. Capitol security guards, reinforced by squads of Glassford's Metropolitan Police, ambled freely among the men, pausing here and there to exchange good-natured banter. Across the Potomac at Ft. Myers, regular army units stood in readiness. Earlier in the day all leaves had been canceled.

At about nine o'clock Waters was called inside the Capitol and given the bad news. Returning to the north steps he faced his men with his arm outstretched in what appeared to some to be a Fascist salute. The veterans pressed forward to listen. "Comrades," Waters shouted, "we have just sustained a temporary setback. The Senate has rejected the bill." At this point a Hearst reporter leaned over to him and whispered: "Tell them to sing America." Waters nodded. "Let us show them that we can take it on the chin," he told the men. "Let us show them that we are patriotic Americans. I call on you to sing America." They did, and then after a half-hearted round of boos for President Hoover, bestirred themselves and headed back to camp. "The conduct, discipline, and loyal attitude of your men has been remarkable," Glassford told Waters as they walked across the Capitol lawn. "Well," replied Waters, "we're not licked yet. We're going to stay around until those guys change their minds."

The bonus marchers remained in Washington for nearly six weeks after the Senate's defeat of their bill—or at least some of them did. Waters claimed that he was able to keep his army virtually intact until it was finally routed by force on July 28, but the truth seems to be that by the time Congress adjourned on July 16 the BEF had already dwindled to no more than 12,000. To hasten the shrinkage along, in early July Congress appropriated $100,000 to help pay the veterans' fares home—with the stipulation that the money was not to be a gift to the men, but an interest-free loan against their 1945 bonus payment. According to government figures, nearly 6000 veterans availed themselves of the offer, but Waters scoffed at this, claiming that the men simply took the money as their due, rode as far as the District line, and then came back.

However many actually remained, it would have been better if they hadn't. The one-sided rejection by the Senate in mid-June had clearly spelled the doom of the bonus bill, and the morale of the men, which had never stood very high, was quick to reflect this fact. Waters fought back, and by praising, cajoling, threatening, and sometimes lying a little, managed to keep his men more or less in line during the weeks immediately following the Senate defeat. When all else failed he ordered them to turn out for close-order drill, as a reminder that they were still soldiers and were expected to act as such.

Still, disturbing signs began to appear: panhandling increased. So did drinking and public loitering, and there were reports now of scattered incidents of hooliganism, especially in the Negro districts adjacent to the downtown camps. The people of Washington, who after their initial misgivings had warmed to the bonus marchers, now seemed less sympathetic toward them, and in some cases even resentful. Donations from within the District began to dry up. So did those from outside benefactors. With each passing day Waters' dwindling army found it more difficult to make ends meet. "Cash on hand," read one evening's report from headquarters at this time, "thirty-five cents. Please be governed accordingly." Even the Hearst press, a rarity among the nation's newspapers for its staunch support of the bonus marchers, turned noticeably cool toward them after the Senate vote and urged them to break camp and go home.

As Congress neared the end of its session, a strange figure appeared center stage and temporarily stole the play from Waters. Only recently arrived from California with a contingent of 450 men, ex-sailor Royal Robertson was clearly the most colorful character of the entire ill-starred bonus venture. Warm-natured, high-spirited, and weighed down by a heavy steel brace supporting his broken neck, he was, in the opinion of his friends, only a little insane. Once many years ago, before the movies could talk, he had played in a film with the great Rudolph Valentino, and had ever since fancied himself as having a special flair for the theatre, which, it soon became evident, he meant to use against Congress. During his brief but memorable stay in Washington, he studiously avoided having anything to do with Waters or the BEF, whom he looked upon as a bunch of do-nothings. "We didn't come here to eat soup and sleep in the jungle over at Anacostia," he declared contemptuously. "We came here to get our bonus." Waters scarcely knew what to make of him. At first he suspected him of being a Communist, but soon changed his mind and marked him down as "just another screwball."

On Tuesday morning, July 12, four days before Congress was set to adjourn, Robertson, "speaking for the great army of veterans standing at your door hungry and broke," presented himself before Vice President Curtis and Speaker Garner in their Capitol offices and personally handed them a number of petitions in support of the bonus. "'Tis simple! 'Tis just! 'Tis human! And for it we humbly pray ere we die." When, not surprisingly, nothing came of this, Robinson ordered his California following to begin marching around the Capitol.

Working in two shifts of about two hundred each, Robertson and his men kept up a steady parade around the Capitol building. "I have no plan, no program, no philosophy whatever. I'm simply going to keep going until Congress quits." During the night hours some of the men fell asleep on the move and crumpled to the ground in a strangely graceful way, and in the heat of the day, which was often above ninety, dozens toppled in their tracks, only to have their places and placards taken over by others. In back of the Capitol, near the Library of Congress, a field kitchen would appear from time to time with soup and beans. And as for other

natural needs—"Those toilets in there belong to the American
people, and that's us. Use them all you want. And don't be in any
hurry. If some Congressman wants to get in and you happen to be
there, well that's too bad, isn't it."

It was an eerie sight to behold—these bedraggled, exhausted
men keeping up their grim procession around the Capitol of the
world's richest and most powerful nation. The newspapers called
it "the march of death" and most of them denounced it as an in-
excusable badgering of the United States Government by a handful of ill-mannered, smelly malcontents. Others, more charitable,
dismissed it as a harmless nuisance. Most everybody, including
probably the marchers themselves, doubted that any good would
come of it, and they were right. But nothing bad came of it either.
With Robertson in firm control of his men, and a full force of
Capitol security guards aided by a hundred of Glassford's police
keeping watch, there was never much likelihood of trouble. Still,
on Thursday afternoon, in a moment of panic or petulance Vice
President Curtis issued an emergency order for two companies of
marines to move in. Fortunately, Superintendent Glassford immediately intervened and managed to get them sent back to the Navy
Yard. "I am really fed up with hysterical meddlers," Glassford
snapped, in what one newspaper called "quite a show of temper."

On Saturday, July 16, at 11:10 in the evening, Congress adjourned without having taken any further action on the bonus.
And that should have been that. The battle of the bonus was over,
and the veterans had lost. Now, surely, they would go home. It
made no sense not to. Still they stayed, however—at least most of
them. Nobody knows for certain, but of the 12,000 or so who had
remained until Congress adjourned, probably as many as two-thirds
of them were still around at the time of the eviction twelve days
later. Why? Were they really serious about their pledge to "stay till
they pay," or could it have been that, confused, discouraged, empty bellied, and having nothing better in view, they simply succumbed to inertia and stayed put?

After Congress had adjourned, the character of the BEF
rapidly deteriorated. Now, without any real semblance of hope to
sustain them, the men grew decidedly more slack and morose, and
sometimes hostile. Drifters, some of them nonveterans, flocked to
the encampments, bringing disease and bad habits with them.
Crime began to show an increase, both inside the camps and out.
Especially disturbing were reports of gangster groups said to be

operating out of Anacostia and several of the other billets. Meanwhile, as the Washington summer hovered at its sultriest, the health
hazard mounted. Always fearful of the worst, city health officials
now grew almost hysterical and issued daily predictions of doom
for the camps, and perhaps the rest of the District as well.

Patiently and unobtrusively, Superintendent Glassford kept
watch over the BEF, and although less than pleased with some of
the things he now saw, still felt that there was no cause for alarm.
Others thought differently, however, and pressures began to
mount to remove this malignant blight from the city. It was hard
for people to understand why the veterans were still hanging
around. What could they hope to accomplish, now that Congress
was no longer in session? Why didn't they go home, or somewhere? If the truth were known, probably ninety-nine out of
every hundred Washingtonians now wished to be rid of the whole
lot of them, one way or another. And the sooner the better.

They didn't have to wait long. The final chapter of the bonus
march was about to begin in one of those condemned buildings
on lower Pennsylvania Avenue that had been home to several hundred veterans for the past two months. On July 21 Superintendent
Glassford was ordered by the District Commissioners to clear a
number of these buildings of their occupants in order to make way
for demolition and new construction. And then on the following
day the order was rescinded, reissued, and rescinded again, the
problem being that Glassford was proving to be his usual troublesome self. "As Superintendent of the District Police I simply have
no authority to evict anyone from United States Government
property," he announced. And of course he was right. But if not
Glassford, then who? Finally it was agreed that a small number of
government agents would take charge of the actual eviction, while
Glassford's police stood by to preserve order, which, obviously,
did fall within his authority. With that matter settled, the eviction
order was again issued, to take effect July 28.

At about ten o'clock on the morning of the appointed day
(later referred to by some as "Bloody Thursday"), 100 uniformed
policemen showed up at the corner of Pennsylvania Avenue and
Third Street, and proceeded to rope off the area surrounding the
building that housed what remained of the BEF's Sixth Regiment,
probably at that time not more than 120 men. The police then
took up positions about eight feet apart outside the ropes and
waited for the government agents, who appeared shortly before

11:00. Meanwhile, the crowd of onlookers, most of them BEF members from nearby billets, had grown to nearly 2000, but showed no sign of surliness. When the government agents entered the building, Waters, who had been kept informed by Glassford and had promised an orderly evacuation, called out to the men to leave peaceably. They did, with one exception who was eventually dragged out by the agents amidst a torrent of obscenities.

Suddenly, with the eviction all but completed, a disturbance arose at the rear of the building, where a group of forty or so veterans tried to crash through the police cordon, or (others say) the police started roughing up a few of the buddies who had come too close to the rope. Fists began to fly; so did bricks and clubs. One veteran knocked a policeman to the ground with a piano leg. Soon Superintendent Glassford appeared on a raised platform along the backside of the building. "All right, boys," he said calmly, "let's quit now for lunch." As if waiting for an excuse, the combatants separated, and there the scuffle ended with no real harm done. Half an hour later Glassford met with the District Commissioners and assured them that his men could handle the situation "unless the field of operation is to be expanded."

After lunch, evacuation was begun on another building nearby, this one little more than a shell with much of its outer wall missing. Here the occupants were more defiant, and sometimes had to be prodded a bit by the government agents. On the second floor a legless man sat with his stumps extended over the edge, swearing at the police and daring them to come up and get him. Shortly before two o'clock another minor skirmish broke out. Glassford, just returned to the scene, got off his big blue motorcycle and with two of his men entered the roped-off area and began climbing an exposed stairway at one end of the building in order to get a better look at what was going on.

As the superintendent neared the top, he heard someone directly below him shout "Get him!", or maybe it was "Get them!" Shots followed immediately, six in all. Glassford whirled and shouted: "For God's sake, put down those guns!" Too late. At the bottom of the steps one veteran lay dead and another dying. How did it happen? Who knows? It was one of those episodes, like the Boston Massacre and the Haymarket Riot, that give rise to different versions of the truth. Probably, in his terse, businesslike way, President Hoover came as close as anyone to what actually took place, when years later he noted in his memoirs: "Two policemen beaten to the ground were forced to protect themselves and killed two marchers."

After that there was no further trouble. Stunned and saddened, the veterans looked on with strange detachment as an ambulance arrived and carried away their fallen comrades. Meanwhile, on Glassford's order, the police had abandoned their cordon around the building and had fallen back to the sidewalk, where they were joined by several hundred reinforcements. For the next couple of hours the two sides faced one another solemnly over a distance of fifty feet or more. For so many people, there was surprisingly little movement, and even less noise. If there were anger or apprehension on either side, no one showed it. Only sorrow and disbelief. Shortly after four o'clock a newsboy came down the street, hawking the Hearst evening paper. Its eight-inch headlines read: "U.S. TROOPS ORDERED TO OUST MARCHERS!"

They first came into view at about 4:45, 600 of them in all, moving slowly down Pennsylvania Avenue from the direction of the White House. At their head, thirty riders abreast and extending the full width of the street, were four troops of cavalry, including one from Custer's old regiment. Following at a close distance were four companies of infantry in steel helmets. A block from the trouble spot the troops halted and shifted positions so that units of infantrymen could take up the point and forward flanks. Upon command, sabres were drawn, bayonets were fixed, and gas masks tugged into place. Along the curbs an orderly crowd of perhaps two thousand spectators, mostly veterans, watched with quiet interest.

A staff car drove up and General Douglas MacArthur and his aide, Major Dwight Eisenhower, got out. For several minutes the general stood with his hands on his hips, surveying the situation and saying nothing. Meanwhile, four or five trucks arrived and disgorged several baby "Whippet" tanks. Tanks? Sounds of disbelief and anger began to arise from the crowd. A few yards away two soldiers mounted a .30-caliber machine gun on the back of a weapons carrier.

At about five o'clock someone gave an order and the troops began to advance, the tanks and cavalry herding as much of the crowd as possible up the side streets, while the infantry pressed forward along Pennsylvania Avenue, prodding loiterers with their bayonets and canisters of tear gas. One after another the occupied buildings were cleared from top to bottom, and then, despite all later disclaimers, many of the adjacent shanties were set afire.

Slowly and methodically the troops pushed ahead, sweeping everyone before them. "It was a distressing sight," recalled an eyewitness a generation later, "but in some ways it was also rather
comic."

> In order to have the various movements carried out with precision, it
> was necessary to keep contact between the cavalry and infantry. Ac-
> cordingly, a mounted dispatch would ride furiously about seventy-five
> feet over to the infantry, salute, wheel around and gallop seventy-five
> feet back, reining in his horse with a great shower of dust and stones.
> At least a dozen messages were interchanged in about fifteen minutes
> this way. It would have been simpler, of course, for the commander of
> the cavalry to yell, "Hey, Bill," to the commander of the infantry, but
> it wouldn't have been so military.

By 5:40 the derelict federal buildings had been completely
evacuated. The government could now proceed with its announced
plans for demolition, and the army could congratulate itself on a
job well done. But the end was not yet. For reasons that are not
clear, and probably never will be, the soldiers continued to press
on, driving several hundred fleeing veterans before them in a broad
counterclockwise sweep southward toward the Anacostia River.
By 6:30 they had overrun and destroyed a second BEF encamp-
ment. Next, at 7:15, came Comrade Pace's Communist camp on
13th and B. And still the soldiers pushed forward, moving thirty
or forty feet forward and then pausing to reform their lines. Now
and then General MacArthur could be seen standing at the periph-
ery of the action, conversing with fellow officers while Major
Eisenhower took notes. There were those who found it strange,
and perhaps a little ridiculous, that the chief of staff of the United
States Army should personally take charge of the trifling and not
very edifying business of putting ragged, unarmed men to flight.
Later, reporters and historians would say that he simply couldn't
resist the temptation to strut before the news cameras in his new
English breeches. Actually, he went along with the troops because
President Hoover asked him to. There is nothing to suggest that he
particularly relished the assignment—or that he particularly didn't.

By all accounts the veterans offered practically no resistance.
Occasionally they would hurl a few bricks or toss back a gas canis-
ter, but for the most part they simply cussed and jeered and then
backed off as soon as the army got within fifty feet of them, or

they caught their first whiff of gas. South of Maine Avenue, as the soldiers paused momentarily to realign, it appeared for a time as if the veterans might make a stand, but as soon as the army began to come on again, their nerve failed and they fell back in noisy disarray toward the river. By 9:30, after having funneled the greater part of the fleeing mob over the Anacostia Bridge, the troops halted on the near side of the river, and MacArthur rode off in his staff car to report to the White House. A few minutes later, ten or fifteen at the most, they started moving again, this time across the river against the veterans' main camp at Anacostia Flats.

They reached Camp Marks at 10:14. In anticipation of their coming, the camp's occupants had begun firing it. Although they would later deny it, the soldiers immediately took up where the veterans left off, and for the next hour or so proceeded to put the torch to virtually everything in the area, including the $10,000 worth of tents and other equipment that Glassford had borrowed from the army and National Guard. The scene quickly became one of unimaginable confusion and panic. Thousands of men stumbled wildly toward the camp's extremities, seeking an escape from the flames and tear gas and the bayonet-wielding soldiers. Others remained behind in the midst of the holocaust, hoping to save something of their few precious belongings, or to steal someone else's. Mothers scurried frantically about in search of their children. Husbands, struggling with mattresses and bedsprings on their backs, shouted for their wives to hurry on without them. Babies screamed; ambulances wailed; gas canisters hissed; men gagged and cursed. Back near the bluff someone was playing "Springtime in the Rockies" on a harmonica.

At about eleven o'clock Glassford rode up on his motorcycle and dismounted. He had called off his police several hours earlier, as soon as the troops had appeared, and now he had come to Anacostia to witness a scene he had done his best to prevent. One of the veterans recognized him, standing alone, and went over to him:

> He looked pale and tired. He said he was sorry all this was happening.
> It grieved him deeply. He said it so nicely. He was every inch a man.
> It was reassuring to see such a man on such a night.

By midnight Camp Marks had been completely evacuated. Most of its former occupants had fled to the poplar bluff at the rear of the camp, from where they watched the flames light up the sky for miles around. "They might at least of waited until daylight," someone said sadly. Suddenly the troops began to advance against the bluff, lobbing a few gas canisters ahead of them. Again panic, screams, and angry obscenities as the crowd scattered in all directions. "We wanted to push that bunch all the way back to Maryland," an officer later explained.

But there would be no further pursuit. There was no need. After two troublesome and unsightly months the BEF had been thoroughly routed, and its camps destroyed. "Law and order has returned to Washington," announced Secretary of War Patrick Hurley when he heard the news. And, at least as far as the army's part in it was concerned, it had all been accomplished without a single casualty. Well, almost. Somehow during the melee a veteran had managed to lose an ear lobe. Some reports claimed it was sliced off by a cavalry saber; others said it was bitten off by a friend in a drunken brawl. Far more serious was the case of two-month-old Barnard Myers, a bonus baby who, according to his parents, was gassed during the army's attack on Camp Marks and had soon after fallen violently ill. When the infant died in a Washington hospital twelve days later, the story was picked up and embellished by the Communists and certain elements of the press. A subsequent hospital investigation revealed, however, that the baby's death was due to severe gastroenteritis, from which he had been suffering "for some time." An autopsy showed no trace of gas anywhere in his body.*

Many years later in his memoirs Hoover would claim, with neither rancor nor dismay, that General MacArthur exceeded his orders in conducting an all-out assault against the BEF, and there can be little doubt that he did. The President's directive, issued through the secretary of war, read simply: "Surround the affected area and clear it at once. . . . Use all humanity consistent with the due execution of this order." Presumably this meant that the veterans were to be ousted from the vicinity of 3rd and Pennsylvania where the recent trouble with Glassford's police had occurred. Nothing was said about going on to the other camps or driving the veterans from the city, and certainly nothing was said about firing their billets. Still, there is no indication that President Hoover was

---

*And yet, to this day the story of the "gassed baby" persists, even among many reputable historians.

very upset over the way MacArthur handled the matter. In fact, if the truth were known, the President, who from the first had been outraged by the presence of the bonus marchers, may have been grateful that the general had gone all the way and rid the city of the lot of them once and for all. At any rate, MacArthur was never officially reprimanded nor even called to account for his excessive zeal.

This still leaves unanswered the question of why the troops were called out in the first place. The official account is that Glassford asked for them. In a sworn statement to the attorney general the District Commissioners declared unanimously that Superintendent Glassford had come to them with the admission that the situation was out of control, and had "implored" them to ask the President to call out the troops. Glassford himself, however, vigorously denied ever having done so: "I did not call for the Army to come in. I have several times stated that I didn't consider it necessary." In a somewhat different version, General MacArthur claimed that Glassford had approached him personally and asked for help from the army—all of which Glassford angrily dismissed as "so much nonsense." About all that is known for certain is that the written request originated with the District Commissioners, and that it appealed directly to the President to send in federal troops in order to prevent further bloodshed and restore order to the city. By all accounts, it was with great reluctance and only after a prolonged period of soul searching, that Hoover complied. "The President played it pretty fine in waiting until the last minute," MacArthur later commented.

Once the decision had been made, however, the President saw no reason to apologize for it. Quite the opposite. On the following day he announced with obvious satisfaction:

> A challenge to the authority of the United States has been met swiftly and firmly. . . . Government cannot be coerced by mob rule. . . . Order and civil tranquility are the first requisites in the great task of economic reconstruction to which our whole people are now devoting their heroic and noble energies. This national effort must not be retarded even in the slightest degree by organized lawlessness. The first obligation of my office is to uphold and defend the Constitution. This I propose always to do.

As the President saw it, from its very beginnings the BEF had been a scruffy, ill-behaved mob of malcontents who had no business being in Washington in the first place. But since the defeat of the Patman Bill, and especially since the adjournment of Congress, it had degenerated into something much worse: namely, a wolf-pack of hoodlums and Communists. At Hoover's instigation various governmental agencies had for some time been giving a close look into the nature of the bonus army, and what they had learned was not very reassuring. Out of 2000 "veterans" checked, fewer than one-third had ever belonged to any branch of the armed services. The others were mainly youngsters, hoboes, and Communists. Nearly half the total number were ex-convicts. An FBI investigation based upon fingerprints on file, revealed that out of 4723 authentic veterans, 1069 had criminal records. The same investigation disclosed that the BEF was riddled with racketeers who were using strong-arm tactics to collect "protection" money and other forms of tribute, principally among the Negro neighborhoods. "Caponeism of the most naked sort," commented Attorney General Mitchell. "This is probably the greatest aggregation of criminals that was ever assembled in the city at any time." As for the Communists, at the request of the President a federal grand jury was summoned to inquire into the degree of their involvement with the BEF, and although the jury's findings were inconclusive, the President seemed satisfied: "A glaring example of Soviet interference in the United States," he exclaimed.

Of course, there were those who saw things differently, including Waters and Glassford, both of whom insisted that the BEF was composed almost wholly of veterans, at least two-thirds of whom had served in France. In this they were supported by Director of the Veterans Administration, General Frank Hines, who concluded (from what evidence is not clear) that ninety-four percent of the BEF were indeed bona fide veterans. Insofar as criminals and Communists were concerned, it had to be admitted that there were some of both. But not many. During the two months that the bonus marchers were in Washington, there were only 362 arrests among them, and only 12 of these were for serious offenses. Furthermore, of those 1069 veterans reported by the FBI as having criminal records, only 800 had ever been actually convicted of anything, and most of those for vagrancy or drunkenness. The Communist presence was even more negligible. "Never close to 300," claimed Glassford. Waters agreed.

Criminals and Communists or not, the deed was done. "Once

again," a British newspaper commented, "the cannon has proved
to be the final arbiter of human dissensions." The country on the
whole seemed to heave a sigh of relief. Good riddance to the bonus marchers and all like them who dared attempt to intimidate
the government of the United States. A "portent of revolution"
had been eliminated. President Hoover had done the right thing,
the only thing. "They picked a bad way to urge what was at best
a questionable cause," remarked William Allen White's *Emporia
Gazette.* "Riffraff," snorted the *Boston Herald* and then went on
to explain that naked force was the only kind of treatment some
people could understand. Declared General MacArthur: "Had the
President not acted as he did, it would have been a sad day for
the Country."

Following the rout at Anacostia, the bonus marchers made
their way out of Washington as best they could, all but a few of
them that same night, stumbling and swearing as they retreated
through the darkness along unfamiliar streets. By dawn they had
crossed over the District line and could be seen strung out for
miles along the main arteries leading away from the capital, most
of them heading northward into Maryland. Once again Governor
Ritchie rose to the occasion and used trucks to help speed the veterans out of his state. A week later what remained of the BEF
(Waters put the number at 8000, but it was probably no more
than half that) reached Johnstown, Pennsylvania, some 300 miles
from Washington. There they took over an amusement park in
response to an earlier invitation from the city's red-headed mayor,
Eddie McCloskey, ex-prize fighter and friend of man. Actually
McCloskey had expected only Waters and his staff, but what he
got was another Johnstown flood. Still, he was glad to have them.
"God must have sent you," he said, and to those who felt otherwise, including the City Council and most of the townspeople:
"To hell with all of you." Thus, amongst the teeters and shoot-
the-chutes of the Ideal Amusement Park the bonus marchers had
found a new home. They named it Camp McCloskey and vowed
to stay there until Congress reconvened in December.

Meanwhile, Waters himself had stopped over in Catonsville,
Maryland, where a sympathizer had given him a twenty-five-acre

tract of woodland. Here, it occurred to Waters, a new home might be erected for the bonus marchers, a self-sufficient community where chickens and vegetables could be raised and perhaps a few head of cattle. It could even serve as a model for other, similar camps throughout the country—not only for veterans but for other down-and-outers as well. The more he thought about the idea, the better he liked it. With a few of his men he set to work clearing away the brush and trees from the shores of a small pond that was to serve as the camp's water supply. Soon the others could move down from Johnstown.

The project never stood a chance. Scarcely had work begun when the camp was declared a potential health hazard and ordered closed by the state of Maryland, which, as Governor Ritchie later remarked, already had enough jobless men without taking on more. Angry and frustrated, Waters left for Johnstown, denouncing, as he went, the lackeys of Wall Street who had betrayed the nation, and calling for the American people to join him in a khaki-shirt movement "to clean out the high places of government"—the way Mussolini had.

Back in Washington, with the drama now ended, various members of the cast were about to be phased out in one way or another. On August 7, eleven days after the eviction, the two slain bonus marchers, William Hushka, 35, from Chicago, and Eric Carlson, age unknown, from Oakland, were buried with full military honors at Arlington National Cemetery. They had finally found federal property from which they would never be evicted. And something else: by law they were now entitled to the rest of their bonus. A week later, while answering a call on F Street, Patrolman Shinault, who had been responsible for killing one (and possibly both) of the veterans, was himself shot to death, only a few days after he had been acquitted of any wrongdoing by a coroner's jury. Somewhat later, Superintendent Glassford was fired from his job. So was President Hoover.

In New York City, Comrade John Pace, fresh from Washington, was summoned before a meeting presided over by Earl Browder and attended by a few other Party functionaries, including a squat, dark-haired stranger who spoke with a heavy accent and was referred to by the others as C.I.Rep (Communist International Representative). After receiving commendation for his "working-class leadership," Pace was ordered to leave immediately on a speaking tour of the country. "Tell them what you saw in Washington," he was told. "Yes," said C.I.Rep. "Refer to Hoover as 'the murderer of the veterans' and MacArthur as 'the tool of the Fascists.' "

As for Camp McCloskey, the less said, the better. For a few days about 4000 bonus marchers, including 300 women and children, lived mainly on apples and slept huddled together under picnic tables and baseball bleachers, while the people of Johnstown looked on with growing resentment and gave precious little help of any kind. Realizing the hopelessness of the situation, Waters soon ordered the camp abandoned, and furloughed his troops to fend for themselves until such time as the BEF would march again. "We'll go back," they told one another. "They haven't seen the last of us yet." And then, dirty, discouraged, and hungry, they set out for home, if they had one. This time, though, they would travel in style—by train, as regular passengers. They never did find out who put up the money for the fares. Rumor had it that it was Herbert Hoover, but this seemed highly unlikely.

Incident at San Jose

I T PROBABLY wouldn't have happened if times hadn't been so bad. But in 1933, the fourth full year of the Depression, times were very bad indeed—worse, perhaps, than ever before in the history of the nation: fifteen million Americans, a third of the total work force, unemployed, and millions of others living in daily fear of being laid off. The entire country seemed stuck on dead bottom. The people were apprehensive and angry. Some had grown desperate.

In San Jose, California, conditions were about the same as elsewhere in America. Like other places, great and small, the town had suffered the ravages of a foundering economy. But there was this difference: in San Jose the Depression was not only a calamity; it was also an incongruity. How was such a thing possible in paradise?

Located about an hour's train ride southeast of San Francisco, Santa Clara County in those days presented a beautiful panorama of luxuriant agriculture. Dairy farms dotted the rolling landscape, and truck gardens that provided fresh produce for the markets of San Francisco, and beyond, numbered in the thousands. What was most special about the area, however, were its lovely orchards with their colorful assortment of apricots, cherries, plums, and citrus fruits. In the midst of all this was the shire town of San Jose, population 60,000—a solid, self-satisfied place of white stucco houses and steady habits. In the days before the Depression it had bustled with commerce and light industry, but now, although the cattle continued to graze and grow fat in nearby fields and the orchards still sagged with fruit, freight cars stood empty in the yards of the Southern Pacific, stores and canneries had closed, and the very soul of the town seemed to be wasting away.

By the autumn of 1933 Jack Holmes' world was in tatters. A tall, nice-looking young man with a winsome, outgoing manner, he was generally well thought of, although some of his friends were at times put off by what they called "his swaggering ways." Women liked his smile, and he obliged them by smiling a lot. Ten years earlier he had graduated from San Jose High and gone on to attend a local college. After two semesters he left, however. He was not a particularly good student. Perhaps he could have been if he had tried. His teachers found him bright enough. But with his good looks and ready charm, a college education must have seemed a waste of time for the sort of goal he had in mind: namely, early success easily arrived at. Eventually he got a job as a salesman for the Union Oil Company, and for a while did very well for himself. But then the Depression came along, and like millions of others in the early '30s, he suddenly found himself out of work, for reasons that he could neither accept nor understand.

Meanwhile, he had fallen desperately in love with a childhood sweetheart, who now happened to be married to one of his closest friends. To what degree the feeling was reciprocated is not clear, but Holmes was convinced that the only thing that stood in the way of her running off with him to a mountain paradise they had often talked about was lack of money. As the passion grew and his savings dwindled, the gap between desire and reality became more painfully apparent—especially in view of the fact that Holmes already had a wife and two children to support. What could he do? With no job and none in prospect, his situation was all but hopeless. In September of that year he separated from his wife and moved into a cheap downtown hotel. It was not long after this that he first approached Harold Thurmond on a matter of some importance.

Thomas Harold Thurmond was a different case. About a year younger than Holmes, he was the son of a respected San Jose tailor. Described by neighbors as "a good boy," he had grown up in a religious home, had attended Sunday school regularly, and

later become a member of the First Baptist Church. His older
brother was a minister in Chico. His sister sang in the choir. Un-
married, Thurmond lived with his parents in their modest home on
the outskirts of town. He had never given them any trouble. True,
it had come as a great disappointment to them when he dropped
out of high school, but there was no denying that Harold had
always done poorly with his studies. Eventually he found work in
a downtown filling station, a job he managed to hold onto despite
the Depression. Although he and Holmes must have known one
another at San Jose High, it was probably at the filling station,
during Holmes' stint as an oil salesman, that the two men became
friends.

Clearly, Harold Thurmond was something out of the ordinary.
His appearance alone was enough to set him apart. A muscular
young man of medium build, his body seemed uncommonly taut,
as if set to spring out against something or someone. His face was
strong and rather handsome, but at the same time undeniably odd-
looking. For the most part his features were regular and unremark-
able, although his ears were perhaps a mite smaller than they
should have been and protruded a bit from his head. It was his
eyes that made the difference. Steel-gray and fiercely penetrating,
they glared out at the world in anger, or perhaps bewilderment,
from beneath dark, bushy eyebrows. The overall effect was strangely disturbing. Some said he was dull-witted. His own mother called
him insane, and blamed his condition on a fall he had suffered as
a youth. As late as the autumn of 1932 his parents had talked
about having him put in an institution—not because he had done
anything wrong, or even threatened to, but because of "his increasingly strange behavior." On the other hand, there were those
who found him perfectly normal, including his employer and customers at the filling station, where Harold was well liked and respected as a good worker.

During the autumn of that year Thurmond and Holmes saw a
lot of each other. The one a bachelor and the other a man recently
separated from his wife and children, they leaned on one another
for support against their loneliness. Thurmond too had love problems, and like Holmes he blamed his misery on lack of money.
One thing led to another, and then one night in early November,
as the two of them were leaving a local movie house, Holmes came
up with a solution to their problems.

It was not a very original idea. Since the still unsolved abduc-

tion of the Lindbergh baby a year and a half before, kidnaping—
like jigsaw puzzles—had become an American craze. Each morning's paper seemed to carry the report of another abduction or
another ransom demanded and paid. Apparently nobody ever got
caught, and the payoff was immense, provided, of course, a wise
choice of victim were made. "Let's snatch Brooke Hart," Holmes
said to Thurmond, or Thurmond said to Holmes, depending upon
which one's confession is believed.

This was obviously an excellent choice because, as the owner
of San Jose's largest department store, Hart's father was one of the
richest men in town, and it was well known that he put great stock
in his son. The old man would pay high. There were certain draw-
backs, however: for one thing, Brooke was no babe in arms. He
was twenty-one years old. Besides that, he had a nodding acquaint-
ance with both Holmes and Thurmond. "Well," Holmes told Thurmond, "the only thing to do is snatch him and then kill him."

Brooke Hart was almost too good to be true. Those who
knew him well called him a model boy. He was considerate of his
parents, polite to his neighbors, and loyal to his friends—a pleasant
young man who seems to have got along well with everyone. Inclined to be on the quiet side, he drank very little, gambled not at
all, and showed a healthy but proper interest in girls. He was not
handsome, mainly because of his slightness of build and almost
effeminate features. In fact, with his bright blue eyes, fair com-
plexion, and curly hair, he came close to being pretty. At nearby
Santa Clara University he had been a member of Delta Sigma fraternity, where he was highly regarded by the brothers.

After graduating from the university in the spring of that
year, Brooke had returned to live with his family in their handsome mansion on The Alameda. Besides Brooke, there were three
younger children living at home, two girls and a boy. There was
also a married half-sister somewhere. Of the lot, Brooke was clearly the favorite, at least as far as his father was concerned. Considerably older than his wife, Alex Hart, then in his sixties, doted on
his first-born son. Only a few months before, he had taken Brooke
into the store as a vice president, and was looking forward to the
day when he could turn the entire operation over to him. "His
grandfather would have been so proud of him."

At 5:55, Thursday evening, November 9, Brooke Hart left the store and entered the parking lot at the rear. He was intending to pick up his friend, Charlie O'Brien, and then attend a public speaking course at the DeAnza Hotel. It was already dark, but the parking-lot attendant recognized him as he headed toward the far exit in his Studebaker roadster. When the car slowed down to enter Market Street, Jack Holmes jumped into the front seat and ordered Hart to drive out of town. Hart immediately recognized Holmes and at first thought he was joking. He soon discovered otherwise, however, when Holmes poked what felt like a gun (but wasn't) into his ribs.

With Thurmond following a short distance behind in Holmes' two-door sedan (then called a "coach"), Hart was forced to drive to a back road about seven miles out of town. There the roadster was abandoned and the three men rode off in the coach in the direction of the San Mateo Bridge, some thirty miles to the north. Holmes was now at the wheel, with Thurmond beside him in the front seat. Hart, who had not been tied or gagged, was alone in back. Not far from the little town of Alviso he rolled down the window and shouted for help at a passing car. No one heard him. Thurmond then reached back and put a pillowcase over Hart's head. He also took his wallet.

The kidnapers' car entered the San Mateo Bridge from the east at about 7:15. Some distance across, Holmes stopped the car and Thurmond helped Hart out, telling him that they were going to switch cars again. While Thurmond removed the pillowcase from Hart's head, Holmes took a brick from the floor of the front seat. Coming up behind Hart, he smashed the brick down hard on the back of his head. Hart staggered but remained standing and cried out for help. Not far away on the San Mateo side, two beachcombers who were searching the shore for firewood heard the cry but thought nothing of it. An instant later Holmes struck again, and Hart crumpled at his feet. At about this time a car sped by on its way to the East Bay.

Propping Hart up against the railing of the bridge, Holmes bound his arms to his side with baling wire. Then with Thurmond's help he weighted him down with two twenty-pound building blocks that Thurmond had bought the day before in a San Jose lumber yard for ten cents each. "Do you think two is enough?" Thurmond asked. "Hell yes," Holmes replied. "Forty pounds would hold a horse on the bottom." And then, according to Thurmond:

> Holmes told me to take hold of him. He took the upper part of Hart's body and I took him by the legs and we lifted him on the rail of the bridge and tossed him into the bay. As I recall, he struggled slightly. . . .

At a few minutes before 7:30, Holmes and Thurmond started back to San Jose. On the way they divided the money from Hart's wallet between them. It figured to an even $3.75 apiece. Back in San Jose, Thurmond borrowed his father's car and headed north again, this time for San Francisco to make the ransom call to Hart's parents. Holmes immediately got in touch with his estranged wife and then his girl friend and her husband, and arranged a friendly foursome for the movies. They decided to go to the Hester Theatre to see *The Three Little Pigs*, the first feature-length animated cartoon. Holmes was his usually cheerful self—only more so. He laughed uproariously at the movie. Meanwhile Harold Thurmond had arrived in San Francisco, where at 9:30 he entered a public phone booth in the lobby of the Whitcomb Hotel on Market Street and placed a long-distance call to the Harts. The line was busy.

At the Hart mansion in San Jose, young Charlie O'Brien was doing his best to convince Brooke's mother that there was no cause for worry. He had dropped around after speech class to find out why his friend hadn't shown up, only to discover that there had been no word from Brooke since he had left the store three hours before. At nine o'clock Mrs. Hart phoned her husband who was attending a Chamber of Commerce banquet at the San Jose Country Club. He came home immediately, reassured everyone, and then waited. At 10:30 the phone rang. Brooke's teenage sister, Miriam, took the call. "Do you want your brother?" Thurmond asked. "Yes," the girl answered. "Do you know where he is?" At this point Alex Hart took the receiver, just in time to hear: "It'll cost you $40,000 to see him alive. If you notify the police it will be just too bad."

After getting his call through, Harold Thurmond left the hotel and started toward the Ferry Building. According to plan he was to take the ferry to Oakland and drop Brooke Hart's wallet in the middle of the bay. But the more Thurmond thought about it, the less he liked the idea. It worried him having to carry the wallet around on his person. Besides, it was getting late and he was tired and wanted to go home. Driving to the Embarcadero, he got out of his car, walked to the end of the pier where the Associated Oil tanker *Midway* was docked, and threw the wallet as far out as he could. By shortly after midnight he was back in San Jose.

Immediately after receiving the ransom call, Alex Hart notified the San Jose police. Since the call had come long-distance, the police were able to trace it to the Whitcomb Hotel, but could find nobody who remembered having seen who made it. At the same time a search was begun for young Hart's car. Somehow, within hours, the press got hold of the story and flashed it out over the wires in time for the early morning edition of practically every major newspaper in the country. Alex Hart begged the reporters not to mention anything about the ransom, but most of them did anyway.

By midday Friday, only twelve hours or so after the ransom call, a major manhunt was in progress. Hundreds of people from San Jose and surrounding towns, including a large number of employees from the Hart store and students from Santa Clara, joined the police in scouring the area. The search was centered in the Milpitas region northeast of San Jose, where Hart's abandoned car had been found by a rancher early that morning. It was thought by some that young Hart had been taken beyond that point into the wild and hilly country near the Calaveras Dam and was being held prisoner there. The police were skeptical, however. Although they kept it to themselves, they were inclined to believe that Hart was already dead, mainly because of the age factor. An infant, perhaps, or even a child, might come out of it alive. But a mature adult who would be apt to provide important evidence against his abductors? Unlikely.

The abandoned car was taken back to San Jose to be dusted for prints and gone over for other possible clues. At the same time a rundown was begun on young Hart himself. Girl friends, bank accounts, clothing, and the possibility of suicide or a self-engineered abduction were methodically checked out. People from as far away as Sacramento, some who had known the victim only slightly or not at all, were questioned. Meanwhile there was a tremendous outpouring of sympathy for the family. Letters and phone calls came in by the hundreds, offering help of one kind or another, including money, which was the one thing the Harts didn't need. An awful thing had happened, and people in all parts of the country were profoundly moved. That Sunday at San Jose's First Baptist Church the minister called on God for the safe and speedy return of the boy to his aggrieved family. Near the front of the congregation, only a few feet from the altar, sat Harold Thurmond with his head bowed in prayer.

On Friday afternoon a deckhand on the tanker *Midway* walked into the San Francisco Police Station with an interesting find—Brooke Hart's wallet. It had landed not in the bay, as Thurmond had intended, but on the guardrail of the tanker. Because the *Midway* had been fueling the Matson luxury liner *Lurline* the night before, the police theorized that the wallet had been thrown out of one of the liner's portholes. This could mean that the kidnaper (or more likely kidnapers) and possibly young Hart himself were aboard the ship. Since the *Lurline* had left that noon for Los Angeles on the first leg of its passage to Hawaii, San Francisco detectives flew south and were on hand to meet it when it docked at San Pedro. With the cooperation of the Los Angeles police, the liner was immediately quarantined. From the ship's officers the police learned that two suspicious-looking men had boarded as visitors in San Francisco, and had not been seen leaving. A thorough search was conducted. For hours dozens of policemen covered the entire ship and checked out all the passengers and crew. They found nothing out of the ordinary except Babe Ruth, who obliged them with autographs.

By this time the kidnapers had made their next move. At 7:00 Friday evening, twenty-four hours after Hart had been dumped into the bay, Thurmond left in his father's car for Sacramento to mail a ransom note prepared by Holmes. The note, a chatty one of some 150 words, assured the elder Hart that his son was all right, but wouldn't be for long if the police were notified of any more developments. Instructions were given concerning the number and denomination of the bills to be used for ransom, but there was no mention of a time or method of payment. After mailing the message Thurmond returned immediately to San Jose. On the following morning Holmes sent him to San Francisco to mail another note. This one, of about 70 words, instructed Alex Hart to display a large numeral 1 in his store window if he wanted to proceed with the negotiations.

Both notes reached the Harts on Monday morning, but were kept secret from all but the police. However, because the press was so relentless in pushing for information, Hart felt compelled to give out some kind of statement. At eight o'clock that evening, ten hours after receiving the ransom notes, he appeared before a cluster of reporters and photographers at his home on The Ala-

meda. Ashen and drawn, he declared that he had received no further word from the kidnapers, and then, in order to allay suspicions, handed reporters copies of an appeal that he hoped they
would run in their next edition. It asked simply that the kidnapers
renew contact. The questions then turned to the subject of Brooke
himself. "Brooke is an exceptional character," his father stated.
"We have been wonderful pals. Why, many times," his voice broke
and he paused for a moment, "why, many times the boy offered
to take me to the football game instead of going with his young
friends." Upstairs, overcome with anxiety and on the verge of nervous collapse, the boy's mother was confined to bed under the
care of her doctor.

On Monday morning, immediately following Alex Hart's receipt of the ransom notes, the FBI entered the case. Although up
to this point federal agents from San Francisco had been quietly
"helping out," they had done so without legal jurisdiction, because kidnaping had not yet been made a federal offense. It was
not until the ransom notes arrived that the crime assumed a federal
character ("using the mails of extort"), thereby enabling the FBI
to play an official role. Working closely with local police, the federal agents fine-combed the entire Bay Area for leads, and checked
out the typical flurry of reports that Brooke Hart (invariably described as "in a daze") had been spotted in a dozen places from
San Francisco to Waco, Texas. At the same time agents maintained
a constant vigil inside and outside the Hart house, waiting for the
mistake that was bound to be made.

There were rumors abroad that the Hart kidnaping was the
work of bigtime desperadoes. Pretty Boy Floyd was often mentioned by the newspapers. So was "Handsome Jack" Klutas, a
highly polished, university-educated hood from the Midwest who
specialized in extortion, kidnaping, and murder. But San Francisco
Bureau Chief Reed Vetterli, a seasoned professional who was personally overseeing the FBI part of the operation, knew better. This
was clearly an amateur job. The ransom notes left no doubt of it.
Both of them were unnecessarily wordy; they were handwritten,
rather than composed of newstype; and, least professional of all,
they had failed to arrange for the payoff. Four days had passed
since the kidnaping, and still no time or place had been set for the
drop. Obviously the whole business was being badly bungled.

On the following morning the two kidnapers strolled by the
Hart store and saw a large number 1 in the window. Early that

evening as young Charlie O'Brien was leaving his father's restaurant, Thurmond jumped onto the running board of his car, stared in at him for an instant and then disappeared. An hour later O'Brien received a phone call instructing him to have Alex Hart drive south along the Coast Highway toward Los Angeles. Hart was to leave at once, go alone, and carry $40,000 with him in the front seat. Somewhere along the way he would be met by a man in a white mask, to whom he was to hand over the money.

Immediately after their phone call to O'Brien, Holmes and Thurmond parked a short distance from the Hart house and waited for the elder Hart to drive off. When by 8:45 he had still not left, they drove downtown and phoned him to find out why he hadn't followed instructions. "I can't drive," Hart told them. "I have never driven a car. I don't know how. I want to play fair and do what is necessary to assure Brooke's return, but in this instance I cannot comply with the demand made." One more thing: would they give him some guarantee, before he paid them the ransom, that they were the real kidnapers? This was a reasonable request, and one that professionals would have anticipated by being prepared to produce a piece of clothing or one of the victim's personal effects. In this case, however, the kidnapers had failed to keep anything belonging to the boy before dumping him into the bay— except of course his wallet, which they had subsequently thrown away. "You'll just have to trust us," they told the boy's father.

Listening in on an extension line was a federal agent. Another agent tended two special lines that had been installed in the Hart house soon after the kidnaping. One went directly to the sheriff at the county jail; the other, to the telephone company's central switchboard. All this represented a relatively new police technique, called "phone tracking," which at that time was little known and less understood by the general public. Since he had entered the case, Reed Vetterli had been banking on the likelihood that sooner or later the criminals would again phone Hart directly, as they had on that first night. The guess turned out to be a good one, but on this occasion they had hung up before the trace could be completed.

Early the following morning Jack Holmes wrote yet another message to Hart and mailed it at the downtown San Jose post office to insure afternoon delivery. In what must figure as one of the strangest of all ransom notes, Holmes half-apologized for the delay in making arrangements. There had been "some confusion," but he saw no reason why the matter could not now be brought to a satisfactory settlement without further complications. If Mr. Hart wished to proceed with the negotiations, he was to post the numeral 2 in his store window at closing time. Then, with Charlie O'Brien driving, he was to leave home at 7:30 that evening and follow the same instructions as before. The note was polite and at times almost deferential. It was also more than four hundred words long. Thus far the kidnapers had written approximately six hundred and twenty-five words and made three phone calls. And there was more to come.

Shortly after dark, the two kidnapers began cruising around the Hart neighborhood in Holmes' car, killing time until Hart left for the drop. At 7:10 they phoned Hart from a public pay phone to remind him of his date with them. The line was busy. Five minutes later they tried again from a different phone. Still busy. They then drove down to the center of town, and Thurmond, wearing a faded blue cardigan sweater and laced high-top boots with his pant-legs tucked inside, went into the Plaza Garage and placed a call from the paybooth while Holmes drove around the block. The phone rang several times before Alex Hart answered. "You had better get a move on," Thurmond told him, "if you want to see your son alive." This was absolutely the last chance, Thurmond warned. No more fooling around. Just do what he'd been told and everything would be all right. Etc., etc.

They caught him still talking. Good police work, but not remarkable, for the Plaza Garage was located right beside the sheriff's office. Once the word had arrived from the FBI, the police had less than fifty yards to travel to get their man. "It was perfect," Sheriff Emig later explained when describing the capture. "If he had phoned from anywhere else except right next door, we'd probably never have got there in time."

The veil of secrecy is here mercifully drawn over what then befell Harold Thurmond. Suffice to say that he was taken next door to the county jail and was, as they used to say in the days before the courts showed much interest in such matters, "wrung out." After six hours he was ready to tell all. As for Holmes, after driving around the block several times and failing to find Thurmond, he stopped off for a bite to eat at the White Front Tavern and then returned to his room at the California Hotel and went to bed as if nothing out of the ordinary had happened. At 2:15 Thurmond knocked on his door. "Jack, it's me." When Holmes opened the door, the police grabbed him without a struggle.

The news spread fast. By daybreak 200 people had gathered in front of the jail and had begun making ugly noises. Sheriff Emig knew trouble when he saw it. At seven o'clock he ordered the prisoners moved to San Francisco for their own safety. As they were smuggled out the back, Thurmond appeared very nervous. He was chewing gum fiercely and from time to time his face twitched. Holmes seemed almost jaunty. He had eaten a good breakfast, whistled a lot in his cell, and refused to break under questioning. Even when confronted with Thurmond's confession, he continued to proclaim his innocence and smile pleasantly. On the way to San Francisco the police stopped for a few minutes at the San Mateo Bridge while Thurmond pointed out the spot where a week before he and Jack Holmes had bashed in Brooke Hart's head and dumped his weighted body into the bay.

In San Francisco the prisoners were taken first to the Potrero Street Police Station where, after further questioning, they were presented before newsmen for pictures. Thurmond looked menacing and seemed to resent being on display, but Holmes was pleasant and cooperative. Neatly dressed in a good-looking blue suit, a new light grey hat, a yellow open-neck shirt, and highly polished black shoes, he smiled winsomely for the photographers. Afterward, the two men were taken out separately for lunch at a nearby Italian restaurant. Thurmond, who had been too nervous to eat any breakfast back in San Jose, was famished. He ordered a large steak. "You know," he said as he devoured his meal, "I'm not such a bad guy. Everybody gives me a dirty look as though I was a tough guy. But I ain't. I'm just screwy." He then told about his unhappy romance. He simply hadn't been able to make enough money to hold onto his girl. One day she broke off their engagement. Soon after, she sent him an invitation to her wedding. "And I've been nuts ever since. I listened to everything Holmes had to offer. I just did as he suggested. I was the pawn."

That afternoon Holmes and Thurmond were moved to the San Francisco City Jail. There for the next seven days they were held "en route to San Jose" in separate cells in the felony wing, incommunicado except for occasional visits from close relatives. On Friday morning Holmes' father came to see him. Until then Holmes had remained outwardly calm and composed, but at the

sight of his father he broke down and cried. Later that day he con-
fessed. His version was almost the same as Thurmond's. The main
difference was his insistence that it was Harold Thurmond, rather
than he, who had masterminded the operation. Like Thurmond,
he agreed to turn state's evidence in order to save his own skin.
On Monday the Reverend Roy Thurmond brought his brother a
Bible and urged him to pray. Meanwhile the bay was being dragged
for Brooke Hart's body. On Saturday afternoon grappling hooks
came up with a shred of cloth believed to be part of the boy's
clothing. The next day a hat was found in the mud flats off Alameda. Tearfully Alex Hart identified it as his son's, but refused to
believe that the boy was dead.

On Wednesday, November 22, a federal grand jury sitting in
San Francisco brought in indictments against Holmes and Thurmond on seven counts of using the mails to extort. Later that
same day federal marshals appeared at the city jail with warrants
for the surrender of the prisoners, but were refused on a techni-
cality. The marshals would be back. Not soon enough, however.
Early that evening a call went out to San Jose:

"Listen, 3M, we can't keep your boys here any longer."

"I know. But I sure hate to bring them back just now, the
way things are here."

"Well, that's up to you. You know if the Feds get hold of
them, that's the last you'll see of them."

An hour before midnight Sheriff Emig arrived to take the
prisoners back to San Jose to stand trial under the recently passed
California Kidnaping Act. With him was a convoy of four cars,
carrying a dozen law officers armed with submachine guns, shotguns, sidearms, and tear gas.

Back in San Jose the return of the prisoners set off a new
wave of indignation. The town was in a mean mood. And why
shouldn't it be? Americans everywhere were getting fed up.
Weren't things bad enough without all these murderers and kidnapers and other thugs being allowed to run around loose? Sometimes it seemed as if the authorities just didn't care. Down in
Alabama, for instance, they were beginning the *third* trial for a
bunch of niggers who, everyone knew, had raped a couple of
white girls. Those boys should have been hung long ago, and would
have too if it hadn't been for their smart-ass Communist lawyers
and a couple of soft-headed judges. Down there in Morgan County,
where the trial was being held, 500 people had come out publicly

in favor of putting a swift end to the affair by lynching the niggers. Most of them favored lynching the lawyers too.

If anything, the good people of San José were probably even more upset than the rest of the country over all the lawlessness that had been going on. During the past few months Santa Clara County had experienced a number of particularly brutal crimes, including the killing of a popular rancher by one of his hired hands, and the murder (or at least so it seemed) of a young Mayfield mother whose body was found in the bathtub with her head smashed in. And now this awful Hart business. "Something is owed to public feeling," exclaimed one of the area newspapers:

> The revulsion of horror of the whole people at the unexampled callousness of this crime will find its normal relief in the knowledge that its perpetrators are put promptly out of the way. . . . Their death without delay will relieve the tension of public feeling.

On Friday and Saturday the temper of the people worsened. It was reported that Holmes had retracted his confession and now claimed that he was having dinner with his family at the time of the crime. As for Thurmond, there was little doubt that he would plead insanity. "He is in every sense of the word unbalanced," declared his lawyer. "Moreover it is my opinion that he never had any understandable conception of the part he played in the tragic crime." To an already aroused community these shenanigans acted as a further irritant. Could it be that these two animals, like so many others of their kind lately, would manage to escape what they had coming to them? The rumor going around San Jose was that this was not very likely.

Later, a reporter from the *San Francisco Chronicle* would claim that a secret association of from sixty to seventy "respectable citizens" of San Jose was formed at this time to see to it that Holmes and Thurmond would never come to trial. Supposedly, written pledges were made by the members of the association that as soon as the body of young Hart was recovered, thereby removing all possible doubt of the prisoners' guilt, the two men would be taken from jail and lynched. Whether such a conspiracy did indeed exist is, in the light of the scanty evidence available, somewhat questionable. One thing seems clear, however: by general agreement, stated or otherwise, the community would hold itself

in check until Hart's body was found. After that—who could say?
Sheriff Emig, fully aware of what was apt to happen, tripled the
number of his jailhouse guards and mounted a machine gun just
inside the main door. Meanwhile the newspapers of the area, playing the story for all it was worth, did their bit to keep the public
temper inflamed.

On Sunday morning, November 26, shortly after nine o'clock,
when most people in the Bay Area were still sleeping, getting ready
for church, or mulling over accounts of Stanford's 7-3 win over
Cal the day before, Brooke Hart's body was found by duck hunters
in five feet of water, about a half mile from the San Mateo Bridge.
It was still heavily weighted. Had it not been, it would by now
have surely been washed out to sea, thereby preserving that final
thin thread of doubt upon which the lives of Jack Holmes and
Harold Thurmond depended. In San Jose a family friend notified
the victim's father in the only way it could be done: "Alex, your
boy is dead." The father, who had continued in spite of all to believe that Brooke was still alive, cried out: "Oh, my God—my
God," and then collapsed. At about the same time, the news
reached Governor James Rolph in Sacramento. To the suggestion
that he call out the National Guard, he snorted:

> What! Call out troops to protect those two guys? The people make the
> laws don't they? Well, if the people have confidence that the troops
> will not be called out to mow them down when they seek to protect
> themselves against kidnapers, there is liable to be swifter justice and
> fewer kidnapings.

And then he postponed his scheduled trip to the Governors Conference in Idaho. "If I had gone away," he explained later, "someone else would have called out the troops."

Upon receiving word that young Hart's body had been recovered, the *San Jose News* ran a Sunday extra. Twelve thousand
copies were immediately snapped up. Shortly thereafter, a crowd
began to form in front of the jail and in St. James Park across the
street, where a statue of William McKinley stood looking benignly
out onto the city that had received him so warmly during his presidential visit a generation before. By midafternoon the crowd had
grown to several hundred, including many women and children.
When Sheriff Emig ordered them to disperse, they listened politely,

but wouldn't budge. Later a deputy district attorney circulated among them to give assurances that the arraignment and preliminary hearing would be held within a few days. Again the crowd refused to break up, but continued to be well-behaved and, except for an occasional jeer at the police, who had cordoned off the area immediately adjacent to the jail, seemed surprisingly good-natured. Sheriff Emig was optimistic. "I think we can handle them," he told one of his men.

In the late afternoon, not long before dusk, Jack Holmes was visited by his father. "I know my boy. He wouldn't lie to me," the father later reported. "I took him by the arm and looked squarely into his eyes and asked him if he was guilty. 'Dad, I swear to you,' he said, 'I had no part in this thing. Thurmond is apparently protecting someone. I don't know why he drew me into this.' " Outside, the crowd had suddenly grown much larger, and for the first time was showing signs of agitation. A rumor going around had it that Holmes and Thurmond were to be moved back to San Francisco to stand trial for mail extortion. "Don't fool yourself," one of the crowd called out to a policeman. "They're not going anywhere. We're coming after them, and when we do, you'd better stand aside, mister."

The Battle of San Jose began in earnest at about eight o'clock that evening. By then the crowd, which had grown to more than 5000, had turned surly. Sheriff Emig recognized the signs and put in a call to Oakland for reinforcements. As he phoned he could hear rocks thumping against the front of the old brick building, and the occasional sound of shattering glass. With him in the jail were his deputies and a few members of the San Jose police force, all of them armed with riot guns. Outside, several police and highway patrolmen kept the crowd at a respectable distance, but Sheriff Emig was not deluded. Once the crowd started to move, there would be no stopping them. The jail was an antique crackerbox that lacked most of the modern security equipment and could offer little resistance to a determined assault. As for the riot guns and the machine gun by the door, they were worthless except for their scare effect, if any. Emig had no intention of ordering them into use against his friends and neighbors. Even if he did, his orders probably wouldn't be carried out. That left only tear gas, and, as luck would have it, the wind was blowing in toward the jail.

Outside in front, a flimsy barrier of planks was being erected by County Jailer Howard Buffington and a few of the deputies.

A well-known local architect shouted over from across the street: "Hey, Buff, why don't you go get yourself a cigar! By the time you get back it will all be over." The jailer shook his head and walked away. "That guy is usually one of the quietest men in San Jose," he remarked to a deputy. Farther down the line a policeman was scolding a young couple who had their three small children with them. "Get those kids out of here," he snapped. "Suppose something happens. This is no place for kids."

At 9:20 the crowd began to press forward against the police perimeter. Those in front complained that they were being shoved by the others behind them, which was probably true. There were signs now of drunkenness, and frequent obscenities were heard. For several minutes the police pushed back against the crowd, but eventually had to give ground. The crowd grew noisier, and, as the police fell back, the pressure against them increased. Suddenly there was a muffled explosion, followed by a thumping sound overhead. And then more of the same, as from inside the jail the sheriff's men laid down a barrage of tear gas. Someone screamed "GAS," and the crowd scrambled back in noisy confusion to the park across the street. But it was only a momentary retreat. "The gas did about as much good as cigar smoke," commented one observer. "The breeze lifted most of it straight up in the air. Some of it blew back into the jail through the broken windows." Within a few minutes the crowd had regrouped in front of the jail.

From this point on, the situation rapidly worsened. The crowd snarled angrily at the police and hurled rocks and bottles at the jail. Now and then a few more canisters of tear gas would be lobbed out from inside, but, as before, they had virtually no effect. At about ten o'clock eighteen-year-old Anthony Catalbi left the scene and drove to his father's ranch to get some rope. "Then I went all over town in my fliver roadster and passed out the word: 'We're going to have a lynching at the jail!' " Shortly before 11:00 a sudden surge from the crowd overwhelmed the police cordon, and a group of a dozen or so men began battering on the door of the jail with a long section of eight-inch pipe from a nearby construction site. A few minutes later another group showed up with an identical piece of pipe, and the two teams took turns ramming at the door, above which appeared the Latin inscription: FIAT JUSTITIA, RUAT CAELUM ("Let justice be done, though the heavens fall.")

Inside, Sheriff Emig disarmed his deputies and locked their

weapons in a cabinet in the back room where the mob would be
unlikely to find them. "It was a damned smart thing to do," one
of the deputies later remarked. "Those guns wouldn't have done
any good anyway, and they could have done a lot of harm, especially if some of the drunks in the crowd had got hold of them."
Emig then ordered his men to stand their ground as best they
could, while he himself went to the second floor and put in another call to Oakland. "We can't hold out much longer," he reported to the Oakland duty officer, and just then the old iron
door of the jail buckled and gave way. Within seconds, dozens of
wildmen had reached the second floor and forced the flimsy door
at the top of the stairs. When Emig tried to block their way, he
was hit on the head with a piece of pipe and pushed unconscious
down the stone staircase.

"They're up there on the third floor," someone shouted, and
the mob hurried up another flight, roughly shoving aside the few
guards who tried to stop them. At the head of the third-floor corridor Jailer Buffington, the last man to stand in their way, faced
the mob and ordered them to get out. They responded by demanding his keys. When he refused, they beat him to the floor and
took them. With a wild whoop they started down the corridor,
looking for their prey. "Thurmond's down there," someone said
and pointed to a cell occupied by young Tony Serpa, who had
recently been convicted of manslaughter and was awaiting transfer
to San Quentin. The mob gave out another whoop and converged
upon Serpa's call. "For Christ sake, that's not him," somebody
said, and they moved on. "Man, oh man," Serpa exclaimed to reporters the next day, after having been removed to the San Francisco Jail:

> I don't ever want to see San Jose again. My attorney wanted to appeal
> my case, but I fired him. To hell with the appeal. I'm ready to go to
> San Quentin right now. I can't commence to tell you how I felt. First
> I heard the people shouting. Then I heard a crash. Then that rickety old
> joint shook like an earthquake.

The mob found Holmes first and then Thurmond, who had
managed to hide for a time by suspending himself from the ceiling
of his toilet. As the prisoners were about to be yanked out of their
cells, a voice rang out above the din: "Brothers, let us pray."

Growing suddenly quiet, the members of the mob took off their hats and knelt down: "Oh, Heavenly Father, forgive these sinners," said a man holding a rope. "Amen, Brother Ben," someone interrupted. "Now let's get the sons of bitches!"

The two men were dragged from their cells. Thurmond clawed at the ceiling "like a rat in a flooded bunker," cried out for mercy, and then fainted. He never came to. As he was carried out of the building, his pants were torn off and he was beaten several times on the face and body. In the park across the street somebody threw a rope over the limb of a mulberry tree. A noose was slid over Thurmond's head and he was hoisted about eight feet off the ground and suspended there. The onlookers cheered, jeered, and applauded. A few prayed. "What do you think of kidnaping now, Harry?" one of them shouted as he looked up at Thurmond.

Holmes was another matter. He fought fiercely to the very end. While being jostled down the stairs and out of the jail, he was pummeled and clawed at by the mob. At the bottom of the outside steps he was taken by the heels and dragged across the street, his head thumping up and down on the pavement. By the time he reached the park, he was stark naked and badly beaten, especially about the face. But he was still conscious. At the north end of the park a large elm tree was chosen, and a man with a rope shinnied up to examine the crotch. "It's no good," he called down. "Well, keep going until you find one that is," someone shouted back. At about 11:25 the noose was placed around Holmes' neck and he was hauled up. However, he managed to grab the rope above the noose and support the weight of his body with his arms. He was lowered and beaten and then hauled up again. This time he was somehow able to insert his fingers between the rope and his neck. Once more he was brought down and beaten. On the third try the hangmen succeeded and the onlookers applauded, while nearby autos honked their approval and played their lights upon Jack Holmes, whose naked body kicked now and then in a grotesque little dance of death as it dangled ten feet off the ground.

By now the downtown movie houses had let out and the crowd had swollen to (some say) over 7500. For blocks around the streets were clogged with people and stalled automobiles, many of them with their horns blaring in frustration, and others abandoned by their drivers who, having despaired of making any headway, had decided to join in the excitement. In the park itself thousands of people milled about, pausing now and then to chat with friends or watch newsmen take flash photos of the two dangling bodies. From time to time someone would faint, causing a momentary commotion, but on the whole the crowd seemed remarkably unruffled and matter of fact. Not far from where Holmes was hanging, a young child could be seen perched on his father's shoulders. Several other children, some of them no older than eight or nine, ran unattended through the crowd. "I touched the rope," one of them boasted to a reporter. In the center of the crowd a dozen or so young toughs stood clustered about the mulberry tree that held Thurmond. They were talking loudly and taking turns drinking from a bottle that was going the rounds. Every so often one of them would flick a cigarette butt up at Thurmond. Finally one of the butts lodged itself inside his jacket, and before long a slight wisp of smoke could be detected curling out from under the dead man's collar.

From across First Street several policemen watched the crowd with detached interest. Occasionally one or more of them would move loiterers away from in front of the jail, or make vain attempts to unsnarl the traffic. None of them ventured across the street into the park. Shortly after midnight the Oakland police finally arrived on the scene. About thirty in number, they made several unsuccessful attempts before finally managing to wedge their way into the park. "It was about as dense a mob as I've ever seen," commented the officer in charge, "but pliant, very quiet." Arriving at the hanging trees, the police pressed the crowd back a few yards and threw up cordons to protect the victims' bodies from possible mutilation or abuse by souvenir hunters, some of whom had already removed several strips of bark from the trees. The bodies were then gently lowered to the ground, while the crowd looked on, passive and silent. "Not even a hoot or a cat-call," one of the officers later recalled. Soon the county coroner arrived and, after putting out the smoldering fire in Thurmond's clothing, pronounced the two men dead. The crowd parted as the bodies were carried from the park on their way to the morgue, where they would be laid out beside the badly decomposed corpse of the young man they had so callously murdered two weeks before.

On the following morning in Sacramento, Governor Rolph issued what the press called "a striking statement." In it the dapper Sunny Jim, now well along in years but still full of fire, left little doubt about where he stood:

With all the sorrows we have, why should we add the sorrows of kidnaping? It is about time that people in their homes have the comfort of knowing that their children will not be kidnaped or murdered. People are so worried that they are taking the law into their own hands. Sorrowing parents have been victimized by money extortionists for too long a time. Since the Lindbergh case conditions have been so bad that men, women, and children throughout the nation are fearful. Mothers fear to let their children play in the streets. There is fear in all homes. . . .

The fine, patriotic citizens of San Jose have done a good job, and I hope this lesson will serve in every state of the Union. This is the best lesson California has ever given the country. We show the country that this state is not going to tolerate kidnaping.

And then, as a parting shot:

I do not think that there will be any arrests in the San Jose lynching case. If there are any, I'll pardon them all.

The American Civil Liberties Union saw things differently. So did the *New York Times*, President Roosevelt, and a goodly number of the nation's clergy and college professors. For several days the air was rent with angry protest, especially that part of the air east of the Mississippi and north of the Mason-Dixon Line. The lynchings were "unamerican," "humiliating and shameful," "thoroughly shocking," and "outrageous." The lynchers were "outlaws," "degenerates," "drunken bums," and "barbarians," who had "set back the clock by decades."

But it was the outspoken Rolph who received most of the fire. "The Governor's action is a betrayal of his trust and an affront to the State of California and the people of the United States," declared the Episcopal Bishop of New York. "He should retract his statement at once and publicly apologize for it, or he should be removed from office." From his home on the Stanford campus, Herbert Hoover, not long out of the White House, publicly criticized Rolph's statement, calling it "subversive of the very foundations upon which the State and all civilized society is built." And in Emporia, Kansas, America's favorite editor, William Allen White, fumed with indignation: "Southern Governors at least have the brains to be ashamed of their lynchings," he wrote in his *Gazette*, "which is more than can be said for Rolph."

And so it went. But Sunny Jim held his ground. To Hoover, Rolph fired back that as the one responsible for turning the guns on the bonus marchers, the former President was hardly in a position to lecture others on how to react to mob action. (A mean thing to say, Hoover retorted, and there the exchange ended.) As for the others, most of them were liberals, and to Governor Rolph it didn't make a damned bit of difference what they thought anyway. He had never cared much for liberals, nor they for him, especially since his recent refusal to pardon the imprisoned anarchists Mooney and Billings. "As far as I'm concerned," he was said to have remarked, "the whole bunch of them can go piss up a stump."

Besides, the governor was confident that the great majority of the American people felt pretty much as he did, and he was probably right. "The public reaction is one of almost universal approval," claimed the *Portland Oregonian*. "The temper of modern America, besieged by criminals and outraged by their crimes, demands certainty and directness of punishment." The *Denver Post* couldn't have agreed more. The lynchings were "goodly, righteous, and necessary," and Governor Rolph was to be commended for his stand. "Millions of red-blooded Americans envy California their Governor."

In Oakland, the Alameda County district attorney, while not exactly approving of what had happened in San Jose, didn't exactly disapprove either, at least not publicly. Said he:

> The lynching is merely a manifestation of the lack of confidence which people have in the administration of justice. There is so much crime going on in the country that is unpunished, that the people are losing confidence in their institutions.

This was hardly the sort of reaction to be expected from Earl Warren, whose later opinions as chief justice of the United States would mark him as one of the nation's foremost civil libertarians. But, of course, at the time of the San Jose lynchings he was still in the elective phase of his career and had his political future to think about. Not so with Rolph. His enemies accused him of exploiting the San Jose affair for his own political advantage, with an eye to the 1934 gubernatorial election. But they were wrong. Early in the following year Sunny Jim announced his retirement from politics. A few months later he died without having budged an iota:

Ask yourself this question. How would I feel if my own son were done to death and demand for ransom made upon me after he had been fiendishly murdered? . . . These criminals no longer fear the law. The one thing these cowardly criminals fear is an aroused citizenry.

It took a while for San Jose to get tidied up after its big night, but within a couple of weeks the town seemed pretty much back to normal. Sheriff Emig, after having spent some time on the critical list with a bad concussion, had been released from the hospital and was back on the job. Jailer Buffington had more or less recovered from his beating, and Alex Hart had returned to work in the store he had hoped to turn over to his son. When cornered by reporters, Hart refused to comment on the lynchings, except to say: "What difference does any of it make anyway? Brooke is dead." A grand jury hearing was held, ostensibly to inquire into the lynchings with a view to criminal proceedings against the leaders. But the hearing was strictly pro forma. No names were mentioned; no information sought or volunteered; and, of course, no indictments returned. "It is a closed scene," remarked an observer, "a fallen curtain. Nothing will be done about it."

On the Thursday evening following the lynch party, the San Jose City Council voted to remove the hanging trees, despite the argument from some of its members that the trees should be left standing as a reminder to all criminal types. That Sunday a crew of city workmen felled the trees, cut them up, and carted them away for firewood. During the operation a sizable crowd gathered in the park to watch, and carry away chips and twigs as souvenirs. Some took leaves for their scrapbooks.

Meanwhile, a group of county officials had examined the jail for damage. The outside was pockmarked from the rocks and other missiles that had been hurled against it; most of the window panes were broken; and the inside of the building was a shambles. It was estimated that the repair bill would run upwards of a thousand dollars. This was no small sum in the deep depression year of 1933. But then, as one of the county commissioners remarked at the time: "That's a damn sight less than a trial would have cost."

Me and Paul

They can talk of Grove and Hubbell,
But when the team's in deep-down trouble,
You're a better man than they are,
Dizzy Dean.

(Anonymous)

IN 1934 the nation's newest folk hero, John Dillinger, was gunned down outside a Chicago movie theatre by Melvin Purvis and associates; Alcatraz became a federal penitentiary; and the American cruise liner *Morro Castle* burned off the New Jersey coast, with a loss of 134 lives, as thousands looked on in fascination from the shore. Navy flyers piloted a seaplane all the way from San Francisco to Pearl Harbor, some 2900 miles, in less than twenty-five hours, while, not to be outdone, three army officers ascended in a giant balloon from Rapid City, South Dakota, and reached an altitude of nearly twelve miles before a tear in the bag forced them to bounce down in a corn field outside Loomis, Nebraska. Once again drought and dust storms scourged the Midwest, destroying crops, animals, and human hopes.

1934 was also the first full year of the New Deal. People in Washington kept saying that the corner had been turned, that things were beginning to look up. Maybe they were a bit, but to those millions of Americans who continued to be unemployed (some of them now in their fifth straight year) and millions of others working half-time or less, there still wasn't much to cheer about. Blue Eagles were everywhere, proclaiming "We Do Our

Part" in the windows of filling stations and First National Stores, on the mastheads of newspapers, and on the screen of the local Bijou between the newsreel and the previews of coming attractions. It was a good year for the movies: *The Barretts of Wimpole Street, The Count of Monte Cristo, The Thin Man, It Happened One Night,* and *Little Miss Marker,* starring America's dimpled darling Shirley Temple, whose popularity was rivaled only by that of a loudmouthed, wiseacre duck, just recently arrived on the show-biz scene.

It was also a good year for popular songs, in case anyone felt like singing. The harvest had never been more bountiful or better. Songs like: "The Isle of Capri," "Wagon Wheels," "Blue Moon," "I Only Have Eyes for You," "Deep Purple," "Moonglow," "P.S., I Love You," "The Very Thought of You," and "On the Good Ship Lollipop."

But, as any American boy worth his bubble gum cards will tell you, 1934 was most of all the year of the St. Louis Gashouse Gang, the brassiest bunch of roughnecks ever to win a major league pennant. In later years an old pro who had played against them and felt their sting would call them "the best single-season team in the history of the game." They probably weren't, but they were certainly the most colorful and exciting.

Of course in those days bigtime baseball was a far cry from what it is now: only eight teams in each league, with nothing west of St. Louis; travel by train; no night games, or batting helmets, or artificial turf, or designated pinch-anything; and lily-white all the way down to the peanut vendors. On the whole the players were a rough lot, sprung from the nation's farms and mines and city sandlots. Most of them had dropped out of school early, sometimes by choice, but more often because they had to in order to help out at home. A high school graduate was a rarity among them, and a college man a wonder to behold. Many of them, including some of the greatest figures in the game, could barely read a boxscore or write their own names.

They chewed tobacco, took Copenhagen snuff, cussed outrageously, and drank cheap liquor until three in the morning. The thought of hiring a lawyer to negotiate next year's contract never even occurred to them, although perhaps it should have, because most of them were shamefully underpaid. After the remarkable performance in the 1931 World Series by Pepper Martin, who came as close as any man ever has to winning a Series single-handedly, Baseball Commissioner Judge Landis sought him out and congratulated him. "Martin," he said, "I'd give anything to be able to change places with you." "Well, Judge, that sure would be fine with me," replied the irrepressible Pepper. "Let's begin by me taking your fifty thousand a year and you taking my four."

The attitude of the players was different too. They cared more about the game and gave it their all, partly perhaps because baseball was more of a sport then and less of a business, but mainly because, being a simpler breed, they knew nothing else and didn't want to. Remarked an old pro recently:

> Today I see these guys with their restaurants and night clubs and car washes, and their franchises in this and that, and I can't help but think that baseball is just a sideline with them. You ought to see them nowadays when they come down for spring training. They've got a thousand dollars' worth of fishing gear and another thousand of golf equipment. The manager says to them: "An extra hour of bunting practice today, boys," and you'd think they'd been stabbed in the heart. They can't wait to get out there in the boat or on the golf course. Well, I can tell you it wasn't like that with us. With us baseball was our whole world.

And that world revolved not around the sun but around winning. Victory was beautiful, no matter how sloppily won, and defeat, no matter how gallantly sustained, was seldom suffered lightly. Grown men were known to shed copious tears over games that should have been won but weren't. And woe be unto the sportswriter foolhardy enough to ask in the wake of defeat: "What sort of a pitch was it he fanned you with, Joe?" Commented the head Gashouser, Frankie Frisch, a few years ago in reflecting on the old days:

> I read in the paper last winter that a sportswriter had filed charges against a ball player just because the player tried to punch him in the nose. Why, I never had any idea that punching a sportswriter in the nose was against the law. It just goes to show how the game has changed.

Few men since Job have been so sorely tried as Frank Francis Frisch, who in the twilight of his playing career was singled out by owner Sam Breardon and his brilliant assistant, Branch Rickey, to take over from Gabby Street as manager of the St. Louis Cardinals. Somehow, after winning successive pennants in 1930 and 1931, Street had lost his touch, and with it his control over the team. As discipline disappeared, so did morale. More to the point, the Cardinals had developed losing ways, and by the time Frisch took charge in midsummer of 1933, were wallowing in fifth place. By the end of the season the club had done no better than hold its own in the standings, but its new manager had come a long way toward establishing his authority, and that in itself was something. "Oooee, that was some wild bunch!" Frisch would recall years later:

> They were always beating up on each other. I've never seen so many black eyes and missing teeth. It's a miracle somebody didn't really get hurt bad. Why, I've seen guys go after Dizzy with baseball bats and chase him all around the park, hollering "We're gonna kill you, you son of a bitch." My coach Mike Gonzales says to me: "Don you thing maybe we better do something, Frong?" And I says: "Naw, leave them be. Maybe they'll catch him."

Back home in New Rochelle after the season had ended, Frisch took stock of the situation and wondered if he could face another year of riding herd over such a bunch of yahoos. Bumping into a friend from the old days who now had five daughters, he sighed: "All girls. Think of that. All girls. How wonderful."

Actually, Frisch was a good choice for the job. He was tough of mind and body, a real scrapper who could hold his own in any company. At the same time he was a likable sort with an irrepressible good humor (a friend once called him "a jovial fiend") who was pathologically incapable of holding a grudge for more than ten minutes. He was human. He made his share of mistakes both on and off the field, and when the mood seized him he could be just as bull-headed as any of his players. The boys called him Frank, Frankie, "the Dutchman," and "cement-head" (although not to his face). He was also known as "the Fordham Flash," after a college he had once spent some time at somewhere back East. Sportswriters sometimes referred to him as "the town crier" because of his tendency to worry and make mournful sounds when things were less than perfect. "If he wins seventeen out of twenty," someone once said of him, "he'll fret more about the three losses than he'll rejoice over the seventeen wins."

But that was his nature. He hated to lose. It bothered him, perhaps because he hadn't had much practice at it. In 1919, after two years at Fordham, he signed with McGraw's Giants for a $200 bonus. Before being traded to the Cardinals in 1927 he had played in four World Series. Since moving to St. Louis he had been in three more, and although when spring training broke up in early April of 1934 probably not even Frankie himself would have thought such a thing very likely, he was about to be in another— the greatest and sweetest of them all.

This would take some doing, for the world's champion New York Giants, who had won in a walk the season before, were generally conceded to be a shoo-in to repeat. The Cubs might make a scrap of it. But the Cardinals? Who were they? They had finished in the second division the past year, and didn't appear to have helped themselves much since then by off-season trades. They had, however, brought up a couple of promising rookies from their farm system. One was a burly young catcher named Bill DeLancey. The other was Paul Dean, kid brother of the irrepressible Dizzy who at twenty-two (or maybe it was twenty-one) was already the mainstay of the Cardinals' pitching staff. "Now listen, you guys," Frisch snarled in the locker room just before the opening game, "we're not going to let anyone in this league run over us. Do you get that? You've got to win those ball games, especially the close ones. . . . Now, if you'd rather go back to the mines and dig for coal than ride around the country in Pullmans and live in the best hotels at the expense of the club, speak right up. We haven't got any room for softies, and no holds barred. That's the way we're gonna play ball."

"You said more'n a mouthful, Frank," chimed in Dizzy. And then they went out and lost seven of their first eleven. On May 1 they were one game out of the cellar.

In May, though, the club came alive and won twenty-one while losing only six. By the end of the month they were leading the league, a game and a half up on the second-place Giants. And why not? They may not have been the greatest team in the history of the game, but they had their fair share of talent, and then some.

At first base was switch-hitting James Anthony "Rip" Collins, a strong boy from the Pennsylvania coal regions, who had come to the club in 1931 and since then had given the Cardinals much of their punch at the plate. Although no Babe Ruth, he had great power, and his ability to hit to any field made him doubly dangerous. In 1934 he would have his best season by far, with thirty-four home runs (to tie Mel Ott of the Giants for the league lead) and a hundred and twenty-eight runs batted in.

At second was the Fordham Flash himself, a lover of birds and classical music, who although now thirty-five and somewhat long of tooth, was still one of the best in the business. True, he may have been a bit slower rounding the bases than in the old days when he reported to McGraw's Giants without having played so much as a day of minor league ball, but when it came to patroling his position afield, he was still the wide-ranging kid with the magic glove: ("Then there was Mr. Frisch," Casey Stengel would later reminisce, "which went to a University and could run fast besides. He was the first second baseman that didn't pedal backwards when they hit the ball down the line. He'd put his head down and commence running like in a race, and he'd beat the ball there.") And as for hitting, he was as much of a menace as ever. During his playing career of nearly two decades he batted for an average of .316. Like Rip Collins he was a switch hitter and could stroke to any field. His speciality was hitting with men on base. He loved the game. He loved everything about it—even managing the Gashouse Gang. "They were a bunch of real gentlemen," he said of them many years later. "Good law-abiding citizens who liked nothing better than to help little old ladies across the street."

And then there was the shortstop—Leo Durocher, man of many parts, all five-foot-six of him. Acquired from Cincinnati the year before, Durocher provided the Cards with great skill afield and a remarkably loud mouth, out of which flowed a constant torrent of profanity and abuse against umpires, rival players, and sometimes his own teammates. At bat he seldom soared above .250. For him a walk and a scratch single represented a great day at the plate. Sportswriters called him "the All-American Out." Among the players, though, he was known more widely as Leo the Lip, or just plain Lippy. With his abrasive, terrierlike ways, he was not an object of great affection among his fellow players, including the Cardinals themselves. Still, he was a valuable man to have around, for he was one of the game's greatest hustlers, the kind who could be counted on to give a complete effort—like getting hit by a pitch to help fire up a late-inning rally, which for Leo wasn't hard to do because pitchers seemed to love to throw at him. "Why is that?" Frisch asked one of them one day. "You let the big guys like Collins and Medwick stand in there and swing away, and then when Leo comes up, who can't hit the ball out of the infield, you knock him down. I don't understand that at all." "I'll tell you why," came the answer. "Because Leo is a mean little son of a bitch. That's why."

John Leonard "Pepper" Martin, the Cardinals' third baseman, was one of the most colorful figures ever to play the game. The thirty-year-old Oklahoma farm boy had come to the club in 1928, riding the rods of a freight train. Since then he had been the main sparkplug of the team. It wasn't that he was such a great hitter, although save for one bad year among his fifteen in the majors he never dipped far below .300. Nor was he the picture of grace in the field, where he specialized in stopping ground balls with his chest. It was as a baserunner that he terrorized the enemy and earned his immortality as "the wild horse of the Osage." Fast? An old friend remembers him as a youngster back on the Oklahoma range. "Even then Pepper was a great runner. He used to scoot alongside a bunch of rabbits and every so often he'd reach for one and heft it for size. If it scaled a little thin he'd put it down again; if it felt nice and fat he'd drop it in his bag."

But there was more than speed to Martin's amazing performance on the bases: he had a way of getting a long, tantalizing lead on pitchers, which sometimes rattled them and threw them off stride (so much the better for the man at bat), and he was a master of the hard slide, especially the head-first, diving variety that became his hallmark. "Pepper's the only guy I know," said a teammate, "who when he walks dust comes out his ears." In the World Series of 1931 he stole five bases. He also tied a Series record and broke two others by getting twelve hits for a total of nineteen bases and an overall batting average of .500. All in all, he put on one of the most impressive one-man shows in the history of World Series competition. Clearly this was his greatest moment of glory. And yet for Pepper, whose brassiness could never quite conceal an inner nobility, there would always be a sour note to it:

> Now, I'm not a dignified man myself, but when I look back over the World Series between the Cardinals and Athletics in 1931, I always remember how the fans booed President Hoover in the first game in Philadelphia.
>
> They cheered me; me, a rookie from Oklahoma who could run a little, and booed the President of the United States. It just didn't seem right, and I sure felt sorry for Mr. Hoover and I was kind of put out

with the fans because, after all, being President of the United States is a
pretty big job and should command respect.

Frisch, years later: "Did I have favorites? Sure I did. I never *played*
favorites, but I had a few. I liked Pepper Martin. You couldn't
help but like John Leonard. Let me tell you that there was some
guy."

The Cardinal outfield that year was no great shakes. In right
and center field respectively were Jack Rothrock, a seasoned jour-
neyman acquired during the off season from the White Sox, and
Ernie "Showboat" Orsatti, former stunt man and one-time stand-
in for Buster Keaton. Both were good enough ball players, but not
very likely to end up in the hall of fame. In left field was Joe
"Ducky" Medwick, a stocky youngster about to begin his second
full season with the Cardinals. At twenty-two he had not yet come
to full flower, but he was already well on his way to greatness.
Tough, rough, and muscular, he was not to be trifled with—on the
field or off. When his temper flared, as it sometimes did, he would
just as soon punch a person as look at him, especially if that person happened to be a sportswriter. During the 1934 season he
would bat a robust .319 while knocking in 106 runs—three more
than Rothrock and Orsatti combined. He was particularly dangerous on bad balls. He may, in fact, have been the best bad-ball hitter of his day, or any day. Some said he was too dumb to tell the
difference; others claimed he simply knew what he liked and went
after it. At any rate, it was not unheard of for him to reach far
across the plate and, with his great strength, rattle a pitch-out off
the left field fence.

The catching for the Cardinals was shared by the veteran
Virgil "Spud" Davis, a solid .300 hitter acquired recently from the
Phils, and the rookie sensation Bill DeLancey. The latter, with his
quick bat and superb skill behind the plate, was already being
acclaimed as the greatest catching find since Gabby Hartnett. Perhaps he was. There wouldn't be time enough to tell for sure, for
after only two years with the Cards, during which he batted .300
and played his position to near perfection, he came down with
tuberculosis and had to quit the game. He died in 1946 at the age
of thirty-five.

On the other end of the battery was a pitching staff made up,
for the most part, of fading greats and respectable second-raters,
principal among whom were the venerable Jesse "Pop" Haines,

"Wild Bill" Hallahan, Tex Carleton, and ex-Giant Bill Walker. And then, of course, there were the Dean brothers, Dizzy and Paul. "Your worries is over now, Frankie," Dizzy announced when he learned that his brother was being called up from Columbus for the opening of the 1934 season. "Why, me and Paul will win you fifty games between us this year." This was an exaggeration. Actually they would win only forty-nine.

Naturally Dizzy's real name wasn't Dizzy, although it probably should have been. But everyone called him that (including his wife Pat) except Frankie Frisch, who called him Jerome. "Why don't you call him Dizzy, like other people?" Pat used to ask. "Because I like the name Jerome," Frankie replied. "It sounds nice." Besides, that was Dizzy's real name: Jerome Herman Dean, except when it was Jay Hanna Dean, or Hannah, or Hanner. Much depended on how Dizzy felt on a given day, or whom he happened to be talking to. He was born in Lucas, Arkansas, or Holdenville, Oklahoma, or some place in Texas, on January 16, or February 22, or August 22, 1911. "I really don't recall exactly when it was. But I'll tell you this. It wasn't February 22nd. I just say that to give George Washington a little boost." No matter. Whoever he was, or wherever from, he may well have been the greatest pitcher of them all. Certainly he thought so himself, and he set out to prove it by winning 120 games in his first five years. It is interesting and a little sad to speculate on how high he might have soared (he was only in his mid-twenties; his career was just beginning) had it not been for that freak accident in the 1937 All Star Game—but that's another story.

The son of an itinerant cotton picker, Dizzy didn't have an easy time of it as a boy. "My mother died when I was three years old and me and Paul had to go out and pick cotton to keep the fire up." There wasn't much chance for schooling. "If I had of finished the second grade, I would of went a year longer than my old man. . . . I reckon that's why I come up with an 'ain't' once in a while." As soon as he could, he joined the army. It was probably the first time in his life he had slept in a clean bed or worn a whole pair of shoes.

In the army he pitched for one of the camp teams at Ft. Sam Houston, where he soon came to the attention of the town fathers of nearby San Antonio. So impressed were they with what they saw of this big, good-looking youngster, that they offered him thirty dollars a week to pitch for their local semipro team once he got out of the army. Somehow or other an early discharge was arranged, and in 1929 at the age of eighteen Dizzy began work as a regular, salaried ballplayer. After winning sixteen straight games for San Antonio, he was signed by the Cardinals and in the spring of the following year sent to their St. Joseph farm club in the Western Association.

At St. Joe he got into a few scrapes with the law. Nothing serious: reckless driving, racing with traffic cops, and a few too many beers now and then. But more to the point, he pitched brilliantly. After seventeen wins he was called up to the Cards' main farm club at Houston in the tough Texas League, where he went on to win eight more games. On the morning after his first win at Houston (a 12-1 rout) he went to the club office, cap in hand, and apologized: "I'm awful sorry about what happened last night, Mr. Ackerman. I promise if you give me another chance it won't never happen again. Can you imagine them bums getting a run off of me?" On the last day of the season he got his first crack at the majors, when the Cardinals called him up to pitch against the heavy hitting Pittsburgh Pirates. He shut them out on three hits. This was 1930. He was nineteen years old.

There was no question now that Dizzy was something out of the ordinary, and he suddenly found himself the object of considerable acclaim, especially among the St. Louis sportswriters. His head was not turned by any of this, however. He had known for some time that he was a great pitcher, and he was surprised it had taken others so long to find it out. "That ain't braggin," Dizzy would say. "The way I see it, braggin is where you do a lot of poppin off and ain't got nuthin to back it up with." And in his case he had plenty. A rugged six-footer with the stamina of an ox and the grace of a ballet dancer, he was a superb natural athlete. He probably could have excelled at any sport, but he had a particularly fine instinct for baseball that helped make it his special game. He also had a good, sharp-breaking curve, outstanding control, and a fast ball (his best pitch—he called it his "fog ball") that at times was virtually unseeable. "My God," exclaimed a scout on first seeing Dizzy at work, "that kid can throw a ball through a two-inch plank!"

None of this would have amounted to much, however, without that rare quality of total composure so essential to all great athletes. Dizzy abounded with it. Although off the diamond he was a bundle of nerves, once on the pitcher's mound he was in

complete control of himself and king of all he surveyed. A bases-
loaded situation or the rhythmic clapping of the fans didn't bother
him at all. He knew that in his strong right arm he had the means
to set things right. And on those infrequent occasions when the
arm threatened to falter, he could always count on the help of the
Lord. As a boy he had listened to the preaching of his uncle, the
Reverend Bland Dean, self-ordained fundamentalist minister of
the gospel, and since then he had never really been far out of
touch with the Holy Spirit: "The Lord He had His arms around
me all the time," Dizzy declared after an especially tight game.
"Yes He did. Like to of choked me, He held me so tight. Whenever
I was gonna go wild, He just patted me on the head and the next
guy popped up." When all else failed (including the Lord) Dizzy
would terrify the batters by throwing at their heads.

If Dizzy had a weakness as a pitcher, it was that he often
failed to take the game seriously enough. An incurable showboat,
he loved to fool around on the mound, swapping insults with the
batters and teasing them with fat pitches. "You guys don't have
to worry none about my curve today," he shouted over to the
Braves' bench one afternoon before the game. "I ain't gonna
throw nuthin but fast balls." He was as good as his word and still
won. On another occasion, with his team only one run up on the
Giants in the ninth inning, he deliberately walked a man so that
he could end the game by striking out the mighty Bill Terry with
the bases loaded. He did it on three straight fast balls right down
the middle. Sometimes, though, Dizzy's clowning cost him. Once
in Brooklyn, Frisch cautioned him: "Now, remember, whatever
you do, don't give Cuccinello a high fast ball. He'll powder it
every time." Frisch should have known better. Here was a challenge that was just too much for Dizzy to resist. He delivered the
first pitch to Cuccinello fast and letter high, and then watched him
loft it into the bleachers. "Say, Frankie, you was right about that
Cuccinello fella," Dizzy said when he came back to the dugout.
"He sure can hit a high fast ball."

Besides being frolicsome, Dizzy was sometimes inclined to be
a little lazy, or at least nonchalant, out there on the mound, especially in games against second-division clubs. Overconfidence
("There ain't many of us really great pitchers left.") caused him to
let up a little now and then, and thereby lose games he could have
won. After Dizzy's spectacular season in 1934, Frankie Frisch
took him aside and lectured him on the subject: "You ought to be

ashamed of yourself. You're no thirty-game winner. You're a forty-game winner. But you loaf around out there. With your stuff you ought to pitch nothing but shutouts."

In the spring of 1931, after his great rookie year in the minors, Dizzy reported to the Cardinals' training camp at Bradenton, Florida. On the third day, after a night on the town, he failed to show up for morning practice. When Manager Gabby Street found him still in bed, Dizzy growled: "Let them other clucks work out. I don't need to. Nobody can beat me." This did not get him off to a very fast start with either Manager Street or the other players—which was too bad, because Dizzy was a friendly fellow who liked people and wanted them to like him. In fact, he went out of his way that spring to instruct his teammates on what they were doing wrong and how they could improve their game.

Dizzy also managed to get off on the wrong foot with the front office. He arrived in Bradenton that spring virtually penniless—not an uncommon condition for one of such profligacy. Since his salary was not to begin until the start of the regular season, he was faced with the prospect of several weeks of free room and board, baseball, and little else. Not even a trip downtown for a glass of beer. He soon discovered, however, that all he had to do to get around this difficulty was to cash IOUs against the credit of the club. This worked very well until the chits began to reach the top, where Branch Rickey exclaimed "Judas Priest!" and put a stop to them. On Rickey's orders Dizzy was put on an allowance of a dollar a day. This was a humiliating state of affairs for a big star like Dizzy, but he didn't have much choice in the matter. Each morning he would report to Gabby Street, draw his money, and sign a receipt for it: "Received [date] from St. Louis Cardinals—$1.00, Dizzy Dean." On the first day he lost the whole amount in a slot machine before breakfast. The second day was better: his dollar lasted till noon. Finally he got so that he had enough left over after supper to buy a bottle of orange soda pop before going to bed.

When training camp broke up that spring, Dizzy was cut from the roster and sent back to Houston. He was crestfallen and at a loss to account for what had happened. So were the St. Louis sportswriters who had been covering the training camp and had seen how brilliantly the youngster had pitched. "A new world's record," groaned one of them. "This is the first time a club ever lost thirty games in one day." "A thirty-game winner? Sure," re-

plied one of the coaches. "But he would have wrecked the club."
And he probably would have. Everybody knew Dizzy was great.
The players knew it, Rickey knew it, and even Gabby Street (whom
Dizzy drove half crazy) knew it. But he was also brash, arrogant,
and undisciplined—a dangerously disruptive influence. It was generally understood that he was being sent down for another year in
the minors not to learn how to pitch better, but to be tamed.

The treatment may have done some good, but not much.
When he came back up to the Cardinals to stay in 1932, he was
still an abrasive, loudmouthed prima donna, given to childish displays of temperament and exhibitionism. "He was," said a sportswriter in describing Dizzy at that time, "typical of the boy who
had not grown out of an uneasy childhood, where his only hope of
matching his fellows is through almost tearful bragging, lying,
fighting, inventing of romantic backgrounds and adventures that
never took place." At times he was almost hysterical in his boast-
ing. He told stories about himself that nobody in his right mind
could have believed, and he made promises he couldn't possibly
keep. But he won ball games for the Cardinals, lots of them, and
as he grew more established and secure he began to mellow a bit—
just enough to reveal an occasional glimpse of his real self: beneath
all that bluster was a sensitive, highly intelligent youngster, who
also happened to be remarkably good-hearted, well-meaning, and
anxious to please. He was, remarked someone who knew him well,
"an exceedingly sweet boy."

In his rookie year he led the league in innings pitched and
strikeouts, while winning eighteen games for a club that finished
a poor seventh. In the following year he won twenty games as the
Cardinals moved up to a still disappointing fifth. He also led again
in strikeouts and tied a modern record in that department by setting down seventeen in one game. "Why shucks, I wasn't even
countin. If I'd of know'd, I would of bore down a little and
fanned three or four more." By the time his brother Paul joined
the club in the spring of 1934, Dizzy was already being spoken of
one of the top pitchers in the game, and Dizzy himself saw no
reason to disagree.

In physical appearance Paul Dean was strikingly similar to his
more famous brother. On the mound it was hard to tell them apart,
because not only did they look alike but they also pitched alike.
Both threw halfway between an overhand and a sidearm, and both
had a smooth, flowing delivery (sportswriters today would call it

"fluid") that made their pitching seem almost effortless. In most other respects the brothers were about as different as two people can be. Paul was quiet, stable, and unassuming. He seldom said or did anything out of the ordinary, and he was a paragon of tranquility. "Dizzy is all nerves," remarked a friend. "Always raring to go. Never still a minute. But set Paul down in an easy chair and he'll stay there for hours." Sportswriters, who had struck a rich vein with Dizzy and hoped to do the same with Paul, soon took to calling him "Daffy." Paul didn't mind, but the name never caught on with anyone who knew him. It simply didn't fit.

The brothers were uncommonly fond of one another. Paul, the younger by some two years, idolized Dizzy, believed everything he said, laughed at his jokes, and never doubted for an instant that his big brother was the greatest man alive. As for Dizzy, he fretted over Paul like a mother moose, jealously watching out for his interests (he once threatened to quit in order to get Paul a better contract), and forever singing his praises as a pitcher: "Why, criminy, Paul's even better than me." He also tried to educate his kid brother in the ways of the world—an undertaking that might better have been left to others, for despite the lofty heights to which he had soared, in some ways Dizzy himself was not so far removed from the cotton fields as he liked to think.

One day in September of 1934 when the Cardinals were in New York, Pop Haines approached St. Louis sportswriter Frank Stockton, one of Dizzy's closest friends, and pointed out a shady-looking character skulking around the hotel lobby. "I'll bet that buzzard's waiting for Dizzy," says Pop. "And I hope he don't see him. He's given rubber checks to half the boys in the league and I bet he wants to sign up Dizzy for some barnstorming, and I'd hate to see the kid come up with a bouncer." When Dizzy came in, Stockton took him aside and told him what Haines had said. "Now remember," he warned, "don't sign anything with him."

"Who me? Not ole Diz. But I know that guy. He borrowed two bucks off me night before last and he's here to pay it back. Don't worry about me. I'll just get my two bucks and be right back."

Five minutes later Dizzy returned, all smiles.

"All right, what did you sign?" Stockton asked.

"Ole Diz ain't so dumb," he replied. "I got one of my two bucks back, and look at this here—a check for fifteen hundred dollars, all for ten exhibition games."

"That check isn't worth a nickel, Dizzy."

"Doggone it. It's gotta be good. He said he'd write it on any bank I picked and the hotel clerk told me that this was his own bank and it had plenty of dough in it."

Stockton phoned the bank. There was no such account.

"Well, criminy," Dizzy fumed, "why didn't you warn me?"

The problem was soon resolved and Dizzy, having had time to think about it, was very contrite. Never again. No sir. Ole Diz had learned his lesson. And then he disappeared into the hotel restaurant. A half hour later, when he met Stockton again in the lobby, he was waving a hundred-dollar bill. "I would of called you about this, but I was afraid the guy would get away." This time he had contracted to do a radio commercial. "All I gotta do is talk for five minutes on how I learned to pitch." That same night over network radio he told millions of fans how he started pitching as a sophomore at Oklahoma Teachers' College. "I think I'll be a college boy from now on," he explained to Stockton.

Without the Dean brothers it's not hard to imagine where the Cardinals would have finished the 1934 season: somewhere deep in the bowels of the second division. Together Dizzy and Paul were the salvation of an otherwise shaky pitching staff. Sometimes working after only a single day's rest, they were a host in themselves—easily the best one-two punch in the league. Even so, winning was not easy for the Cards that year. The Cubs and Giants were both strong clubs, especially the latter with such outstanding pitching as Hubbell, Schumacher, and Fitzsimmons, and the great hitting of Mel Ott and player-manager Bill Terry. After their hot streak in May the Cardinals played only .500 ball during June, July, and early August. Seemingly stuck in neutral, they had fallen from the league lead and were now floundering about in third place, three and a half games behind the Cubs and an uncomfortable seven and a half in back of the front-running Giants. And then something happened that gave every promise of turning a merely bad situation into a disastrous one: the Deans went out on strike.

On Sunday, August 12, during a hot, high-tension series with the Cubs in St. Louis, Dizzy and Paul lost both ends of a doubleheader before a stunned capacity crowd of 32,000. Not only were they beaten; they were routed—and it's not unlikely that their vanity suffered somewhat in the process, especially Dizzy's. That evening when the time came for the team to leave for an off-day exhibition game at Detroit, the Deans were missing. It was later learned that they had gone to a barbecue.

A barbecue! Frisch was furious. Like every other manager and most of the players he resented exhibition games. But they went with the job, and everyone was expected to show up, if only to wave at the fans and sign autographs. To Dizzy, though, it didn't make much sense for a big star like him to have to be on hand for a game that didn't count for anything, especially when, having just pitched, he knew he wouldn't be called on to play. A year earlier he had skipped one in Pittsburgh and got away with it. But that was under Manager Street. Things were different now, as Dizzy was about to learn.

From Detroit the next day Frisch fired off a few choice words to Dizzy, ordering him and his brother to report back to the team immediately, and slapping him with a hundred-dollar fine; Paul got fifty. Dizzy responded by tearing up his uniform and announcing: "I ain't gonna play no more ball till that Dutchman apologizes." Paul tore up his uniform too, but said nothing except to confirm that it was his twenty-first birthday.

"That's all right with me," Frisch growled when he learned of this, and suspended both of them without pay until further notice.

"Well, I guess maybe me and Paul will just get in a little fishing down in Florida," Dizzy told the press.

"Let them go," snapped Frisch. "I don't care if we finish in last place. There's going to be discipline on this club." And then he added: "Of course we won't really finish in last place." But he would have had trouble convincing many people of that, most of all himself. Of the sixty-three games the Cardinals had won up to that point, the Dean boys had accounted for more than half.

Dizzy and Paul didn't go fishing in Florida or anywhere else. As Dizzy explained to the press: when on August 15 they went to pick up their checks (their last, for a while at least), they discovered that the fines had already been deducted, and their salaries were so small to begin with that he and Paul would have been hard put to make it as far as Kansas City on what was left over. This was a well-deserved slap at Sam Breardon, the most tight-fisted club owner in either league, who at the time was paying the Deans a total of $11,500 between them. With the Cubs or the Giants they would have been getting at least twice that much; probably more. In addition to the fines, the club had deducted thirty-six dollars for the torn uniforms. "I don't think that's fair at all,"

Dizzy complained. "Them uniforms could of been mended."

The real reason Dizzy and Paul didn't go fishing is that they wanted to play ball, and they most likely expected that the devastating effect of their absence from the mound, plus pressures from the fans, the front office, and the players themselves would soon force Frisch to come to them on bended knee. They should have known better. The Dutchman would have killed himself first. Still, Manager Frisch notwithstanding, they might have got their way, had it not been for a remarkable turn of events: suddenly the Cardinals started winning ball games. Showered from all quarters with predictions of doom, the team rallied around their manager and played like demons, especially the hard-pressed pitching staff, which somehow managed to keep going without their two aces. To ease the strain, Pepper Martin helped out on the mound a little by pitching two scoreless innings of relief against the Braves. ("I fooled a few of them with my fast ball, I guess.")

During the week following the exhibition game at Detroit the team won seven out of eight, and in the excitement of winning, the Deans were all but forgotten by players and fans alike. Meanwhile the Cardinal front office had come out squarely in support of Frisch. So had National League President John Heydler and Commissioner Landis. Things looked bad for Dizzy and Paul. At the end of the fourth day, after consulting his big brother, Paul surrendered and was permitted to return to the club, and the payroll. ("I knowed I was wrong all along."). Three days later, following an apology of sorts to Manager Frisch and a letter of regret to the Detroit Tigers for having missed their exhibition game, Dizzy, $486 poorer and perhaps a little wiser, was also reinstated. He celebrated the occasion with a shutout against the Giants.

There's no question that for the Cardinals the strike was the turning point of the 1934 pennant race. From then until the end of the season they would lose only twelve games, while winning thirty-three. Surprisingly enough, the strike left no bitter aftertaste. Quite the opposite: the whole affair appears to have given a great boost to the team's morale. The air had been cleared. Frisch had convincingly established his authority by demonstrating that as long as he was manager he would also be the boss, and that nobody, not even the Great One himself, could expect special treatment. "We're all in this together," he announced to the press. "Nobody is bigger than the team." By and large the players couldn't have agreed more. Most of them were fond of Dizzy, more or less, but they were nevertheless openly pleased that he had been taken down a peg or two. In the past he had been allowed to get away with too much too often. As for Dizzy himself, he took his licking in stride, and after his week's vacation came back stronger than ever, and every bit as humble and unassuming.

The race was now on in earnest. The momentum the Cardinals had picked up during their Deanless days stayed with them, and, save for a jarring double defeat by the Pirates on Labor Day, they continued their winning ways. Dizzy and Paul were little short of sensational, their most spectacular outing coming on September 21 in a doubleheader at Brooklyn's Ebbets Field, where a weekday crowd of 18,000 was on hand to witness one of baseball's most remarkable afternoons of pitching. As usual, Manager Frisch held a pregame briefing for his pitchers, including Dizzy, who was scheduled to go in the first game:

> Frisch: Now this guy you've got to keep the ball high and outside to. He'll hit it over the fence if you get it inside.
>
> Dizzy: That ain't the way I pitch him. I give him nuthin but low inside stuff and he ain't got a hit off me yet.
>
> Frisch: And this next fellow, nothing but curves. He'll slap a fast ball every time.
>
> Dizzy: That's mighty funny. I never have bothered to curve him yet, and he's still trying for his first loud foul off ole Diz.

And so it went, down the list, until finally:

> Dizzy: Now look here, Frank, this is pretty silly, ain't it. I mean, I've winned twenty-six games already this year, and it don't look exactly right for an infielder like you to be telling a big star like me how I should pitch.

A few minutes later, while waiting for the umpires, Frisch chatted for a while with Brooklyn Manager Casey Stengel by home plate:

"Casey, you don't know what it's like. Those guys [meaning Dizzy and Paul] give me nothing but trouble."

"That so?" says Casey. "How many games they won for you?"

"Forty-two."

"You wanna swap 'em? I got a couple who've lost forty-two."

That afternoon Dizzy went out and blanked the Dodgers on three hits, all of them coming after two were out in the eighth. Paul did even better by hurling a no-hitter, which missed being a perfect game by the slim margin of a first-inning walk. Paul was quietly pleased. Dizzy was nearly hysterical. "What'd I tell ya? What'd I tell ya? He's even better than me." And then, about his own performance: "I let up a little toward the end. Why, if I'd of knowed that kid was gonna pitch a no-hitter, I would of bore down and pitched one too."

All well and good, but in order for the Cardinals to capture the pennant it wasn't enough that they win ball games; it was also necessary that the front runners lose a few. The Cubs had been very accommodating in this respect and by early September had dropped quietly into third place. Bill Terry's Giants had been less obliging. Although failing to keep place with the torrid Cards, they had played well enough to preserve what was generally thought to be a safe lead for so late in the season. At the start of the final week, with all of their remaining schedule at home, the world's champions were still two and a half games in front. And then, for no apparent reason, the mighty Terrymen simply fell apart. Of their last seven games they lost six—the final four against the lowly Phils and Dodgers.

Meanwhile the Cards, also at home, continued their relentless drive. On the final Monday they beat the Cubs, 3-1, behind Bill Walker. On Tuesday, while Lindbergh kidnaper Bruno Hauptmann was being indicted by a Bronx County grand jury, Dizzy defeated the hardhitting Pirates, 3-2, for his twenty-eighth win. Next morning, with the Cards now only one game behind and the tension almost unbearable, Leo Durocher got married. Frisch had pleaded with him to put it off for just a while longer, but Leo groaned that he positively couldn't exist for another day without his Grace. Finally Frisch relented: "All right. For Chrisake, go ahead and do it. Maybe it will clear your head." That afternoon, with Durocher at his usual shortstop position and Grace in the stands, the Cards were shut out on two hits by the Pirates' venerable Waite Hoyt. Grace wept.

On the following day, Thursday, the Cardinals came back to win, 8-5, over the Cincinnati Reds, and on Friday shut them out, 4-0, behind Dizzy, to go into a tie for first place. Paul took charge on Saturday to win 6-1, and put the Cards one game up. At this point, with the Giants and the Cardinals each having one more game to play, it was still possible for the race to end in a tie and a sudden-death playoff. Since a St. Louis win on the final day would clinch the pennant no matter what happened in New York, and was therefore greatly to be desired, Frisch sent Dizzy back in on Sunday after only a single day's rest. Again he blanked the Reds. It was his fourth victory in ten days, his third shutout. The Cardinals had ended the season by winning twenty of their last twenty-five games and had once again hoisted the National League pennant over Sportsman's Park.

As for the Giants, who had almost miraculously managed to snatch defeat from the jaws of victory, the last few days had been pathetic, predictable, and (some would say) preordained. Commented the *Times* on the morning after New York had been dropped into a first-place tie by Brooklyn fireballer Van Lingle Mungo: "Struggling feebly, as if weighed down by the utter futility of it all, the world's champion Giants yesterday toppled to within a step of completing one of the most astounding descents in the history of major league baseball." What made that descent all the more humiliating was the fact that the coup de grâce had been delivered by the despised Dodgers, of whom Bill Terry had asked not so many months before: "Brooklyn? Are they still in the league?"

"You know, Casey," Terry said to Stengel after it was all over, "if you had played all season the way you played the last two days, you wouldn't have finished sixth."

"Bill," Casey replied, "if your Giants had played all season the way they played the last two days, you wouldn't of finished second."

And yet, in the recurring nightmares that must have disturbed Manager Terry's slumber for some time to come, it is likely that the awfulest apparition of all was neither the sharp-tongued Casey, nor the lightning-like Mungo, nor any other of that insolent Brooklyn bunch that had finally done him in—but rather the firm of Dean and Dean. Of the Cardinals' pennant-winning ninety-five victories, the Dean brothers had accounted for forty-nine—thirty for Dizzy and nineteen for his baby brother. Of the last eighteen games of the season, the Deans had won twelve. All this was bad enough, but what was especially hard for Terry to take was the outrageous way they had treated his Giants. During the course of the season "me and Paul" had beaten the world's champions twelve times.

Thus, in about the most dramatic fashion imaginable, the Cardinals had come on to win in the stretch. In the bedlam that was the St. Louis clubhouse after Sunday's game, Dizzy took time out from leading cheers to assure reporters that, although he was mighty happy, he wasn't at all surprised. He had knowed all along that with him and Paul the Cardinals just couldn't lose. "Ain't that right, Frankie? Didn't I say that?" And then: "You know, I really love that Dutchman." The World Series? "There ain't much question about that, is they? Me and Paul will win four games. Who won the pennant? Me and Paul. And who's gonna win the Series? Me and Paul."

In the American League the race had ended in a yawn. For the first time in twenty-five years the pennant had been won by the Detroit Tigers. Under the inspired leadership of their tough new catcher-manager, Mickey Cochrane, the Tigers had fought their way up from a fifth-place finish the year before and, after taking over the lead in early August, had coasted home, seven full games ahead of the second-place Yankees. They were a strong, versatile team with plenty of power at the plate, including their famous "G-Men," Greenberg, Gehringer, and Goslin; and an impressive pitching staff headed by twenty-four-game winner Lynwood "Schoolboy" Rowe, who, among his other feats had rung up sixteen straight victories that season, and little Thomas Jefferson Davis Bridges, whose wide-breaking curve and great heart had won him twenty-two. As the Series opened the odds hung at nearly 2-1 for the Cards, but both Frisch and Cochrane knew better. The teams were much more evenly matched than that. It was anybody's Series.

The great best-of-seven face-off opened in Detroit on Wednesday, October 3. The city was wild with excitement, and, despite the odds, aglow with expectations of winning its first world's championship since 1887. Area newspapers and radio spoke of little else, and freely predicted that Tiger hitting would prove too much, even for the Deans. More than twenty-four hours before the opening pitch, fans began to queue up outside Navin Stadium, so as to be on hand when bleacher tickets went on sale the following morning. By midnight their number had swollen to nearly three thousand. Men, women, and children of all ages (a few of them

babes in arms) huddled in blankets or clustered around small sidewalk fires to take the edge off the early autumn chill. Some
roasted wieners on sticks and heated coffee and beans in tin cans.
Two hundred policemen, pretending not to notice the illegal fires,
moved amongst the crowd on the lookout for trouble, but there
was none. People had more important things on their minds. Besides, they might lose their place in line.

At 1:53 the next day, twenty-three minutes late because of
a massive tangle of customers at the turnstiles, the Tigers took the
field and amidst a deafening cheer from the capacity crowd of
nearly 47,000, the 1934 World Series got under way. For Detroit
fans there would be precious little else to cheer about on that
crisp, dappled afternoon. "From the moment Mayor Frank Couz-
ens threw out the first ball," commented one sportswriter, "it
suddenly became painfully patent to one and all that these Cardinals were decidedly very ferocious birds, who will snap your hand
off if you slip them a crumb." And the Tigers slipped them quite
a few. Obviously suffering from a severe case of the jitters, they
committed five errors in the first three innings, which helped the
Cards jump off to a lead that they proceeded to improve upon as
the game progressed.

While his teammates were hammering away at three Detroit
pitchers for a total of eight runs, Dizzy Dean had no trouble holding the Tigers to three. It was not one of Dizzy's better performances. He was obviously tired. During the final two weeks of the
pennant race, he had lost twenty pounds. Since then he had been
so doggedly pursued by sportswriters, photographers, and auto-
graph hounds (all of whom he goodnaturedly obliged) that he had
found little chance to rest. Besides, he was bothered with a head
cold.

But he pitched well enough to win, and that, after all, was
the main point. That night in a radio interview beamed by short
wave to Admiral Byrd in Little America, Dizzy admitted that he
had not been up to his usual level of performance: "Hello, big
Byrd down there in Little America. . . . That game today, I want
to say was a hard-pitched game, although, I want to say that I
didn't have a thing out there on my fast ball or my curve. I finally
staggered through and won the game 8-3, but I can pitch better
than that." And later to a sportswriter: "Look, I know me and
Paul is gonna win four games in this here Series—if Detroit is
good enough to win a couple when we ain't pitchin—and you

might just as well be honest and tell the public all about it. They pays our salary and it's only fair that we tell em just what's gonna happen."

The second game also played in Detroit, this one under a mainly sunny sky, was a different story. Although the Cardinals' Wild Bill Hallahan and his reliever Bill Walker pitched well enough to win any ordinary game, they were clearly outclassed by the "Arkansas Express," Schoolboy Rowe, who after a shaky start settled down to hurl a masterful 3-2 twelve-inning win in which he allowed only one Cardinal to reach base after the third. Even Dizzy was impressed: "Criminy, with a wind behind him that Rowe fella's almost as fast as Paul." On the following day, back in St. Louis, Paul Dean set Detroit down with eight hits to win handily, 4-1. Things seemed to be going about as Dizzy had predicted. And then suddenly the Tigers came alive.

On Saturday, October 6, Detroit evened the Series at two-all by hammering St. Louis, 10-4. It was a bad day all around for the Cardinals: five pitchers mauled, five fielding errors, a costly wild pitch—and a near disaster on the base paths: In the fourth inning, when the score was still close, Dizzy went in as a pinch runner for the slow-footed Virgil Davis who had just singled. Later when called upon by the press to explain why he had so nonchalantly exposed his great pitching ace to the hazards of the base paths, Manager Frisch was reported to have defended his decision with: "Well, we were out to win, weren't we? Dizzy is a fine base-runner, I'll tell you that, and I thought that him being in there might give us the lift we needed." Years later, however, Frisch had a different story to tell about how Dizzy happened to be on the bases:

The funny thing is that I never did send Dizzy in. Nobody did. He just went in by himself, although I couldn't very well tell the reporters that without having them think that I'd lost control of the club, which I guess in fact I had because of the way we were crowded in there. In those days, you see, the parks were smaller, and in order to squeeze more people in for the World Series and All Star games, sometimes they'd put in extra box seats right around the rim of the playing field. At least that's the way it was at Sportsman's Park.

So there we were, sitting right in the middle of the fans, and there was so much confusion that it was hard to see and keep track of what was going on out on the field. All of a sudden Mike Gonzales tells me Dizzy has gone in to run for Davis, I think it was, who was pretty slow.

"All right, let him go," I says, and I remember thinking to myself (and this is a fact), "If he gets hit in the head it won't hurt him any."

But it did, at least for a while. When the next batter, Pepper Martin, slashed a grounder to Gehringer at second, Dizzy took off on the dead run. Gehringer ("the mechanical man") came up cleanly with the ball and flipped for the force-out to shortstop Billy Rogell, who in turn whirled and fired to first to double up Pepper. His throw caught the onrushing Dizzy flush on the forehead at point-blank range, and dropped him in his tracks. Moments later before a stunned home crowd of 38,000, he was carried from the field on a stretcher. The rumor quickly spread that he had suffered a serious concussion.

Before he reached the locker room, he regained consciousness:
"Where'm I at?"
"You're all right, Jerome," Frankie answered. "You got hit."
"Say, that's a fact, ain't it. Hey, Frank, I guess I done broke up that double play pretty good."
"Yeh. Great."

Early that evening, with Paul along for company, Dizzy was taken to nearby St. John's Hospital, where he was pronounced in sound condition and ordered to remain until morning so as to get a good night's sleep. When Paul got back to the hotel, several of the players were waiting for him in the lobby. "Hey, Paul," one of them asked, "what did the X-rays show in Dizzy's head?" "Nuthin,'" said Paul and went to bed.

For the better part of twenty-four hours Frankie Frisch was the most reviled man in St. Louis—and perhaps the entire country. The sportswriters were outraged. So were the fans. It was generally supposed that Dizzy would be out for the remainder of the Series. Some said he was through in baseball. It came, therefore, as something of a surprise for the near capacity crowd in Sportsman's Park the next day when who should take the mound for the Cardinals but the Great One himself. He lost, 3-1, to Tommy Bridges, whose curve that afternoon was at its tantalizing best. After the game the hometown reporters tried to excuse away the defeat. "Your head must have been bothering you out there, Diz. Right?" But Dizzy, who could be as noble in defeat as he was insufferable in victory, would have none of it. "No such thing. Didn't bother me a'tall. You can't hurt me none by hittin me on the head. I just got beat, that's all."

And so now the Cardinals found themselves in a very precarious situation. Detroit needed only one more win, and the final two games were set for Navin Stadium, the Tigers' home turf. In the Detroit locker room after the game, Mickey Cochrane was ecstatic. "That's the one we needed," he kept shouting as he slapped his players on the back and hugged Tommy Bridges before the newsreel cameras. "Yes sir, that's the one. We've got them on the run now. Tomorrow we'll give them Rowe and that will end it." The bookmakers agreed. After Dizzy's defeat in the fifth game on Sunday, the odds shifted to 3-1, Detroit.

Both teams arrived back in Detroit early the following morning to find the city in a state of mass hysteria. Thousands of cheering fans packed the area in and about the railroad depot. Thousands of others jammed the public square in front of the Book Cadillac Hotel where the two teams were staying. By midmorning Michigan Avenue from the center of town out to Navin Stadium was one huge, hopeless tangle of automobiles and pedestrians. Along the route and outside the Stadium dozens of vendors peddled peanuts and hot dogs and pennants and tieclasps shaped like miniature bats, while scalpers worked their way among the crowd and, hard times notwithstanding, sold $5.50 reserved-seat tickets for as much as $18.00 apiece. Elsewhere across the depression-ravaged country, millions of other Americans dropped what they were doing (if anything) and tuned in their radio sets. For the first time ever the World Series was being broadcast coast to coast, courtesy of NBC, CBS, and Henry Ford who paid $100,000 for exclusive advertising rights.

The sixth game was by far the most exciting and hard fought of the lot. The Cardinals, smarting from their two recent defeats and not at all relishing their new role as underdog, roared into Navin Stadium in an angry mood. "To hell with that Rowe," Frisch shouted at his players in their pregame briefing. "We're the better ball club. We pulled out the pennant and we can pull this out."

"That's a fact, Frankie," seconded Dizzy. "Paul will take 'em today and then I'll set 'em on their cans after that."

Actually, until just before game time Frisch was undecided whether to go with Paul or Wild Bill Hallahan, who had pitched well in the second game and was the more rested of the two. "Bill hasn't won so many games for us, but he has a way of coming through on the big ones," Frisch announced, and then chose Paul.

A wise move, for not only did Baby Brother continue his mastery over the Detroit batters, but he also knocked in the game's winning run.

Although a tight 4-3 game, the outcome was never in doubt, for it was obvious that the Cardinals had no intention whatsoever of losing. At the very outset they took charge. They were the aggressors and the Tigers the aggressed-against. Jumping off to an early one-run lead, they forced Detroit to play catch-up ball, and although the Tigers twice managed to come from behind and tie the score, each time the Cardinals soon forged ahead again. What was most surprising was that the Tigers were able to stay as close as they did. Even behind their great Schoolboy, they were outplayed all around, especially on the bases, where the Gashouse Gang more than lived up to their reputation. As seen by one more or less neutral reporter:

> Literally and figuratively the Cards simply swept the Tigers off their feet. . . . They tore around the bases like men possessed. They bowled over whoever came in their path, nor did they pause to make apology for or inquire of the damage they left in their wake. Cochrane, the mighty Mickey, and most of his infielders seemed to be doing nothing but picking themselves up off the ground.

Meanwhile the St. Louis dugout was busy needling the opposition. This was nothing new. All season long the Cardinals had distinguished themselves as the loudest, rudest, crudest bunch of bench jockeys in the business. With the likes of Pepper Martin, Leo Durocher, and Dizzy on hand, how could it have been otherwise? "Hey, Freddie," they would shout out at an opposing pitcher, "how come your tits bounce up and down like that when you throw?"

"That's a fact, Freddie. You done gottin fat. You know that?"

"Yeh. Maybe that's why you don't pitch so good any more. You gonna have to get yourself a brassiere. Bumpity, bumpity."

Or:

"Say, Johnnie, you wanna come round after the game and see some dirty pictures Pepper's got?"

"Yeh. Of your wife!"

This time they zeroed in on the Schoolboy, whose childhood sweetheart, Edna Mary Skinner, had come up all the way from Eldorado, Arkansas, to see him pitch in the Series. A few days

earlier, when being interviewed on a Detroit radio station, Rowe
interrupted his remarks with a playful "How'm I doing, Edna?"
That was all the Cardinal bench jockeys needed. A thousand times
that afternoon, or so it must have seemed to Rowe, the St. Louis
dugout erupted in unison with "How'm I doing, Edna?", usually
accompanied by a "Yoo-hoo" and dainty wave of a handkerchief.
Forty years later an old-time Detroit fan who had watched the
game that day from just behind the Cardinal dugout, was still
bitter: "They never should have allowed that Edna business to go
on the way it did. The umpires should have put a stop to it. Or
the Commissioner. He was there and heard it. That wasn't baseball.
You can't expect a man to pitch with that sort of thing going on.
That's what cost Detroit the Series, right there." Maybe so, maybe
not. At any rate, three days later the Schoolboy and Edna were
married in a simple ceremony at the Detroit Leland Hotel before
heading home for Eldorado. Tiger right fielder Pete Fox was the
best man. None of the Cardinals were invited.

After the game the St. Louis locker room was complete bedlam. The Cardinals had won the big one. They had beaten the best
the Tigers had, and in so doing had not only survived but had
clearly regained the momentum. Dizzy was like a wild man. Wearing a white pith helmet and brandishing a small rubber tiger by the
tail, he rushed excitedly about the room, proclaiming Paul the
greatest pitcher in the history of the world, and stopping now and
then to thump his teammates on the head and assure them that
the Series was as good as won. He'd go out there tomorrow and
finish it up himself.

"What about that, Frankie?" the reporters asked. "Is it going
to be Dizzy again tomorrow?"

"If I live until tomorrow, maybe. It'll be Dean or Wild Bill
Hallahan."

Later that afternoon, shortly before leaving the stadium,
Frisch sent for Dizzy and told him he'd decided to pitch Hallahan.
The Great One was outraged: "Here you got the greatest pitcher
in baseball, and you gonna go with a second-rater like Hallahan?"
he screamed at Frisch.

But Frankie was in no mood to bicker with Dizzy or anyone
else. He was a tired old man of thirty-five who had just set a new
record by playing in his forty-ninth World Series game, hadn't had
a decent night's sleep in weeks, and was living on the raw edge of
his nerves: "You know something?" he shouted at Dizzy. "You're

crazy. You know that? And I'm not going to pitch a crazy man. That's why I'm going with Bill."

Dizzy growled and retreated to a bench in the far corner to sulk, while Frisch glowered and banged things around in his locker. Before long, Leo Durocher, who had overheard the angry exchange, came over to Diz and urged him to go back to the Dutchman and apologize. Maybe then he'd get to pitch, after all. "And we need you out there tomorrow, Diz. You're our best."

Leo was right. It wouldn't be easy for the Great One, but he'd do it. Approaching Frisch, he put his arm around his shoulder: "Why don't you stick with me Frankie?" he said. "I'll make you the greatest manager in the game." As apologies go, it wasn't much of one, but it was good enough. "I guess I knew all along that Diz would pitch it," Frisch later admitted. "He had a terrible cold and only two days before he'd been conked. But—well, he was my boy. I knew it."

And so the word was out that Dizzy Dean, coming back after a single day's rest, would make his third start in the Series. This was all the Detroit fans needed to round out their circle of gloom. Whereas only a few hours before there had been dancing in the streets, now the air hung heavy with despair. After Rowe's defeat, most people seemed to sense that the Series was lost and the final game would be only a formality. They were right.

On the following day, while scalpers scurried about frantically to unload their treasures for as little as fifty cents on the dollar, a subcapacity crowd of fewer than 40,000 filed into Navin Stadium to witness the sad demise of the once mighty Tigers. Overnight the weather had turned cold and most of the fans wore jackets or topcoats. Some carried blankets. A brisk wind gusted in from right field toward home plate, causing occasional eddies of dust along the edge of the infield. In the radio booth, behind the backstop, Ted Husing and Graham McNamee described the pregame scene to millions of listeners, while on the field the two teams took their turns at batting practice. Over by the first-base grandstand Dizzy spent fifteen minutes or so signing autographs. As game time approached he strolled back toward the Cardinal bench, passing by the handsome Tiger slugger Hank Greenberg en route. "Hey boy," Dizzy called out to him, "what makes you so white? Why, you tremblin like a leaf. Must be you heerd ole Diz is gonna pin your ears back today." Back in the dugout, he paused for a moment on the top step as if to sniff the air, and then went in and sat down beside Paul. "Just a couple of runs, you guys," he said as he pounded the ball into his glove. "That's all. Ole Diz is gonna shut 'em out this time."

For the first two innings it was a contest. After that it was a rout. While his mates pounded six Detroit pitchers for eleven runs, Dizzy, working like some well-oiled machine, blanked the hapless Tigers on six scattered hits. For Detroit fans it was a humiliating and monotonous performance, enlivened only briefly late in the game when, after some rough play on the base paths, the hated Joe Medwick was ejected from the game (by Commissioner Landis himself) amidst a barrage of fruit, pop bottles, seat cushions, and obscenities from the frustrated bleacherites in left field.

Oddly enough (or perhaps not) in the Tiger ninth with the game all but won, Dizzy narrowly missed being lifted. Not that he was weakening. In fact, he was getting stronger as the game progressed. But with one out and a man on first, he was suddenly seized with his old compulsion to clown, brought on perhaps by the appearance at bat of Billy Rogell, who had beaned the Great One just three days before. Apparently determined to make Rogell look bad at the plate, Dizzy began to pitch cute to him. Rogell responded by slapping a single to right field. Next came the mighty Greenberg, whom Dizzy proceeded to tease with a tempting assortment of fat pitches. Frisch, recognizing the familiar symptoms, trotted in from second:

"All right, Jerome, you've had your fun. Now cut out the fooling around or I'll yank you."

"Now that would be kinda crazy in front of all these folks, wouldn't it, Frankie. Here I got em down 11-0 with only two outs to go and you gonna take ole Diz out?"

"I mean it. So help me."

"Criminy, I couldn't believe it," Dizzy later recalled. "I looked up and seen he had four pitchers in the bullpen. Why, I thought we must be gettin ready for the 1935 season."

By this time Durocher had come in from short. "What the hell, Frank. Let him have his fun."

"No. There's too much at stake. You lose Greenberg, Jerome, and you're out."

And so, convinced that Manager Frisch meant business, the Great One bore down and struck out Greenberg for the third time that afternoon. Four pitches later, at 4:49 Eastern Standard Time, the final batter grounded into an easy force-out, and the St. Louis

Cardinals became enthroned as the new champions of the baseball world. It had happened to them before—twice, in fact, since 1926 —but never so sweetly. Almost hopelessly behind in early September, they had come roaring through to capture the National League pennant in one of baseball's most thrilling finishes. And now they had once again shown their mettle by bounding back to win the final two games and the Series from the formidable Tigers. It was a glorious and altogether fitting finale for a remarkable team that just wouldn't quit, and it had happened pretty much as Dizzy had said it would: "me and Paul" had won all four games.

During the weeks immediately following the Series, while most of his teammates were recuperating at home, Dizzy was busy traveling the glory road. Smartly attired in a new tuxedo that Paul helped him pick out, he attended the annual banquet of the Baseball Writers Association as guest of honor to receive the Most Valuable Player Award. After that came a number of other banquets and other awards, all richly deserved by the man who had won thirty games while losing only seven and had led both leagues in strikeouts for the third consecutive year. Mentioned frequently amongst the accolades, but not to be found in any record book, was the fact that Dizzy had won the big ones. He had been at his best when his best was most badly needed—which, in the final reckoning, is what being a champion is really all about. "He may or may not have been the greatest pitcher of all times," Frankie Frisch said of him a generation later. "But I can tell you this: if there was one game I knew I had to win, I'd want Jerome to pitch it for me."

Following the ceremonial banquets came the personal appearances and endorsements of toys, cereals, and sweatshirts, which in the aggregate netted Dizzy some $25,000 and made his face one of the most famous in the country. It was an exciting, triumphant whirl for the one-time cotton picker from Arkansas, or Oklahoma, or maybe Texas. He enjoyed it immensely, savoring every iota of adulation (and money) that came his way. But was he perhaps overdoing things a bit? There were reports that the Great One looked tired. Back in St. Louis the front office fretted about all those chicken croquettes and those late hours. Dizzy quickly put their fears to rest, however: "You don't have to worry none about ole Diz," he phoned them. "I'm in the pink. You can bet I'll be rarin to go when Manager Frisch and the others reports to me at Bradenton next spring."

Peace in Their Time

Wͪᴇɴ ɪɴ ᴀᴜɢᴜsᴛ ᴏꜰ 1934 President Hindenburg went to his final rest and "handsome Adolf Hitler," as he was sometimes called by newsmen in those days, became the sole boss of the Third Reich, there were many Americans who counted this a not altogether bad thing. Of course, Hitler had his faults, but, as he had proved so convincingly since taking over as Chancellor the year before, he knew how to keep the Communists in line, and that was certainly a point in his favor. Not that it really made much difference to most Americans one way or the other. Lord knows, there was enough to worry about here at home, and the farther we stayed away from other people's problems the better off we'd be.

Nevertheless, for a time, early in the following year, it appeared that this country was at last ready to join with other respectable nations by becoming an adherent to the World Court—that is to say, by agreeing to submit its international disputes to the Court's arbitrament. Seven times before, going back to 1923, the matter had come up for formal consideration by the United States Government, and seven times America had balked at the prospect of surrendering any part of its sovereignty to a bunch of foreigners, "most of whom," cautioned a Southern Senator, "can't even speak English."

Now, though, as the new Congress opened for business in January of 1935, there was little doubt that the Court's time had come. How could it be otherwise? Riding high after the Democrats' lopsided victory in the congressional elections of the previous autumn, President Roosevelt had pronounced the Court an issue of "paramount importance," and had let it be known that he expected the party faithful to support it. With the Democrats holding an almost three-to-one advantage in the Senate, approval for the Court seemed a foregone conclusion, even without the help of those several Republican senators who were already on record as favoring it.* "It looks to me," announced Court-enthusiast Eleanor Roosevelt in mid-January, "as though we were about to take another step toward doing away with war."

The Court resolution was reported out of the Foreign Relations Committee on January 14 with a "do pass" recommendation, and, had the Administration been so inclined, could have cleared the Senate without much difficulty within a few days. There would, of course, have been a good deal of squawking from those grizzled old isolationists, like Hiram Johnson and William Borah, who had fought so doggedly (and successfully) fifteen years earlier against America's entry into the League of Nations, and who for the same reasons would fight against the World Court, which, after all, was the creature of the League. But these once powerful "sons of the wild jackasses" had long since seen their numbers dwindle to insignificance, and it was unlikely that they could any longer cause much trouble. "The Court has a comfortable margin of support," the President was assured. "It can be passed with no difficulty."

That being the case, the President ordered the leadership to dangle the resolution before the Senate, while at the same time not permitting it to come to a vote. The purpose of this was to keep the Senate occupied until the Administration could finish preparing its upcoming legislative program for submission to Congress. As one observer noted, the President was obviously providing an oratorical bone for the senators to gnaw on, thereby enabling them to give the impression to the home folks that they were gainfully employed. And gnaw they did. For nearly two weeks Court speeches, pro and con, took up most of the Senate's agenda, and at times it was only with considerable difficulty that the Democratic leadership was able to prevent the excitement of the debate from forcing the measure to a vote. When asked if he

---

*Since it would involve the nation in international commitments, the Court resolution was considered to be in the same category as a regular treaty. This meant that a two-thirds vote of the Senate was needed for ratification.

minded so much talk and so little action, a Carolina senator answered: "I don't mind at all. This argument has been going on for twelve years and I'd just as soon keep it going for twelve more if it meant we could stay clear of the Court."

The first intimation that the Court might be headed for trouble reached the President on the final Friday of the month when Senate Majority Leader Robinson informed him that signs of defection were being detected within the ranks of the pro-Court forces. These he attributed not so much to the prolonged debate in the Senate as to the increasingly savage anti-Court attacks that had been appearing recently in the *Chicago Tribune* and the Hearst chain, and to the stepped-up efforts of the well-oiled Hearst lobby at the Capitol. In Robinson's opinion there seemed little question that the Court would pass, but the margin would probably turn out to be more thin than comfortable. "Perhaps we shouldn't put it off any longer," he suggested. And the President agreed: "Because of indications of growing antagonism . . . a favorable vote should be obtained as soon as possible." According to Robinson, that would be on the following Tuesday, or Wednesday at the latest.

But that Sunday afternoon, January 27, the situation was dramatically altered by the Reverend Charles Coughlin, who, on his weekly broadcast from The Shrine of the Little Flower in Royal Oak, Michigan, unleashed a withering attack against the Court. For those who weren't around during the early and middle thirties, it is hard to imagine what a powerful influence Coughlin wielded. For an hour, beginning at 4:00 Eastern Time every Sunday afternoon, America stopped moving, and, enraptured by the extraordinary magnetism of this radio priest with the cherubic face and Wurlitzer voice, listened while he explained in very simple and understandable terms why the country was in such a mess and what should be done to clean it up. To many of the better educated he was an unprincipled rabblerouser who deliberately played to the baser passions of the masses. But to most Americans he was, during his brief moment of glory, the very incarnation of wisdom and courage—a man with commonsense answers who wasn't afraid to take on the big shots. And a patriot through and through (even though he was a Catholic and a priest) to whom the United States of America should feel deeply indebted for his repeated warnings against the conspiracies of Communists, international bankers (read: Jews), and other alien interests.

As for the Court, in Father Coughlin's considered judgment, it was a devilish device controled by foreigners, who would like nothing better than to suck America into the embroils of their senseless, vicious squabbles, which had been going on over there since the beginning of time and would probably continue forever. Besides that, the great American eagle could expect to get plucked clean by "that fraudulent tribunal . . . , that den of international thieves . . . , that Frankenstein monster raised by international bankers." There was no question at all that one of the first things the Court would do if this country joined would be to cancel all war debts, thereby stealing $12 billion out of the pockets of the American workingmen.

On that particular Sunday the Reverend Father clearly out-did himself, which is saying a great deal, for even at his ordinary best he was probably the greatest spellbinder in the country. "I appeal to you," he called out in cathedral tones to his nationwide audience, "to every solid American who loves democracy, who loves the United States, who loves the truth . . . to keep America safe for Americans and not [make it] the hunting ground of inter-national plutocrats." Let the people not be deceived by the prom-ises of false prophets that adherence to this foreign tribunal would mean peace. Just the opposite: "Since the Court was organized war has been waging almost continually among and between the members of the Court. Some of these have been waged within the very shadow of the Court itself, and the Court has done nothing either to end or prevent these wars." By getting America involved in the bickerings of Europe, the League Court would bring war, not peace, to this Country.

"If you want to keep peace in America," came the warning from The Shrine of the Little Flower, "keep America clear of the Court." And the people of this great nation could, if they chose, do exactly that. They need only let their voices be heard. "I beg of you in the name of the God of Peace and Justice to wire your Senator in Washington," Coughlin urged his millions of listeners. "Today, whether you can afford it or not, telegraph your Senator this simple, vital message: Vote 'no' on the World Court." As was his custom, Father Coughlin concluded his program that afternoon with a prayer, this one from the 83rd Psalm:

> Oh, God, Thy enemies have made a noise . . . . They have taken a malicious counsel against Thy people . . . . They have said: Come and

let us destroy them, so that they be not a nation, and let the name of Israel [America] be remembered no more. For they have contrived with one consent: they have made a covenant against Thee.

That evening an aroused Eleanor Roosevelt, who had made the Court one of her pet projects and had spoken out publicly in its favor on several occasions, managed to obtain some last-minute air time on NBC. Escorted only by her private secretary, the First Lady walked the half-dozen or so blocks to Washington's station WRC, where, "speaking as a private citizen" (but not paying as one, for her air time was free), she reaffirmed her belief in the Court and made a final plea in its behalf. Like Coughlin, she urged her fellow Americans to get in touch with their congressmen. "Tell them," she said, "not to be afraid to take this step toward peace." Mrs. Percival Pennybacker, Exalted President of the Chautauqua Women's Club of America, was deeply moved by what the First Lady had to say and felt that "Her message to the nation will have a widespread salutary effect." But this seemed rather unlikely, because although a woman of many gifts, as a public speaker Mrs. Roosevelt left much to be desired. Besides, by the time she had started talking it was already a quarter to eleven, and in those days most Americans were already in bed by then. It is a fact, however, that on the morning following her appeal, the faculty of Mac-Alester College in St. Paul, Minnesota, voted 40-1 in favor of the Court.

Meanwhile, earlier that same Sunday evening on the Good Gulf Gasoline Program, America's beloved humorist Will Rogers had turned serious, to give his views on the Court. He was against it. Always had been and always would be. He was against it for just about every reason he could think of, and some he couldn't. But mainly he was against it because of the way those foreigners had been treating Americans during recent years. For one thing, they just didn't appreciate what we'd done for them—winning the war and all that:

We have shown the people of Europe in a billion ways that we care. We have had our men killed or crippled; we have lent them money; but if we said tomorrow that they didn't owe us a nickel, they wouldn't appreciate it. I told them in Paris that we didn't resent it so much because they hadn't paid us but because they didn't show appreciation for what we had done . . . .

Now, any way you sliced it, lack of appreciation was hard to take, but those people over there were downright onery about it. They had taken to calling America "Uncle Shylock" and "Uncle Sham" and saying how awful it was that those greedy Americans wanted their money paid back to them. And that wasn't all:

> They blame us for everything, I don't care what it is that's wrong with the world; we done it. Whether it's famine or pestilence, acne or tight underwear.
>
> When I was in Europe they had a little jail break over there, and the newspapers blamed it on us. It's the truth. They said that American motion pictures gave the prisoners the unusual idea of breaking out of jail.
>
> And when I was in Paris, some American tourists were hissed and stoned. But not until they'd finished buying.

It would be a pretty good idea to leave people like that well-enough alone. "If we get linked up with this World Court, I guess it won't be long before they'll be calling us 'Uncle Sucker,' and we'd deserve it too."

The telegrams began to descend upon the Senate even before Father Coughlin had finished his Sunday afternoon broadcast, and they continued to pour in for the next two days, at first by the hundreds, and then by the thousands. Exactly how many there were in all is hard to say. Coughlin himself claimed a total of 200,000, bearing nearly two million names. This may have been an exaggeration, but probably not much of one. Not since the impeachment trial of Andrew Johnson in 1868 had there been such a dramatic outpouring of public opinion on a single issue, and certainly never before in the history of the Republic had the Senate been so deluged by instant instructions from the folks back home, including the Squirrel Hill Station, Pennsylvania, Sunday School Class, which emptied its collection plate that week to join the telegram stampede against the Court. Between them, Western Union and Postal Telegraph were forced to hire fifty extra clerks to help handle the added business.

By closing time on Monday the Senate was in what one member called "an unstable condition" as far as the Court was concerned. Majority Leader Robinson informed the President that the telegrams were having a powerful effect. By his reckoning the Administration still had a slight margin, but there was no telling what

might happen before the measure came to a vote, probably sometime the following afternoon. At Robinson's urging the President
brought his personal influence (and charm) to bear by having an
intimate breakfast meeting at the White House the next morning
with four known-to-be-shaky senators, three of whom (all Democrats) proceeded to vote against the Court later in the day, despite
what one of them called "attractive offers from the President."

At opening time that Tuesday, January 29, there was an excitement about the Senate Chamber seldom seen in recent years.
With the word out that the Court would finally be coming to a
vote, the main galleries were packed with hundreds of spectators,
while dozens of others waited patiently, but to no purpose, outside in the corridors. Dignitaries from half a hundred foreign countries filled the diplomatic gallery to capacity, and in the section reserved for the press, a formidable array of titans of the industry
had assembled, including top executives from Colonel McCormick's
Chicago Tribune and the Hearst papers. On the floor there was
much desk-hopping and general scurrying about in what appeared
to be a last-minute comparison of notes, while at the rear of the
chamber small clusters of senators huddled together in muted ex-
changes. Senator Huey Long of Louisiana, one of the Court's noisi-
est and most implacable opponents and a bitter enemy of the President, was his usual highstrung self, as he paced nervously back
and forth in front of the chamber, his tie askew and his face florid
with anticipation of the upcoming battle. Now and then he would
pause to chat briefly with a colleague or to stare blankly about the
hall while running his fingers through his tousled hair.

Sitting calmly at their desks (for they had gone this route
many times before) were the last of the old Progressives, Borah,
Hiram Johnson, and George Norris—relics of an earlier time, but
giants still, whose integrity and dedication no one dared question.
For them no need for telegrams, or advice from Mrs. Roosevelt.
They would vote "no" on sharing America's sovereignty, just as
they always had in the past. So would Senator La Follette, "Young
Bob," whose father had fought to keep this country out of the
World War and later had done as much as any other man to block
its entry into the League of Nations, because he believed, as did
his son, that American should belong only to Americans. At twelve
o'clock noon Vice President Garner gaveled the Senate to order,
and the day's proceedings got under way.

In keeping with a unanimous vote of a few days earlier, on

this occasion no one would be allowed to speak for more than thirty minutes on the Court resolution. This was only reasonable, for during the past two weeks there had been ample opportunity for everyone to speak at length on the subject (and virtually everyone had), and it seemed unlikely that anything could be added to what had already been said. Still, now that the matter had been formally brought forward for a vote, a few words (nearly six hours' worth, as it turned out) were obviously in order. Senator Pope of Idaho led the way by treating his colleagues to a somewhat discursive survey of American constitutional history, the purpose of which was to show that "the desire of the American people for a world court is too deep and sincere to be uprooted and killed. They will not permit this country long to shirk its responsibilities to promote a world order of law and peace on earth."

This brought Huey Long to his feet (which was not hard to do). The people? It wasn't the people who wanted the Court, but rather "these luncheon organizations that dine on pâté de foie gras and chocolate eclairs and then pass a resolution while they are knocking the foam off the top of a drink. They are great 'resoluters'." (Laughter)

Senator Schall (Minnesota): "Today in my office there are 1500 telegrams from people in my State urging me to vote against our going into the World Court . . . and not one for. I take it that these wires are due directly to the tremendous influence of that great American, Father Coughlin." Senator Schall went on to glorify America at length and denounce the likes of Woodrow Wilson and Franklin Delano Roosevelt for their cynical attempts to surrender America's sovereignty in order to augment their own power. Not content with trying to become dictators of the United States, they had set their sights on becoming rulers of the world by "getting us in over there to help the big international bankers grind us down some more, destroy our standard of living, destroy us, and take away from us, regiment us, lockstep us into a poverty-stricken, humble, cringing manhood and womanhood such as exist in Europe." Well, the plan wouldn't work. America's destiny had already been set along a higher road: "God reared this country of the United States, so as to have a place where men could grow souls and give an example to the rest of the world how to grow and how to come near akin to God, Himself."

The main task of squiring the Court resolution through the

Senate fell to Majority Leader Robinson, who gave a very business-like and estimable performance. But he was clearly no match for the opposition, whose attacks on the Court proved much angrier and stronger than he had anticipated. Early in the afternoon he began to sniff defeat and got in touch with the President, who advised the Court forces to accept a limiting amendment that they had earlier rejected somewhat disdainfully in committee. Robinson, obviously embarrassed, made known the Administration's new spirit of compromise. But it was too late. The opposition had the Court on the run, and they knew it. "How else," asked doughty old Hiram Johnson, "can you explain why you are willing to accept now what you found so hateful a few weeks ago?" Whereupon Robinson was forced to admit that the Court's chances had indeed been weakened by "unfair, unjust, unreasonable, propaganda carried on during the course of this debate, carried on by agencies outside the Senate. . . . I have in mind an address made by Father Coughlin."

Senator Schall (interrupting): "I am wondering if the address by Mrs. Roosevelt did not offset that of Father Coughlin."

Robinson: "I am not going to yield to the Senator from Minnesota to make one of his characteristic attacks on Mrs. Roosevelt."

Senator Long (standing beside his desk and occasionally pounding on it, by way of punctuating his remarks): "We are being rushed in pell-mell to get into this World Court so that Senor Ab Jap or some other something from Japan can pass on our controversies."

Schall: "Together with Europe and the rest of those nations."

Long (again): "I do not intend to vote for this infernal thing that is being offered here, and it does not make any difference what kind of soothing syrup, salve, or sweetening is put on it. I could not go back to the hills and bottoms of the State of Louisiana and tell the good, honest citizens down there that I have voted their rights away to be American citizens unless some Japanese, British, or French citizen or envoy owing us money is willing to approve it. That is my logic, and that is my offering, and that is how I stand on the matter." And then, in one of the most moving moments of the entire debate, Senator Long, as he often did, perhaps came closest to what was the real crux of the matter to most Americans by reminding his colleagues that this country had plenty of problems right here at home:

We who are down there [he was speaking of Louisiana but his remarks could have pertained equally as well to many other parts of the
nation], starving to death from lack of milk that you are pouring in the
creek because you have too much, we who are down there with our
children crying for something to wear while you are burning up the
cotton to keep them from having too much, we who are down there
while you are shooting the cows and killing the hogs because you do
not want an oversupply, with everybody crying for something to eat—
until some of these things have been destroyed, until America has better
taken care of Americans, we hope you will postpone this undertaking
to go over and adjust European affairs.

At six o'clock, amidst cries from the floor of "Vote! Vote!",
the clerk began to call the roll. Suddenly the chamber became very
businesslike, as senators ceased their milling about and returned to
their desks to vote, some said, on the very future of America, and
perhaps mankind. In the galleries newsmen kept a running tally,
while spectators outstretched one another to see and hear what
was going on below. Halfway along it became clear that the vote
was running against the Court. Doubtful senators, watching from
the bottom of the alphabet as the roll call progressed, went with
the tide, and in the end the Court was beaten, yet again—this time
by a vote of 52-36 (seven short of the necessary two-thirds), with
a surprising total of twenty Democrats breaking Party ranks to
vote "Nay." "Thank God! This will end forever any thought of
the entry of the United States into entangling alliances," exclaimed
Senator Borah. "Wonderful! I'm delighted," said Hiram Johnson.
In the galleries a wild cheer went up from the partisan crowd when
the vote was announced, and reporters stumbled over one another
in their rush for telephones. So did several senators, at least fifteen
of whom phoned their congratulations to the Reverend Father in
Detroit. "Our thanks go out to Almighty God that America has
retained its sovereignty," declared the radio priest.
    A half-hour after the vote had been taken, a feature writer
for TIME magazine glanced in at the Senate floor: "It was empty
except for some charwomen standing hesitantly around the walls
and a lone Senator bent over his desk with head in arms. Lifting
his head with a start, Leader Robinson glanced at the waiting charwomen, gathered up a bundle of papers, and trudged wearily out."
Outside on the Capitol steps a small group of anti-Court visitors

were still savoring the victory with excited chatter, broken now
and then by loud choruses of a current hit song that, with slight
variation, seemed especially suited to the occasion:

> No, no, a thousand times no!
> You can not buy our caress.
> No, no, a thousand times no!
> We'd rather die than say yes.

Four More Years

WHEN IN THE AUTUMN of 1936 President Roosevelt nosed
out Republican challenger Alf Landon by 11,000,000 votes and
thereby entrenched himself for another four years in the White
House, there were those among his countrymen who were less
than thrilled. A Florida druggist closed his shop and emigrated to
South Africa; in Chicago the manager of a dry-cleaning plant shut
himself in his room for three days and read *Anthony Adverse.* In
Maine and Vermont, the only two states that voted for Landon,
merchants hung out crepe to mourn the occasion, and in New
York City a popular columnist suggested that a lot of true-blue
Americans would have felt better if, instead of the usual congratulations, Landon had wired Roosevelt: "Your re-election is the big-
gest calamity since the introduction of the Japanese corn-borer.
All I hope is that it will hurt you as much as it hurts the country."

Nowadays, the passing of the years having mellowed some of
his critics and permanently silenced others, it is sometimes easy to
forget that Franklin D. Roosevelt, in addition to being one of the
nation's most beloved Presidents, was also one of its most hated.
To millions he was the champion of the poor and the downtrod-
den, the Great White Father who put food into starving bellies and
saved the family homestead from the hands of the moneychangers.
To millions of others (a distinct minority, to be sure, but still a
substantial number) he was the ruination of the country, the de-
stroyer of the American dream, and (some said) an unprincipled
demagogue whose only true commitment was to his own lust for
power. Besides that, he was a devious, supercilious snob.

It was hard not to have strong feelings about the President, one way or the other. It wasn't just the things he stood for, but also the way he stood for them. Never before had a President of the United States advocated such a drastic departure from the old ways and values, and never before had a President identified himself so prominently with the programs he was trying to sell. Add to this a personality that, while exuding great charm, also (alas) bore certain traces of arrogance, duplicity, and at times utter ruthlessness, and it becomes understandable why in most mixed company the subject of FDR was usually good for a spirited discussion, and sometimes a punch in the nose. The battle lines transcended class, section, and often party as well. It was not necessary to be a Wall Street Republican to hate Roosevelt (although it probably helped). Some of his fiercest opposition came from the nation's lowly, like George Evarts of Harrisburg, Pennsylvania, a letter carrier and long-time Democrat.*

Evarts was basically a kind man. If anyone had charged him with being short on Christian charity, he would probably have been deeply hurt. As a regular, church-going Baptist, he prided himself on living by the Golden Rule, and while he readily admitted that he couldn't quite bring himself to love his enemy in the White House, he was certain that he didn't actually hate him. And yet, he did. For years, whenever he came across a picture of the President in a newspaper or magazine he would spit on it. "I remember how he was always referring to FDR as a traitor and a dictator and the worst thing that ever happened to the country," his son remarked many years later. "He said it would be an act of great patriotism if someone shot him."

George Evarts had many reasons for feeling as he did about Roosevelt, but all of them were probably rooted in his belief that he was being personally put upon by the President. First came the 25 percent cut in his salary, not long after Roosevelt took office in 1933. The fact that the cut was soon restored made little difference. Evarts had been put on his guard, and as time passed he saw plenty of other signs that he was being taken advantage of.

It seemed to me [he recalled nearly forty years later in a taped interview] that more and more people on my route were getting hand-

*There was such a person, but in order to protect his identity I have changed his name and place of residence.

outs for doing nothing. Of course, a lot of them had lost their jobs and
tried to find work and couldn't. Well, that was all right, I guess, or at
least I could see why maybe they should get some kind of help. But
there were plenty others, and everyone knew who they were, who'd
never done an honest day's work in their life and I don't think ever intended to if they could get out of it. Loafers, you know, that's all they
were. Now, you tell me why people like that should be given a free ride.

By early 1934 there were 28,000,000 Americans on relief, more
than one out of every five. George Evarts might not have been
very smart about economics, but he understood enough to know
that sooner or later the money for all this would be coming out of
the pockets of workingmen, like himself, who were keeping the
country going. This didn't seem right, and the more he thought
about it, the more it rankled:

> From time to time I'd hear about these families with a houseful
> of kids on the east side who were getting over two hundred dollars a
> month relief from the government. Now, there I was out carrying mail
> all week long in all kinds of weather and, mind you, getting forty
> dollars a month less than they were! And there were jobs available, too.
> But, you see, people like that didn't want them. I remember reading
> about this restaurant owner in Baltimore, I think it was, wanting to hire
> some negroes for kitchen help but he couldn't find any who would go
> off relief. I don't blame them. Why should anyone go to work when the
> government pays you to sit around and do nothing? Even a nigger has
> more sense than that.

After the WPA arrived in 1935 Evarts, in making his rounds,
regularly passed by the new Community Center project where he
saw work gangs standing around doing nothing. Often he would
notice a half-dozen or so men waiting in line to take turns digging
in a hole barely big enough for one worker at a time. Newspaper
cartoonists had great fun lampooning the WPA. Invariably its
members were depicted as leaning on their shovels, and a new
word, "boondoggling," was born. Roughly translated, it meant doing the least possible amount of work in the greatest possible
length of time on a project of no consequence at the highest possible cost to the taxpayers. About the shovels, it was true: the men
did lean on them—a lot. "Better than leaning on rifles," declared a
friend of the President in reference to what was going on in many

places overseas. Well, yes. But what was wrong with having them go out and find some honest work? Sometimes, especially during the Christmas season, when, weighted down like a mule he put in upwards of fourteen hours a day, it seemed to George Evarts that he was the only person in the whole country who was really working for a living.

By 1936 Evarts, with the help of his favorite newspaper and certain oracles of the airways, had finally come up with the answer: Roosevelt was deliberately making the people dependent on him so that he could take over as dictator. The results of that autumn's presidential election, which Evarts supposed would be the nation's last, clearly showed that the plan was working. And why shouldn't it? As New York's aging Democratic chieftain Al Smith remarked bitterly, "You don't shoot Santa Claus." Somewhat earlier the *New York Times* had published a parody of "The Night Before Christmas," with Roosevelt cast in the role of Jolly Old St. Nick. Carrying with him a bulging sack of money, Santa slides down the chimney and fills the nation's stockings with money:

> By mantels and chairs he piled dollars so thick,
> For he knew, though devalued, they'd still do the trick.

Finally, his happy work completed, F. D. Claus ascends the chimney and takes off in his presidential limousine:

> And they heard him exclaim, as he flew out of sight:
> 'Merry Christmas to all—and be sure to vote right.'

Just what that consummate Roosevelt hater, H. L. Mencken of the *Baltimore Sun*, had been saying all along. The President was out to change the country of Jefferson into a bunch of lackeys and mendicants. Roosevelt's idea of a proper government for America, charged Mencken, was "a milch cow with 125,000,000 teats." Mencken's solution: crown Roosevelt king and then behead him.

In his well-appointed seventeenth-century home in Old Greenwich, Connecticut, retired Manhattan stockbroker Richard Glencross,* 200 miles and several social strata removed from George

---

*Again, a fictitious name for a real person.

Evarts, was also worried about the erosion of the great American work ethic and the waning independence of the electorate. But to Glencross these were not the result of any nefarious power play on the part of the President; rather (and perhaps even worse) they were symptoms of a serious disease that had already had disastrous effects upon American society and could very well prove fatal if not checked.

The name of the disease was political ineptitude, and it had been growing like a cancer from the time Roosevelt first came into office. Since then, surrounded by college professors and political yes-men, the President had proceeded to embark upon one crack-pot scheme after another, each one seemingly more expensive and more confusing than the one before. "The whole idea of the New Deal was Government planning," Glencross recalled nearly a generation later. "Planning was Roosevelt's flag; he ran it up and saluted it every morning. But planning is dangerous if you don't know how to do it. And he didn't. That was his big problem."

The President's professor friends excused his failures and frequent shifts in policy by calling them "pragmatic," when what they really meant was that nobody knew what was going on. Not long before the 1936 election the Supreme Court simplified matters considerably by declaring much of the New Deal unconstitutional, including the NRA, which, if the truth were known, the President was almost glad to be rid of. "You know, the whole thing has been a mess," he confided to his Secretary of Labor, Frances Perkins. "It's been an awful headache." Thus, after nearly four years in office Roosevelt was back to just about where he had started, or so at least it seemed to Richard Glencross. Meanwhile the national debt had risen to $31 billion, up $576 per family since FDR's coming to power.

This skyrocketing debt was particularly worrisome to Glencross, who, having spent a long and successful career in the money market, recognized that the first rule of economics—be it for an individual, an industrial empire, or the United States Government —was solvency. Deeply troubled by the New Deal's reckless strategy of trying to spend the nation out of the Depression, he couldn't help but recall that Roosevelt had been elected in the first place on a platform of economy in government.

> For three long years [the President had said during the campaign of 1932] I have been going up and down this Country, preaching that

> Government—federal, state, and local—costs too much. I shall not stop
> that preaching. . . . I propose that government, big and little, be made
> solvent and that the example be set by the President of the United
> States and his Cabinet. . . . Stop the deficits! Stop the deficits!

Although hardly in a position to cast stones, perhaps Huey Long
had been right in characterizing the President as "a liar and a fake."

At about this time a story going the rounds told of the diffi-
culties encountered by a make-believe Congressional committee,
set up at some future time for the purpose of finding a suitable
place to erect a monument in honor of President Roosevelt. Several sites were suggested and for one reason or another rejected as
unsuitable. For instance, it obviously shouldn't be too near the
statue of Jefferson because Jefferson founded the Democratic Party, while Roosevelt dumbfounded it. And it couldn't be near Ben-
jamin Franklin's either, because when Franklin did his experiments
he always kept both feet on the ground. And so on. Finally a perfect spot was found for it—right beside that of Columbus, because,
like FDR, Columbus didn't know where he was going when he set
out, didn't know where he was when he got there, and didn't
know where he had been after he'd left. And he did it all on borrowed money!

August of 1934 saw the birth of the American Liberty
League, not to be confused (by any means) with the American
Civil Liberties Union. While ostensibly bipartisan, the League was
in effect a predominantly Republican affair, fronted by a few
prominent Democrats, who for reasons of personal pique against
Roosevelt himself or an allergic reaction to his policies (or both),
had broken with the President. Foremost among these were former presidential candidates John W. Davis and Al Smith.

Although at the time of its inception the League proclaimed
itself politically neutral and concerned only with safeguarding the
Constitution, it wasn't hard to figure out where its real sentiments
lay, since its membership list read like a Who's Who of the nation's
wealthy and well born, including many of the DuPonts and their
aunts and uncles and cousins from the boardrooms of General
Motors, Montgomery Ward, and other corporate leviathans. Of
course (the Leaguers were forever pointing out), it wasn't necessary to be rich to belong to the League. Anybody who loved his
country and the Constitution could join. In fact, as one of Roosevelt's columnist friends remarked, for anyone unable to pay the

initiation dues, the League would be willing to accept first mortgage on his home.

The announced intention of the Leaguers was to keep America safe for democracy. "What they really mean," quipped the President, "is to keep Long Island safe for polo." Although probably never numbering more than 75,000 members, the League from its beginnings until its almost unnoticed demise a few years later, made a considerable amount of noise in its often frantic attempts to turn public sentiment against Roosevelt, whom they saw as a serious threat to traditional American freedoms, especially the freedom of the marketplace. With an almost unlimited treasury the League proceeded to sow the nation knee deep in anti-Roosevelt, anti-New Deal pamphlets, broadsides, news releases, canned editorials, and political cartoons, some of which, it must be admitted, were very cleverly done. In addition the League maintained an impressive stable of public speakers, whose main job it was to appear before various business and civic groups and educate them on what the President was doing to the country, and what was likely to happen if he weren't stopped.

Among the League's most effective weapons, if it can be said to have had any, was doughty old Al Smith, he of the derby hat and the sidewalks of New York, who had labored in the Democratic vineyards for forty years but had cooled on Roosevelt during the early days of the New Deal, some said because the new President had failed to offer him a place in the Cabinet. By mid-1934 Smith, once the darling of the liberal wing of the Democratic Party, had broken openly with the President and found a strange new home among the ultraconservative money barons of the Liberty League. The reason, all personal animosity aside, was that, to Smith's way of thinking, Roosevelt and his professor friends were trading in America's birthright for an alien ideology that could end only in the death of the country's most precious freedoms. Although Smith's views were not always identical with those of the Liberty League, they were close enough, and no one expressed them more directly or with greater eloquence than the now disillusioned and not-so-Happy Warrior who had worked his way up from the Fulton Fish Market to presidential candidate by championing the cause of liberal reform. Attention was due a man like this, but against the roar of the New Deal juggernaut his voice was only an angry whisper in the wind.

According to the Liberty Leaguers, the New Deal was a deal,

all right, but not a new one. It was plain, old-fashioned Marxism, and Comrade Roosevelt would stop at nothing to impose it upon America. No other President had ever resorted to such foul and desperate methods to gain his ends, declared a League spokesman:

> With pious phrases . . . [he] does that most despicable and devastating of all things—incites class against class, plunders the rich to purchase the poor—and thus under the guise of love for mankind kindles fires of hate that bring high and low into the common ruin of dissension, bankruptcy, and revolution.

Meanwhile, the Constitution was being arrogantly shunted aside as old-fashioned and irrelevant to the nation's present needs. ("I hope your committee will not permit doubts as to its constitutionality, however reasonable, to block the suggested legislation," the President had written to a congressional friend in 1935.) Indeed, with Congress in Roosevelt's pocket, all that stood between him and the outright destruction of the Constitution was the Supreme Court, whose members ("those nine old men") were by 1936 being publicly derided by the President for their "horse and buggy" decisions.

> Does any man or woman within the sound of my voice [asked Liberty Leaguer Charles Dawson, himself a Federal judge] doubt that the President hopes, if re-elected, that he will have the opportunity within the next few years to place upon the Supreme Court enough judges holding his Constitutional views to change the whole current of Constitutional construction in this country? Do any of you doubt that if such an opportunity is presented, that is exactly what he will do?

Shortly before the 1936 election, the President's oldest son, James, announced that after his father won he would try to change the Constitution so as to make room for his program. Remarked the President's friend Hugh Johnson, former head of the NRA: "Son Jimmy ought to have a Maxim silencer for a birthday present."

It was obvious where all this was leading—straight to Moscow, with Roosevelt the American Stalin. Speaking before an overflow crowd of American Liberty Leaguers in Washington in January of 1936, Al Smith warned his countrymen that they would soon have to decide which way the nation was to go:

There can be only the clear, pure, fresh air of free America, or
the foul breath of Communistic Russia. There can be only one flag, the
Stars and Stripes, or the flag of the Godless Union of the Soviets. There
can be only one national anthem, the Star-Spangled Banner or the
Internationale.

Actually, as several public figures were quick to point out,
Smith was saying nothing new. Even before the New Deal had
clearly revealed its "Communist" leanings, it had aroused strong
suspicions when, after less than a year in office, the President had
broken with the policy of his predecessors by establishing diplomatic relations with the Soviet Union. For millions of Americans,
especially those belonging to religious and patriotic organizations,
this was unsettling, to say the least. The President had "disgraced
the Country by closing his eyes to moral filth." By "clasping to
his bosom a viper deadlier than death itself," he had opened the
way to the subversion of the free institutions of the United States
and the ultimate triumph of Godless Bolshevik tyranny. "The
President has put himself in league with Communism," a New
York minister warned his congregation. "He has declared war
against God and freedom." From Massachusetts came a petition
bearing 600,000 signatures, imploring the President to reconsider
before it was too late. All to no avail. Recognition of the Soviet
Union would help ease the Depression, the President argued, by
opening promising opportunities for trade with the Russians. As
it turned out, he was wrong: the anticipated trade never amounted
to much of anything. But the subversion did.
    It soon became apparent to those who chose to see it that
way that the President's domestic program was entirely consistent
with his friendship with the Soviet Union. More and more bureaucracy, more and more governmental interference with the lives of
the American people and the free flow of the marketplace, and
more and more leveling legislation aimed at reducing all men to an
identical state of dependency and degradation—the pattern was
clear. At first, critics of the New Deal called it "creeping Socialism." Later it became "galloping Socialism," and before long, just
plain communism. Like Al Smith, Father Coughlin had seen it
coming and from his Shrine of the Little Flower had warned his
huge radio audience Sunday after Sunday as to what was happen-
ing. The nation's most powerful publisher, William Randolph
Hearst, who along with Smith and Coughlin had supported Roose-

velt's candidacy in 1932, was also quick to see the danger and pass
on the word to his millions of readers. In a particularly clever car-
toon that appeared in all the Hearst papers, a huge wolf ("Communism") is shown jumping up against a smiling, bespectacled figure
("New Deal") and licking him affectionately. In the background
a number of elfin characters labeled with various acronyms, which
critics had come to refer to as Roosevelt's "alphabet soup" (the
NRA, CCC, FERA, WPA, etc.), look on approvingly:

"Look," says one, "he loves our Daddy."

"Daddy looks like he loves him too."

"I wanna play with him, Daddy."

"Aren't wolves dangerous?"

"Naw, this is a good wolf."

"New Deal" is dressed in an academic cap and gown. So are the
elves.

To some Americans, the presence of large numbers of Jews in
prominent positions within the New Deal was just so much added
proof that the Administration was taking its cues, if not its orders,
from Moscow. Everybody knew that most Jews were radicals,
which was the same thing as being Communists. People like Mor-
genthau, Brandeis, Frankfurter, Baruch, Benny Cohen, and that
notorious New York Hebe, Fiorello LaGuardia, obviously wielded
great influence with the President. In fact, there were those who
said that Roosevelt himself was a Jew, an allegation they supported
by widely distributed genealogical charts that traced the President's
forebears on both sides back to early seventeenth-century European Jewry. Thus, the New Deal was in reality a Jew Deal, controled by an inner circle of Communist Kikes who had been cleverly inserted into positions of power by their leader, Moe Rosenvelt,
or Rosenbaum, or Rosenblum—depending upon which genealogical
"expert" one chose to believe.

Nowhere was the Communist menace more clearly recognized
and feared than in the South, where to many people the clincher
was the way the New Deal was pandering to the nigras. Never before had an Administration appointed so many of them to important Federal positions, which meant that more and more white
men were having to take orders from them. Worse than that, the
President—and especially his wife—seemed to go out of their way
to be seen mingling with them in public, at times even eating with
them at the same table. All this was more than an affront to
Southern sensitivities; it was a deliberate attempt to stir up race

hatreds—a well-known Communist trick. There was even some talk going around that Roosevelt and his friends had set aside a secret fund for hiring big black bucks to go through the South and rape white women. At taxpayer expense! In Georgia, Democratic Governor Eugene ("Our Gene") Talmadge, sporting his red suspenders and puffing on his cheap stogie cigar, announced in the spring of 1935 that his state might have to secede from the Union again in order to save itself from "that damned cripple in the White House."

"That damned cripple in the White House." Probably not many Americans would have been so blunt about it as "Our Gene," but there was no denying that a lot of them resented the fact that the President of the United States was "only half a man." News photographers made it a practice never to shoot the President below the waist or to show him in his wheelchair or braces, and, except in support of the March of Dimes, editors usually played down the President's affliction. But there it was, nevertheless: The most powerful nation in the world had as its leader, indeed as commander in chief of its armed forces, a person who couldn't even stand on his own two feet without being propped up.

How unfitting and demeaning it was to the national image to have the office once occupied by Washington, Jackson, Lincoln, and Teddy Roosevelt now the property of a hopeless cripple. Even some of those most well disposed toward him had, in spite of themselves, their moments of revulsion. A young pro-Roosevelt reporter recalled years later seeing the President being lifted out of his limousine and deposited into his wheelchair by secret service agents. The President's hat had slipped to one side and he had cocked his head at a ridiculous angle to keep it from falling off. He seemed then a poor figure indeed to be the leader of a great people. "That's one of his problems," commented an anti-New Dealer. "He's locked into that wheelchair. He doesn't have any idea of what's really going on in the Country. We ought to have a man who can get out and move among the people." Someone recommended that in the future more attention be paid to the physical condition of those aspiring to the presidency and that no one should be permitted to hold that office who couldn't make it up the Capitol steps under his own power—or at least, suggested Our Gene, "be able to walk a two-by-four plank."

Millions of other Americans, willing to overlook or forget the President's physical infirmities, saw plenty of other things about the man himself that they found hard to take. What it all came

down to was that, for the most part, those people who didn't like
what the President stood for didn't like the President either. The
one thing far and away most irritating about him was that famous
Roosevelt charm, which, it was claimed with some justification, he
wielded like a weapon whenever he sensed that an advantage might
be gained from doing so. During the incipient stages of his break
with the President, William Randolph Hearst was invited to meet
with Roosevelt and talk over their differences. But Hearst refused.
"I'm afraid I'll fall under his spell," he explained.

That smile, that friendly warmth, that lively sense of humor
with its hearty laughter, that marvellous enthusiasm for the moment ("I am having a perfectly glor-i-ous time," he would say, and
who could doubt it?)—it was all so contagious and charming. But
it was also, in the minds of many, very phony. "Our great American smiler," William Allen White called him. "A slick old thimble-
rigger." The popular writer John Gunther recalls his first presidential press conference in late 1934. For twenty minutes he sat
there entranced by the easy, relaxed, friendly way the President
responded to a wide variety of questions from reporters. A fasci-
nating performance, during which the President's radiance warmed
the room and the hearts of his audience, who left in the best of
moods. "And yet, he *said* almost nothing. Questions were de-
flected, diverted, diluted. . . . I never met anyone who showed
greater capacity for avoiding a direct answer while giving the ques-
tioner the feeling he had been answered."

For those not bedazzled by the President's charm, however,
his personal mannerisms were often annoying and sometimes
downright contemptible. It is a fact, for instance, that the Daughters of the American Revolution failed to appreciate the President's
flippancy when he addressed them at their national convention as
"Fellow Immigrants." It is also a fact that some of those closest to
him were appalled by his occasional acts of cruelty, often com-
mited behind his victim's back to the accompaniment of a smile
and a callous remark. To many of his countrymen what was least
charming of all about the President was his insufferably superior
attitude. A well-traveled joke during those years told of a little
man who reached the Pearly Gates and found a long line waiting
there. "We're a bit behind schedule today," St. Peter explained.
"God has an appointment with His psychiatrist. Recently He's
started behaving like Franklin D. Roosevelt." That silly cigarette-
holder, the pince-nez, and the cape (a cape, mind you!), were all

seen as the props of a complete snob, who, with his oh-so-proper pedigree, obviously enjoyed looking down his patrician nose at the American people—and talking down to them with his private school diction that reeked of condescension. "God, how I hated his patronizing ways!" one of his uncharmed contemporaries later remarked of him:

> Every time he said "My Friends" with that superior tone of his, it was all I could do to keep from kicking hell out of the radio. There were a lot of other people I knew who felt the same way. It was really maddening. You know, the wonder of it is that nobody shot the son of a bitch.

Those who disliked the President didn't, as a general rule, care much for the rest of the family either. The Roosevelt children, all grown, displayed a remarkable proclivity for marital problems and traffic tickets. Two divorces within only a few months, at a time when "till death do you part" was still taken seriously, caused many Americans to view with alarm the moral degeneracy of the nation's First Family. As for the traffic violations, consider the case (or cases) of Franklin Jr., who, although not the only one of the five younger Roosevelts to end up in traffic court, was certainly the most persistent.

In January of 1935, while on his way to a dance in Philadelphia, Franklin Jr., slammed his La Salle coupe into a parked car, causing it considerable damage and shaking up its driver. Although charged with "assault and battery by automobile," he was allowed to continue to the dance in a taxi. Next night in court he explained that he had been blinded by the snow and that his car had skidded. There was a rumor he had been drunk. Less than a month before, while on his way back home from Harvard, where he was an undergraduate, he was arrested near Orange, Connecticut, for driving seventy-eight miles an hour on a wet highway, and going through a red light. A telephone call from the White House got the court appearance postponed until after the holidays, at which time he was fined ten dollars and then had lunch with the judge. Somewhat earlier he had been stopped for speeding in Windsor Locks, Connecticut, and for a similar violation in Union, also Connecticut —not a very good state for young Franklin. In Boston in March of 1934, ten months before his accident in Philadelphia, he ran into a

sixty-year-old woman but, because of the reportedly icy conditions of the roads, was excused without charges by the authorities
after paying a ten-dollar fine for driving with an expired license.
All of this, of course, made great newspaper copy and was excellent grist for the anti-Roosevelt mill.

It was Eleanor Roosevelt, however, who drew most of the
fire, partly because she was the President's wife, and partly because she was—well, she was Eleanor, which is to say that although
a sweet, courageous, and highly intelligent person, she was in
many ways incredibly naive, and, sad to relate, a bit vapid at times.
She was also uncommonly homely, and, for all her genuine warmth,
she could never quite shake loose a finishing-school prissiness that
made her appear to some people to be "putting on airs." Somewhat lacking in humor herself, she soon became the butt of other
people's jokes, some of them good-natured, but most not. Even
her husband joined in the fun. His close friend and advisor Sam
Rosenman ("Sammy the Rose"), who could do an uncanny imita-
tion of the First Lady, would sometimes phone the President late
at night to cheer him up: "Franklin," he would say with Eleanor's
voice, "I've been picked up by the vice squad and they've got me
down here in this goddam jail." And then a barrage of obscenities.
The President would roar with laughter.

Much of Mrs. Roosevelt's trouble, if it could be called that,
came from her almost frenzied mobility. She was, to use one of
TIME magazine's favorite words for her, ubiquitous. One day she
would appear on an Indian reservation, and the next at the bottom of a mine shaft. She enjoyed mingling with the people and
was interested in the conditions under which they lived and
worked, especially the poor. With the heart of a social worker and
the stamina of a long-distance runner, she would often leave the
White House at a moment's notice to visit with migrant farm
workers in California, tour an urban slum, or inspect an automobile assembly line. Her husband called her "Rover," although not
to her face. Her critics (which is to say, by and large, the President's critics) called her a meddling old busybody who didn't
know enough to stay at home where she belonged, and blamed the
President for not being man enough to keep her under control.

For those who remember the First Lady it is easy to understand why for so many years she was America's favorite joke. Even
among many of her friends and well-wishers her ungainly appearance, her often comic ways, her innumerable causes and crusades,

and her occasional simpleminded comments were sometimes just too much to resist poking fun at. So, alas, was her remarkably banal column, "My Day," which by election time, 1936, was appearing in over sixty newspapers throughout the country. In one of his gentler spoofs of Mrs. Roosevelt, Hearst newsman Westbrook Pegler presented the following near perfect parody of the First Lady's hard-hitting brand of journalism:

> Yesterday morning I took a train to New York City and sat beside a gentleman who was reading the . . . Report of the International Recording Secretary of the World Home Economics and Children's Aptitude and Recreation Foundation of which my very good friend, Dr. Mary McTwaddle, formerly of Vassar, is the American delegate. This aroused my interest and I ventured to remark that I had once had the pleasure of entertaining a group of young people who were deeply concerned with the neglected problem of the Unmarried Father. It turned out that the gentleman himself was an unmarried father so we had a very interesting chat until he got off at Metuchen.

If Pegler's parody seems a bit overdrawn, then consider an example of the real thing—a typical excerpt from "My Day" itself: FDR has just learned that the Supreme Court has declared the Agricultural Adjustment Act unconstitutional, and Mrs. Roosevelt goes down to the White House pool to join the President and a few of his friends for what she supposed would be "a rather quiet and subdued swim at six o'clock":

> My husband was already in the water, and before I reached the door, I dropped my wrapper, plunged into the water, and swimming about very quietly, I inquired hesitatingly how they were all feeling. To my complete surprise instead of either discouragement or even annoyance, I was told that everyone was feeling fine, and on that note we finished our swim.

And yet, none of this does much to explain why among a surprising number of her countrymen, most of them basically decent human beings, this kind and generous woman managed to arouse such feelings of intense hatred. Perhaps it was her lopsided passion for the underdog, or perhaps the subversive example she set by ignoring woman's traditional role as homebody. At any

rate, among many Americans, especially the respectable and secure, she was often more fiercely detested and maligned than the
President himself. "She is the greatest argument for mercy killing
I know," declared a Bronxville banker. "She should have been
shot as a child."

Not that any of this would have much effect upon the President's political fortunes—not the erosive dangers of the dole, the
threat of dictatorship, the Moscow menace, the wheelchair, the
Jews, or even Eleanor. When the time came for the American
people to speak out in November of 1936, they paid little attention to such matters. Come what may, they were determined to
rehire the boss, and they acted accordingly by giving him a thumping victory in the nation's most one-sided presidential election
since James Monroe ran unopposed in 1820—all of which seemed
to bear out (among other things) what Henry Mencken had said
earlier: "You can't beat a somebody with a nobody."

And, say what you will, in those days when the frost was on
the national pumpkin, Franklin D. Roosevelt was indeed a somebody, a political phenomenon of the first order who swept everything before him. He was, in the words of his friendly foe, William
Allen White of Emporia, "the most unaccountable President that
this United States has ever seen . . . , a wizard in the White House
[who] casts his weird spell upon a changing world." And yet,
mused White, "how much is false, how much is real, how much is
an illusion of grandeur, a vast make-believe, only time will tell."

The Gang That
Couldn't Think Straight

THINGS HAD BEEN getting steadily worse overseas since Mussolini invaded Ethiopia in the autumn of 1935 and got away with it. Emboldened by Il Duce's success, in March of the following year Hitler sent 50,000 troops into the hitherto demilitarized Rhineland, in direct violation of the Treaty of Versailles. He also got away with it. When civil war erupted in Spain that summer, it didn't take the totalitarian powers long to choose up sides. By early 1937 thousands of Italians and Germans, equipped with modern weapons and aircraft, were fighting alongside General Franco's insurgents, while to a much lesser extent the Soviet Union supported the forces of the Republic. Newsmen and military observers soon took to calling Spain a testing ground for another world war. Maybe they were right.

Americans were deeply disturbed by all this, and, if the truth were known, a bit frightened. The situation in Europe was obviously getting out of hand. Something would have to be done about it. But by whom? Certainly not America. When in the autumn of 1937 President Roosevelt urged that aggressor nations be "quarantined" by the rest of the world, most of his countrymen felt that he would do better to confine his attention to things here at home and not get this nation involved in other people's problems, especially when they could conceivably lead to war. "It's an awful thing," the President remarked to a friend, "to look over your shoulder when you're trying to lead and find no one there." Two months later when the Japanese, who had recently resumed their attack against China, sank the U.S. gunboat *Panay* sent to evacuate

Americans from the war zone, the nation scarcely blinked. The
boat shouldn't have been there in the first place.

Meanwhile, here at home another bunch of bandits were up
to no good.

In those days Bangor, Maine, was not generally regarded as a
place of much excitement. Set off from the mainstream of civilization by great distances and a hostile climate, its 30,000 people
lived lives that were sober, frugal, and for the most part remarkably
serene. The tempo of the town was slow and its future predictable
—or so at least it seemed in those long-gone years of the late '30s
before the world went mad. The days paraded by in single file,
each one pleasant in its way and all but indistinguishable from the
others, while an aura of unflagging Republicanism hovered protec-
tively over the town.

Bangor's banks were solvent. Its business was sluggish but
sound. On Saturday nights, long before shopping centers had
sprung up along the outskirts, farm families from nearby parts
poured into town in their rundown jalopies to buy boots and cor-
duroy pants from the "Jew stores" on Pickering Square. At the
corner of Main Street and Union, the Bangor House, which had
hosted the godlike Daniel Webster on his visit a century before,
served the finest food in the state. The Great Northern Pulp and
Paper Company was as solid as a rock. So was the Bangor & Aroos-
took, one of the few railroads in the country to show a profit
during the Depression.

On outer Hammond Street, where in a few years Dow Air-
base would rise almost magically out of the meadows and alder
swamps, the trolley line ended at the edge of a cow pasture, a hundred yards beyond Fairmount Avenue. A mile in toward town,
new Ford V-8s were priced as low as $495 at Webber Motors, and
at a nearby Tydol station gasoline sold for fifteen cents a gallon,
except during the summer gas wars when the price sometimes
dropped to eight for a dollar. From Union Station on Washington
Street, near where Kenduskeague Stream joins the Penobscot, a
half-dozen or more trains left daily for Boston, only six hours
away. And in his second-floor shop on Central Street, Harry John-

son cut hair for a quarter a head—directly across from Dakins
Sporting Goods Store.

The gang that made the big ruckus in Bangor on that brilliant
autumn morning in 1937 was composed of three men (down from
an original four). All of them were young and undersized, and all
hailed from Indiana, a state that distinguished itself in the years
between the wars by its bountiful production of bigtime hoodlums,
or, as they were then generally called, "bandits" or "desperadoes."
The chief of the trio, and the tallest at 5'5", was Alfred Brady, a
weak-chinned, hawk-nosed misfit who, upon first meeting, was
variously described as "good-natured," "innocent," and "pleasantly
shy." As FBI Chief J. Edgar Hoover later said of him: "He looked
like a common type of easily embarrassed farm boy, seeming incapable of vicious thought."

Brady was born in a rural slum near Kentland in northern
Indiana, only a few miles from the Illinois border. His early years
read like something out of a social worker's casebook. His father,
a dirt farmer who barely managed to grub out a living for himself
and his family, died when Alfred was only four years old. Soon
after that, the boy's mother took him to Indianapolis where she
remarried. In 1926 she died, leaving her sixteen-year-old son to
shift for himself. Alfred then quit school and got a job working in
a clothing store. He also ran errands now and then for the neighborhood merchants. In spite of all this, his spiritual education was
not neglected. He attended Sunday school regularly. By 1930,
when he was twenty, he had become the acknowledged leader of
the young people in his church, where he organized a Christian
Fellowship for teenage boys. At the same time he was busy outside the church organizing another kind of boys' club. This one
stripped hubcaps and other accessories from automobiles, which
young Alfred disposed of through a neighborhood fence.

During the early 1930s Brady graduated from stealing accessories to stealing the automobiles themselves, a much more profit-
able business. But also more risky. By 1934 the law had caught up
with him and convicted him of "grand theft, auto." Ordinarily he
would have been sent to the state prison, but, according to J. Edgar

Hoover, "his mildness of manner and his air of innocence saved him from the penitentiary." Instead, he was given a term on the penal farm, where, Hoover noted, "he so successfully played the role of the dull-witted farm boy caught in the toils of the law that even his fellow inmates nicknamed him 'Dopey.' "

His brief term at the penal farm was time well spent for young Brady. In fact, it was a basic training of sorts, during which he picked up a goodly amount of information that would later prove invaluable—such as the whereabouts of fences, location of hideouts, and the names of crooked cops and political fixers. By the time he was released in the summer of 1935 he had acquired something of the know-how and confidence of a professional. He was sure now what he wanted to make of his life and how to go about doing it. "Before I'm through," he confided to a fellow prisoner, "I'll make Dillinger look like a piker."

Soon after his release from the farm, Brady set about organizing a gang. His first recruit was Rhuel James Dalhover, a sloe-eyed, underwitted little man four years older than Brady (who was then twenty-five) and an inch shorter. Through Dalhover, Brady soon met Charles Geiseking, a twenty-seven-year-old moonshiner from Kentucky, and his nineteen-year-old understudy, Clarence Lee Shaffer, Jr., a swarthy, vacuous-looking boy who had just deserted the girl-mother of his illegitimate child. Of such stuff was the Brady gang composed. During the next two years it would commit between one hundred and fifty and two hundred armed robberies, four murders, and innumerable assaults, to establish what Hoover later called "a record for utter conscienceless criminality."

From the formation of the gang in the late summer of 1935 until February of the following year, the Brady boys averaged four holdups a week. Operating out of Indianapolis, they ranged over most of Indiana and western Ohio. Their specialty during this early phase of their career was grocery stores, most of them small neighborhood types, but some of them early versions of supermarkets, which were then just beginning to appear on the American scene. Many of these jobs netted practically nothing. One yielded a total of nine dollars, of which Brady, as boss, received three and each of the others, two. When Dalhover complained that this was not much of a haul for an armed robbery, Brady replied: "Maybe not, but it all adds up." On one occasion the boys made a daytime raid on a large market in Piqua, Ohio. Brandishing a revolver and a shotgun at the three dozen or so people in the store, Geiseking and

Shaffer emptied $700 out of the cash register and the customers' pockets, while Dalhover waited outside behind the wheel of the car. In the rear of the store Brady was trying to open a safe when a clerk, unaware of what was going on, appeared suddenly through the cellar door. Instantly Brady whirled and fired, and the clerk crumpled to the floor mortally wounded. "Let's get out of here," Brady shouted as he rushed back to the front of the store. "Some stupid bastard tried to jump me, so I plugged him and kicked him down the cellar steps."

As with most traveling men, the boys soon discovered that during their off-hours life on the road was apt to be something of a bore. Still, they managed to make do. Each had his own little pleasures and diversions. Dalhover and Geiseking enjoyed strolling through the various towns they visited, window shopping. Often they would drop into hardware and sporting-goods stores to examine the guns, sometimes purchasing a particularly attractive piece to add to their arsenal, for, like Brady and Shaffer, they had a great passion for firearms of all kinds. They also attended ball games and fights, and amusement parks where they could shoot at little metal ducks. As for Shaffer, mainly he liked to eat, especially hamburgers, of which he could never get enough. His appetite was prodigious. And why not? He was still a growing boy. It was his great ambition in life to open a hamburger stand one day in downtown Indianapolis. He was also fond of shooting off his mouth, and sulking when things didn't go his way. The others sometimes found him hard to put up with. Brady himself was addicted to roller-skating, and he was very good at it, although once at the height of his career he fell down and broke his nose. Wherever he went he carried his expensive skates with him in the trunk of the car, right next to his shotgun.

Besides all this, the gang sometimes read adventure stories, like those in *Doc Savage* and *Argosy*, and enjoyed thumbing through the latest gun catalogues. Movies also rated high. In those days even the smallest town had at least one movie house, and the boys attended hundreds of them during their two years together. Once or twice a month they would pack a lunch and go to some out-of-the-way place to put in a day of target practice. Their favorite spot was a wooded area outside of Greencastle, Indiana, where earlier in the decade John Dillinger had pulled off one of his most spectacular bank robberies.

Then, too, they helped pass the time by playing cards (mostly "Casino" and "Michigan") and by bickering with one another. Brady was particularly abrasive. He had a habit of needling the others in a way that kept everyone on edge. He sometimes called Shaffer "Kewpie" because of the boy's youthful appearance, and made fun of Dalhover's stupidity at cards. Furthermore, as leader of the outfit, he insisted on bossing the others around, and they resented it. Once, after Brady had given them a dressing down for not wearing neckties (Brady was a stickler for neatness), Dalhover and Shaffer decided to kill him by shooting him in the head while he was asleep. When Geiseking refused to go along the idea was dropped, but not until after Brady had been presented with an ultimatum and had agreed to be more considerate of the others' feelings in the future.

Unlike many of their professional colleagues, the Brady boys were not much given to hard liquor. A bottle of beer now and then was about the extent of their drinking. Girls were another matter. In fact, chasing "dames" accounted for much of the gang's off-duty time. Each member had his own methods of pursuit. Brady was most successful at roller rinks, where his graceful gyrations seldom failed to make a hit. Once outside the rollerdrome, however, his luster dimmed considerably, partly perhaps because he didn't believe in spoiling his dates with lavish spending. According to a woman he sometimes went out with in Indianapolis, Brady was the world's greatest skinflint. His idea of a big evening was to take his date on a ride (often in a stolen car), buy her a chicken sandwich, and then bed her down. Dalhover was as generous with his girl friends as Brady was tightfisted, but then, Dalhover couldn't roller-skate.

An hour or so before midnight, early in 1936, Brady and his gang rode into Anderson, Indiana, where they intended to pull a job the following morning. After casing the town, they "ran the streets," that is, they determined the best route of escape and practiced traveling it to make sure they would be able to beat a hasty retreat when the time came—a common criminal procedure that Brady insisted upon before every job. On this occasion the practice session took longer than usual, and it was nearly one o'clock before the boys were ready to turn in for the night. Since it was also a Brady rule never to check into a hotel or overnight cabin after midnight, lest suspicions be aroused, he ordered Dalhover to pull over to the curb on a side street, where the boys loosened their ties and stretched out to doze as best they could.

Sometime during the night Police Officer Frank Levy happened by on routine patrol. "He asked us what we was doing," Dalhover later boasted to a fellow prisoner. "And do you know what I says? I says 'Killing coppers—that's what we're doing.' And then I let the son of a bitch have it." Officer Levy died instantly, without even knowing why.

It was time the boys had a vacation anyway, and this seemed like a good time for one. Soon after the murder of Officer Levy, Brady and the others left for New Orleans to take in the Mardi Gras. There they remained for the better part of two weeks, resting up from their arduous schedule of the past few months, and enjoying the favors of several different women. When the time came to leave, Brady, posing as an FBI agent, persuaded a young married woman to leave her husband and three-year-old child and join him on the road. This arrangement lasted for only a few weeks, however, for, as the woman later testified, she couldn't stand Brady's stinginess. Still, to give him his due, she did concede that on one occasion he presented her in a single afternoon with a beautiful wedding ring, a string of pearls, and a diamond-studded wrist watch (all of which he had stolen only hours before). It was at about that time that she began to suspect that he really wasn't an FBI agent at all.

When the boys returned north in the late winter of 1936, they were ready for bigger game. Although they wouldn't shy away from an easy grocery hit now and then, it was decided that they would henceforth concentrate on jewelry stores. The risk would be the same, Brady argued, and the hauls were bound to be bigger. Dalhover and Geiseking agreed that the time had come to step up. Shaffer, who hated to agree with Brady on anything, grumbled his opposition but in the end went along anyway.

Immediately their new specialty began to pay off handsomely. From the final week of February through April the Brady gang pulled off at least six jewelry heists for a total take of close to $150,000. There was nothing particularly elaborate or imaginative about their style. While one of the gang, usually Dalhover, waited out front with the motor running, the other three walked boldly into the store in broad daylight, wearing neither masks nor gloves. Waving guns at customers and clerks, they would work their way methodically through the store, emptying everything they could lay their hands on into pillowcases. Then, after as long as fifteen or twenty minutes inside, a casual stroll to the car and a fast getaway. All very simple, provided nothing went wrong.

On a day in late April 1936, something did go wrong. Surprised while holding up a jewelry store in Lima, Ohio, the gang became involved in a shoot-out with the police. They finally managed to reach the car, but not until Geiseking had been hit in both legs. After shaking off their pursuers, the boys headed for Indianapolis, where they took Geiseking to the home of a doctor in a residential section of the city. "They told me that the wounded man had been shot by a jealous husband and that they hadn't taken him to the hospital because he wanted to avoid publicity," the doctor later reported. Finding this story a little hard to believe, the doctor managed, through the help of his wife, to notify the police at once. It would have been better if he hadn't, for in the ensuing gun battle a law officer was killed and the Brady gang got clean away— that is, all except Geiseking, who was left behind to serve ten to twenty-five years in the Ohio State Penitentiary.

The gang was now down to three members, all of them very hot, so much so that they decided to split up and lie low for a time. Shaffer went to Indianapolis where he was ordered by Brady to stay out of sight until further notice. Brady and Dalhover returned to New Orleans for another go at the high life. But this time things weren't so pleasant. They now had worries. Big ones. Since their Mardi Gras visit of less than three months before, important changes had taken place. They were no longer the anonymous pikers who had terrorized neighborhood grocers for a ten-dollar bill. They had moved up in the world. Now they were big-time, with several major heists and three killings to their credit, two of them cops. Their names were known. So were their faces. Rewards were out for them in two states.

To make matters worse, by switching to jewelry they had made life more complicated and intrinsically more dangerous for themselves. They had graduated to a much more elaborate and sensitive type of operation. It was no longer enough just to steal; there was now the added problem of merchandising. Fences were needed, and go-betweens, all of whom needed constant cultivation and some of whom where apt to be talkative after a few drinks, with the result that too many people knew too much about the gang's business. This posed dangers from two directions: first, the police were able to pick up information on them through underworld gossip, sometimes relayed to them by paid informers; second, other crooks, aware of what Brady and his friends were up to and how well they were faring, were in a position to muscle in, before or after the fact.

All this had been borne out rather dramatically when, not long before the shoot-out in Lima, a group of ten or more burly thugs hijacked the gang out of $68,000 worth of jewelry they had just stolen from a store in Dayton, Ohio. Brady and his boys bristled, and swore they'd gun down everyone involved, beginning with their trusted go-between Dago Jack, who, they learned, had set them up for the hijackers. Understandably, the Midwest underworld began to stir with apprehension. Word soon reached the police, who persuaded Dago Jack to place himself under their protection. In return he told them everything he knew about the Brady gang, which was plenty. Thus, when Brady and Dalhover arrived back in Indianapolis from New Orleans to pick up Shaffer in the late spring of 1936, they found the police waiting for them. Totally surprised, they were taken without a fight and were hustled away with Shaffer to the Indianapolis jail to await trial for murder.

At this point the gang's brief but busy career of crime should have been at an end. But no. Somehow their lawyer managed to get them transferred from the modern, high-security jail in Indianapolis to a small, rundown crackerbox in the town of Greenfield, twenty miles to the east in Hancock County. There for several weeks they behaved like model prisoners. And then on October 11, with their trial about to begin, they caught the sheriff offguard, and after beating him senseless with his own gun, stole a nearby car and disappeared.

Once again the Brady boys were on the loose. But the road back would not be an easy one. When arrested they had been relieved of all their money and, worse yet, their guns—including six revolvers, four rifles, four shotguns, and a submachine gun. Now they had only twelve dollars, a stolen car, and the sheriff's pistol, which they proceeded to use to good effect. "We went back to doing small jobs," Dalhover later told the police. "Grocery stores mostly. A little bit here, a little there." Once they had accumulated a thousand dollars, they outfitted themselves with a new arsenal, bigger and better than the one they had lost. Suddenly their world looked brighter.

Now they could go about making up for lost time. Grocery stores were meager pickings; jewelry had almost done them in; from here on it would be banks. Banks were where the cash was, and cash was what the gang wanted. No more fences, no more go-betweens. Only the three Brady boys now, and their guns—and lots of money. This was really the big time, the biggest of the big. Just like Dillinger! An exciting prospect indeed, made even more so by the fact that at about this time the gang made its first appearance on the FBI's "most wanted" list. The charge: transporting stolen property across state lines, specifically jewelry and cars, including a supercharged beauty they stole at gunpoint from a gentleman in Chicago who (how were they supposed to know?) turned out to be an FBI field agent.

By late November the gang had settled in Baltimore. There they lived quietly for the next eight and a half months in a pleasant residential district, behaving for all the world like solid, middle-class types, save for an occasional out-of-town trip to rob a bank in the Midwest. It was a new way of doing business for the boys: crime by long-distance foray. A far cry from the early days when they had gone scurrying from town to town, victimizing corner grocers and hiding out in rundown overnight cabins. What they had now was the best of both worlds. Brady even opened a savings account in a Baltimore bank under an assumed name and got a part-time job as a machinist, which he felt would be helpful to him professionally. In the basement of their rented house he set up a modest metal-working shop, and, with Dalhover's help, worked at keeping the gang's arsenal in good repair.

How many banks they robbed during their stay in Baltimore is not known for certain, but they must have averaged better than one a month and accumulated a considerable sum of money. Meanwhile, Shaffer and Dalhover had become so caught up in the spirit of respectability that they got married to a couple of Baltimore waitresses. It all happened very suddenly—a double elopement to Elkton, Maryland, where no waiting period was required. Also no blood test, which was fortunate for Shaffer, since he had syphilis. The double wedding was held at the home of a local justice of the peace, five days after the boys had hit the bank at North Madison, Indiana, for $1600. It was a simple ceremony, joining in holy matrimony Mr. and Mrs. Herbie Schwartz and Mr. and Mrs. Mickey Riley. In attendance as witness and friend of both grooms was Edward Maxwell (Brady), who may have wondered how Mrs. Riley (Dalhover) would react when she discovered that her husband already had a wife somewhere back in the Midwest. Two weeks later the boys took a business trip to Carthage, Indiana, where they "withdrew" $2150 from the local bank.

On May 25, 1937, at 9:30 in the morning, the Brady gang pulled up in a maroon sedan in front of the bank in Goodland, Indiana, a small town close to the Illinois border in the northern part of the state. Dalhover stayed at the wheel, while Brady and Shaffer sauntered casually into the bank. Holding a gun on a woman teller, the only other person in the bank, they waited for fifteen minutes until the time lock on the safe opened. After stuffing nearly $2500 into a bag, they walked out as nonchalantly as they had entered, leaving the terrified teller free to call the police. Within a matter of minutes State Trooper Paul Minneman, who happened to be passing through town, had picked up Deputy Sheriff Elmer Craig and started off in pursuit.

About fifteen miles outside of town, Brady had Dalhover pull off the road and stop beside a crossroads church. The pursuers were too close for comfort, but the boys had foreseen such a contingency and may even have welcomed it. Recently for $175 they had purchased a real machine gun from a bartender in Kentucky. It was a souvenir of the Great War and needed a lot of work done on it. But that was taken care of easily enough. After a few weeks of tinkering in Brady's basement metal shop, the gun was in first-class working condition. Now all that was needed was a chance to try it out.

In the shadows by the far corner of the church, the boys mounted the gun on its tripod and waited. Before long, the patrol car rounded the bend at full speed and came to a sudden stop beside the maroon sedan. The two officers had just started to get out when Brady opened fire with the machine gun. The heavy slugs whapped through the car door as if it were paper, mortally wounding Trooper Minneman. Craig, who would miraculously live to tell the tale, managed to crawl out of the car on the far side, only to be met by a shotgun blast. As he lay semiconscious on the ground, the blood gushing from a deep wound in his throat, he heard someone walk over to him. "You want to finish this one off?" a voice asked. "Never mind about him," someone answered. "Let's get the hell out of here."

Within a couple of hours after the Goodland holdup, an interstate alarm was sounded, and one of the biggest manhunts ever conducted in the Midwest was underway. Roadblocks were thrown up; traffic was stopped; back roads were patroled; and airplanes joined in the search. Still, the gang managed to reach Indianapolis and disappear without a trace in the familiar city. In the process

Brady and Shaffer broke into one of the buildings on the Indianapolis Fair Grounds, trussed up the night watchman, and locked
him in a closet—for the sole purpose of using his phone. And for a
local call, at that. The watchman later reported that from the
closet he had heard Brady shout out: "Della, turn off the engine."
On the strength of this, the police proceeded to check out every
Della in the area. Of course, they came up with nothing, because
what Brady really said was: "Dalhover, turn off the engine."

The boys had every reason to congratulate themselves. Once
again they had scored big, and despite all the police could do, had
got away scot free. Besides that, their machine gun, for which they
had such great affection and hopes for the future, had worked
flawlessly. They would undoubtedly have been even more pleased
had they known that finally, after four murders and a hundred
and fifty or so armed robberies, they had been promoted to the
very top of the FBI's "most wanted" list. They were indeed, as
Brady had promised, beginning to make Dillinger look like a piker.

Back in Baltimore on a rather nice day in early August, two
and a half months after the Goodland Bank job, the Brady boys
were quietly at work a few blocks from home, doing nothing
more out of line than transferring some of their possessions into
a newly stolen car, when they were approached by a police
cruiser out on routine patrol. Most likely they would have been
given no more than passing notice. But why take chances? Within
seconds the boys had riddled the cruiser with .45 slugs and were
racing away in their new car. By some miracle neither of the patrolmen was hit, but their cruiser was so badly damaged that they
were unable to give chase. Later that day the outlaws' automobile
was found abandoned. In it were papers, carelessly left behind,
that provided enough clues to enable the Baltimore police to slowly unravel the mystery of the gunmen's identities, both assumed
and real.

Four days later, on August 11, FBI agents and local police
moved in on the gang's Baltimore hideout, but by this time the
boys were far away. Without bothering to return home after the
shooting, they had stolen another car and fled the city, leaving
two wives and the greater part of their arsenal (including their
precious machine gun) behind. Shortly thereafter, they stopped
just long enough in Thorp, Wisconsin, to pull off a $7000 bank
robbery, and then swung eastward by way of upstate New York
into New England. By early September they were holed up in a

rooming house in Bridgeport, Connecticut, posing as "hardware men." Their landlady would remember them fondly: "I never had more quiet or gentlemanly men in the house. They were well dressed and had a fine command of English, never drank or gave me any trouble." For three weeks the boys lay low, and then, in late September they ventured forth to see what they could do about replenishing their arsenal. Maine seemed like a good place to go, because, being a great hunting state, it was, as Dalhover later told the police, "the only state where they don't want your whole life history when you go in to buy a gat."

On Saturday, October 2, Brady and Dalhover sauntered into Dakins Sporting Goods Store on Central Street in downtown Bangor. Introducing themselves to the clerk as Charlie Harris and Edward Macy of Warren, Ohio, they produced letters of reference from hardware stores in Portland and Augusta where they had made several purchases earlier that week. After a bit of general browsing among the hunting gear, they bought two Colt .45 revolvers and some ammunition. The clerk was impressed by how neatly the two men were dressed, but there was something about their behavior that aroused his suspicion. As soon as they had left, he went out back to the office and told owner Shep Hurd that he thought they might be gangsters. Hurd phoned the police; the police notified the FBI in Boston; and the FBI did nothing. "Insufficient information." Later that same day Dalhover and Shaffer dropped into Rice & Miller's, a hardware store on Broad Street, only a block from Dakins'. There they picked out three .32 automatics. The clerk thought the men looked "hard" and checked with his boss on what to do. "Sell them anything they want," the boss ordered. "What do you care how they look?"

On the following Wednesday the boys revisited Dakins, where they purchased another Colt and ordered a .35 automatic Winchester rifle. As Shep Hurd was ringing up the sale, one of them asked:

"Where can we get a machine gun in this town?"

"We don't handle them," Hurd answered, without looking up.

"Well, see what you can do about getting us a Thompson. Get all the clips you can find too. We'll be back next Monday or Tuesday."

This time when Hurd notified the police he got results. Chief Crowley agreed that not just anyone was apt to come in off the street and order a submachine gun, and when Hurd made a positive identification of Dalhover from the wanted poster, Crowley again got in touch with the FBI Boston office, where things now began to stir.

Meanwhile, the boys were staying in an overnight cabin at Auto Rest Park, a seedy little amusement center about ten miles west of town. The accommodations were not very lavish, but there were amenities aplenty, including a roller rink for Brady, a menagerie of mangy-looking animals, and a fun house filled with coin machines and notions. On the last night of his life Shaffer watched penny movies and tried several times without success to grab a camera with the nickel derrick. Dalhover examined articles at the souvenir counter. Finally he bought a small snapshot book and two crystal fish. "They make good paper weights," he explained to the clerk.

On the Monday following their second visit to Dakins, one of the gang phoned the store to find out if their rifle had arrived. It had. What about the Thompson? That had come too. Would the store be open the next day, Columbus Day? It would. Fine. They would drop around in the morning and pick up the merchandise. "Here as earlier," the *Bangor Daily News* later commented, "they acted with incredible stupidity. In fact, they all but engaged a press agent to let Bangor know what they were up to."

On the following morning, shortly before 8:30, Harry Johnson raised the new shade on the window of his second-floor barbershop on Central Street. Down below, people were already moving about, for in those days most stores opened for business at 8:00 or 8:30. Across the street in front of Dakins, James Seely, one of the junior clerks, was sweeping the sidewalk, an early-morning ritual for Bangor merchants. It was a beautiful crisp, clear day, the sort that causes poets to wax rhapsodic over New England autumns, and makes men think that perhaps life will go on forever, after all. Directly beneath Harry Johnson's shop, in a vacant store next to the Singer Sewing Center, two federal agents stood ready with submachine guns. Above, on the roof of the building, three more lay hidden. In the street below, two black sedans were parked diagonally across from one another, with agents crouched down inside, watching the area in front of Dakins through rear-view mirrors. In addition, thirty Bangor policemen and a squad of Maine state troopers were hidden in scattered vantage points near the store, or were going about their usual patrol and traffic duties in the immediate vicinity.

Inside the store, posing as a clerk, was FBI agent Walter Walsh, a former national pistol champion who specialized in trick shots and was generally conceded to be one of the Bureau's top men with a hand gun. Within easy reach of Walsh was a string that had been fastened to the back of the counter and strung along the wall to a piece of colored cardboard hanging just above the front window. The idea was that when the string was pulled, the cardboard would drop into view as a signal to those outside that the outlaws had entered the store. Crouched behind the counters and hidden out back in the office area were four more agents, all with their service revolvers drawn. Since opening time, a half-hour before, a dozen or so customers had come into the store, but all but one had left when special agent Myron Gurnea, who was in charge of the operation, poked his head in the door: "Get ready," he said, "They've been around the block twice. They should be in soon."

A minute or so later a black 1937 Buick sedan, Ohio license KY 747, pulled up and double-parked a few feet beyond the store. A clean-shaven, neatly dressed little man got out, nodded amiably to the young clerk sweeping the sidewalk, and went inside. It was Dalhover. Shep Hurd picked up a box of film and took it to the other side of the store, where Walsh was standing. "That's him," he whispered to Walsh. By this time Dalhover had spotted Hurd and started toward him. "Say, what about those things you got for me?" Dalhover asked. Walsh reached down and yanked the string. Nothing happened. The line had fouled somehow, and the card above the window failed to drop.

No matter. Suddenly Walsh was standing beside Dalhover with a gun in his ribs. "It happened so fast I couldn't believe it," Hurd said later. "That Walsh was the quickest man I ever saw. Especially with a gun. He pulled that gun out so fast I really didn't see it happen, and I was looking right at him." Dalhover didn't even flinch. He simply stood there with his hands in his pockets and an untroubled, almost pleasant expression on his face, as if nothing out of the ordinary had occurred. "Up with 'em!" growled Walsh. When Dalhover failed to respond, Walsh stuck his foot behind him and slammed him backwards onto the floor.

By this time another agent had joined Walsh, and the two of them jerked Dalhover to his feet. "Where are your pals?" the G-Men demanded. Dalhover said nothing, and then mumbled something that was later described as "sullen and uncooperative." "Talk, you _____ _____ son of a whore!" shouted one of the agents, and slashed the butt of his service revolver diagonally down across Dalhover's face. Dalhover staggered and started to slump, but the agents held him up. "They're out front," Dalhover gasped.

Meanwhile, Shaffer had got out of the car, more to kill time than anything else. At first he wandered a couple of doors down to the Astoria Cafeteria and glanced at the menu posted on the door. Then he walked back past the car to Dakins, where he arrived just in time to catch a glimpse of the commotion going on inside. Immediately he whipped out two pistols and, as he backed into the street, blazed away with both of them through the store window. One of the slugs caught Walsh in the shoulder and sent him spinning against the wall, painfully but not seriously wounded. Almost simultaneously federal agents cut loose with machine guns on Shaffer from the building across the way. Within five seconds he lay sprawled across the trolley tracks, gushing out blood onto the street.

No sooner had Shaffer gone down than an agent from one of the nearby automobiles dashed up behind the outlaws' car. Smashing the rear window, he ordered Brady to come out with his hands up. For several seconds Brady, who was in the back seat, simply sat there, staring to the front and saying nothing, as if weighing his options. And then, calmly: "All right. Don't shoot. I'm coming out." An instant later he sprang from the car and began firing wildly with his automatic. He was dead before he hit the ground. Within ten minutes Dr. Harry McNeil, head of the city's health department, arrived. "This one's still alive," he announced as he examined Shaffer. But not for long. A minute or so later Shaffer too was dead. The autopsy revealed that between them the two men had taken more than sixty .45 slugs.

Before the smoke had cleared a third body got up and checked itself for signs of life. This was the young clerk, James Seely, with broom still in hand, who had been caught in the middle of the shooting. Although slightly scratched from glass splinters and scared half out of his wits, he was unhurt. In fact, remarkably enough, despite the amount of lead that went flying about Central Street that day, there were no injuries except to the outlaws themselves and agent Walsh. This was partly due to the excellent marksmanship of the federal agents, but there was also a large element of luck involved, including the gang's decision to come early in the morning, at a time when there was only a thin scattering of pedestrians and automobiles about. This made it easier for the FBI and safer for everyone, except Brady and his boys. If the action had taken place later in the day, when ordinarily (and especially on a holiday) downtown Bangor would be bustling with shoppers, the affair might have had an even uglier ending, for the FBI had insisted that Central Street remain open to normal traffic, lest the gang sense a trap. Agent-in-charge Gurnea was willing to make one concession to public safety, however: as soon as the colored card dropped in Dakins' window, thereby positively placing the outlaws on the scene, the block would immediately be sealed off. But, of course, the card never appeared. Not that it would have made any difference, for it was only a minute or so after Dalhover entered the store that the shooting started.

Within a quarter of an hour, reporters and photographers from the local papers were swarming about, interviewing Hurd and Seely and other witnesses, and taking pictures of the dead men. A middle-aged woman came forward and pointed to a hole in her coat about the size of her thumb. One of the slugs had passed through it, she claimed. A reporter from the *Commercial* jotted down something and had his photographer snap the woman's picture. By 9:00 an ambulance had arrived, and the mutilated remains of Brady and Shaffer were placed in long wicker baskets by the Bangor police and driven to the hospital for autopsies. There the doctor on emergency duty examined the two bodies and filled in the death certificates: CAUSE OF DEATH: "gunshot wounds, justifiable homicide." Opposite OCCUPATION he wrote on both certificates: "bandit."

At about ten o'clock a fire engine drove up and began hosing the blood down the sewer. By this time a goodly crowd had gathered, including a large number of schoolchildren whom Columbus had freed for the day. Many of the curious clustered about in front of Dakins, fingering the jagged holes in the window and straining to get a peek inside. Others converged upon Harry Johnson, who had come down from his barbershop to tell, time and again, how it had all happened. A cordon of police encircled the bandits' car while FBI agents gave it a thorough search. Among their findings were twelve .38 and .45 pistols, two high-powered rifles, two submachine guns, and enough ammunition for a small war—an impressive arsenal indeed, especially when added to the hand guns the boys had on them. But not impressive enough to satisfy the Brady gang, whose excessive craving for guns had finally brought them down. Later J. Edgar Hoover would call them "the gun-craziest bunch of desperadoes" his Bureau had ever encountered.

By noon the fire department had completed its job of tidying up Central Street; the management at Dakins had finished painting white circles around the bullet holes in the window, thereby calling attention to Bangor's newest tourist attraction; and the crowd had dwindled to a few children and a couple of reporters, still sniffing around for a new lead or a different angle. The brief drama was over. It had ended almost as soon as it had begun. "But it was thrilling while it lasted," commented the *Bangor Daily News.* "We advise all gunmen and other holy terrors to keep away from Bangor."

Meanwhile, Dalhover had been taken to the police station where he was questioned without let-up by the FBI until 3:00 the following morning. At first, he was inclined to be taciturn, but he talked more freely after a federal agent smashed him in the face with his fist. Among other things, he revealed that the gang had not intended to do any bank jobs in Maine ("Your roads here are too damned rotten."). They had planned to return to Connecticut after their shopping spree in Bangor, and pull an $85,000 payroll holdup. "If you hadn't caught up with us, we'd of been on the top of the world in a couple more years." When asked by a local police officer, "But didn't you know they would be suspicious when you wanted a machine gun?", Dalhover shrugged his shoulders: "I guess we made a mistake there."

A day or so later Dalhover was flown back to Indianapolis to stand trial for murder. On November 17 of the following year, at the state penitentiary in Michigan City, he seated himself in the electric chair without the slightest sign of fear or remorse. Shortly after midnight 2300 volts poured through his miniature body, once and then again. A tiny wisp of smoke arose from the top of his head, and at 12:06 he was pronounced dead.

Back in Bangor the undertakers at White & Hayes Funeral Home had finished their work on Brady and Shaffer by the afternoon following the shooting. On Thursday, October 14, two days after his death, Shaffer's body left for Boston on the first leg of its journey back to Indianapolis, where it would be turned over to his father. Ordinarily it would have been sent to his wife in Baltimore, but she refused to have anything more to do with him. "I'm not sorry," she said when she heard the news of his death. "We was afraid they'd come back. They had it coming to them." Shaffer's mother, who had remarried and was living on a small farm outside of Indianapolis, also refused the remains but was glad they were being sent home. "At least I'll know where he is now," she told a reporter.

As for Brady, former Sunday school stalwart who had set out to make Dillinger look like a piker, there was no one to claim the body, and so it fell to his lot to be buried in Bangor, where his string had run out. On the second day following the shooting he was assigned to the Overseer of the Poor for a pauper's burial. At 10:45 the next morning, a grey, wind-swept day, a small crowd gathered at a remote rear corner of Mt. Hope Cemetery, a few miles north of the town. There were no mourners, and no prayers, nor even a minister. Just the funeral attendants, the gravediggers, and a few reporters, who watched from the comfort of their cars parked a few feet away on a narrow dirt road. When the attendants began lowering the coffin, one of the reporters got out and stood beside his open door to get a better look. From his car radio could be heard the faint sound of music. It was Anson Weeks, playing "How Could You?"

"All the World's a Stage"

DURING THE FINAL MONTHS OF 1937 the nation's economy, which had managed to climb haltingly back to its pre-Depression level, suddenly went into another tailspin. It began in the late summer with a slump in consumer spending, and, as before, one thing led to another, until by March of 1938 there were once again nearly ten million Americans out of work. People sadly (and many angrily) recalled F.D.R.'s recent boast that the country was well on its way to total recovery "because we planned it that way."

The President responded to the new crisis as he had in the past—with more federal spending, mainly for relief projects. By July of 1938 the downward trend had been stopped and by December most of the lost ground regained, but the nation's confidence in the New Deal had been badly shaken and would never be the same again. More and more it was being said that Washington couldn't make the country run without resorting to the dole, and while the principle of emergency relief spending was by now acceptable to most Americans, the idea of having the nation permanently dependent on handouts was not.

Abroad, things were even worse. In Europe war was now clearly in the offing. Each day, it seemed, the reports grew more frightening. Madmen were on the loose, brutalizing their own people and despoiling their neighbors. Sooner or later they would have to be stopped. One would think that France and England would be able to see this, and cut the monsters down to size. But no. In March of that year, as the Western powers looked on and did nothing, Hitler simply moved into Austria and annexed it to his Thousand Year Reich. Six months later, in a humiliating scene not soon to be forgotten, France and England caved in completely before Hitler's announced intention to annex Czechoslovakia's rich Sudetenland area. "This is absolutely my last territorial demand," the German Fuehrer assured them, and then in the following spring proceeded to devour the rest of Czechoslovakia. Meanwhile, strange events that defied all comprehension were reported to be taking place inside the Soviet Union: mass arrests of people from all walks of life, followed by automatic confessions of plots against the state, and executions numbering in the hundreds of thousands or more—all very mysterious and sinister. And in Asia the Japanese continued their cruel rape of China. No wonder most Americans were feeling jittery about conditions overseas.

To make matters worse, in addition to the new depression at home and the mounting madness abroad there was the worrisome fact that alien ideologies appeared to be spreading throughout the United States at an alarming rate. Disgruntled and disenchanted by the apparent failure of the nation's traditional institutions to come up with workable solutions, thousands (some said millions!) of Americans had latched onto fascism or communism, and were fanatically engaged in attempting to destroy the American way of life. Encouraged from abroad by financial support and organizational aid, more and more Americans, it seemed, were expressing their dissatisfaction by parading around in black shirts and armbands with swastikas, or peddling Marxism to their friends and fellow workers. These were frightening things to witness. As usual, it was the newsreels that brought them home most forcefully to the American people, who shuddered at the sight of storm troopers strutting down the streets of the nation's cities, or known Communists stirring up the hatred of one group against another.

It was the American Fascists, or more specifically the Nazis, who caused the worst shivers, mainly because they were so conspicuous and because their European sponsor appeared at that time to present the most immediate threat to the nation's security. What American over fifty can ever forget the horrifying spectacle of those sinister-looking, jackbooted figures who called themselves the German-American Bund, assembled at their rallies or health camps, with their Nazi songs and frenzied sieg heils? According to a New York congressman, "There are 25,000 men and women in Nassau County going crazy, dressed in uniforms," and goose-stepping all over the place. In Detroit there were said to be "thousands of little tots ranging from four to six years of age, parading around in the Youth Movement uniform crying 'Heil Hitler' and swearing by the German Government." Reports had it that Bundists were caching arms at different points around the country, that they had infiltrated strategic industrial plants, and that special elite corps were being trained in sabotage.

Under the leadership of their bumptious American fuehrer, Fritz Kuhn, their numbers and arrogance grew progressively greater during the late thirties. So did their fanaticism, to the point where they sometimes forgot the Bund's official line that its members were good Americans first and good Nazis second—although, of course, there was no inconsistency between the two. At a York-ville rally in uptown New York City, after the usual singing of the Star-Spangled Banner (the American flag was always on display above the swastika), 500 Bundists were treated to a Nazi peptalk by one of the organization's out-of-town dignitaries: "Do you want a Government by Hitler in the United States?" he shouted out at one point. "Yes!" the audience roared. "You weren't sup-posed to say that," the speaker screamed back at them angrily. "You were supposed to say no."

In Congress one member claimed that he had it on good authority that there were as many as 480,000 Bundists in the country (actually there were probably never more than 15,000), and they "obviously don't stand for what America stands for." In order to alert the nation, Congressman Dickstein of New York City, a Jew and rabidly anti-Hitler, compiled a list of suspected American Nazis and had it printed in the *Congressional Record*. When a colleague protested that a person's honor and patriotism should not be impugned until after he had been questioned under oath ("I do not think people should be libeled through the Coun-try by mere rumor. It is unfair."), Dickstein brushed aside the ob-jection. There was too much at stake to worry about such trifles. Later when it was discovered that six of those named were entire-ly innocent, Congressman Dickstein said that he considered his overall average pretty good.

While the Bundists made Americans shudder, the Commu-nists made them squirm. This was partly because the Communists were more secretive about who they were and how they operated, and partly because they were—well, less wholesome. Say what one might about the Bundists, they were a cleancut, straightlaced lot who flaunted their intentions in broad daylight, whereas the Communists were apt to be soiled and sneaky and have weak eyes. Unlike the Nazis, who strutted, the Communists slithered. There wasn't much question about what they had in mind, but like the Lord, whom they denounced as a counter-Revolutionary, they moved in a mysterious manner. Besides, it was obvious that many of their leaders were big-city Jews, and if the truth were known, most Americans didn't care much for big-city Jews, or, for that matter, any other kind.

It was hard to say how many real Communists there were. It was thought that there might be a million or more, some of whom were well-known agitators like Earl Browder and Harry Bridges who were very much in the public eye, while others (doubtless the vast majority) operated clandestinely in key positions, waiting for their chance to tear down the United States Government and turn the country over to Moscow. It is known now that their actual membership was very small, probably never more than 100,000, but at the time they seemed decidedly more numerous. This was partly attributable to their great success at enlisting others (usually innocent dupes) to help them in hastening the day of the workers' paradise. Several years later the movie actor Edward G. Robinson explained how this had happened to him:

> I have always been a liberal Democrat. The revelations that persons whom I thought were sincere liberals were, in fact, Communists, has shocked me more than I can tell you. That they persuaded me by lies and concealment of their real purposes to allow them to use my name for what I believed to be a worthy cause is now obvious. I was sincere. They were not. I bitterly resent their false assertions of liberalism and honesty through which they imposed upon me and exploited my sincere desire to help my fellow men. Not one of the Communists who sought any help or requested permission to use my name ever told me that he or she was a member of the Communist Party.

The instrument the Communists found most useful in attracting the unwary was the "front," a seemingly proper organization or cause that in reality was controled and manipulated by the Communists for their own purposes. "I now realize," Robinson complained, "that some organizations which I permitted to use my name were in fact Communist fronts. But their ostensible purposes were good, and it was for such purposes that I allowed the use of my name and even made numerous financial contributions."

In the summer of 1938 a high-ranking defector from the American Communist Party named twenty-eight Communist fronts, of which he himself had served on fifteen. The large majority of them were outwardly directed at combatting poverty and the spread of fascism—certainly worthwhile aims that most reasonable people would find hard to argue with. Small wonder that men of conscience and sensitivity joined or supported these groups by the thousands.

There can be little doubt that most of those attracted to these fronts would have been shocked had they been aware of the true nature of what they had become a part of. Others were aware, or at least suspicious, and went along just the same, generally because they figured they could use the Communists' help while at the same time keeping them under control—often a costly miscalculation. The problem on the outside was to separate the conspirators from their dupes, and this was no easy task, since, as everyone knew, Communists were very sneaky and would just as soon lie as not, even under oath. An American Legionaire from Ohio perhaps had the simplest solution: "If a guy talks like a Communist and acts like a Communist, and hangs around with Communists, then I say he is a Communist and had damned well better be treated like one."

Communist activity in this country had been a matter of official concern to the government since 1930, when New York Congressman Hamilton Fish, one of the first of America's long line of professional Red hunters, persuaded Congress to authorize a special committee to "look into the question of Communist subversion." Although the subsequent hearings failed to produce much in the way of concrete results, they did receive a lot of attention in the press and probably did as much as anything else to alert the public to the presence of the Marxist menace in America.

Since that time, as the Depression ravaged the land and fascism flourished abroad, American communism appeared to have mushroomed in size and influence. Recently it had played a conspicuous role in the rash of sitdown strikes (said to have been a Communist invention), of which there were 147 in Detroit alone from November, 1936, to July, 1937. It was no secret that the nation's labor unions were shot through with Communists, just as it was no secret that schoolchildren and college students were being indoctrinated by Communist teachers, while Communist artists turned out scores of books, plays, and movies, deliberately calcu-

lated to promote class hatred among Americans. Clearly, communism had become a factor to reckon with in the United States, and
just as clearly something would have to be done to stop it. In early
January of 1938 over 15,000 people crowded into the Jersey City
armory to roar their approval when Mayor Frank Hague promised
that "all un-American reds and radicals" would be sent packing
out of the city. Seated beside Hague on the speaker's platform
were prominent politicians of both major parties, together with
business and religious leaders. On the wall in back of the platform
a huge banner proclaimed: "Jersey City 100 per cent American."
Outside in the rain a crowd of 2000 watched and applauded a
parade of veterans carrying anti-Communist signs and shouting
what newspapers called "patriotic slogans." Afterwards a display
of fireworks was put on by a local merchant who wanted to do
something to "combat the Red menace in America."

At the same time, the threat of Communist subversion was
beginning to receive more serious attention among the lawmakers
in Washington:

> Why, Mr. Speaker [declared a New York Representative on the
> floor of Congress], I saw 50,000 people march through our streets with
> the red flag of Communism. . . . We in Congress here are the only ones
> who can do our duty to our established government by investigating
> this monster and stopping this conflagration before it sweeps us out of
> control of our Government. . . . Let us save this Country . . . before the
> hour becomes too late.

On June 7, 1938, the Speaker of the House, pursuant to a 191-41
resolution by Congress, appointed a seven-man committee to investigate subversive behavior in the United States. The House Un-
American Activities Committee, as it came to be called, was to be
headed by a genial giant from Texas named Martin Dies.

Being the creature of a predominantly Democratic Congress
that had been swept into office during the Roosevelt landslide of
1936, the new committee might have been expected to be tilted at
least a trifle to the left. It wasn't. In fact, of its five Democratic
and two Republican members, a majority were of a distinctly conservative stripe and known to be downright hostile to the New
Deal. Foremost among these were Republican J. Parnell Thomas,
a New Jersey stock broker and insurance salesman who would

later be sent to prison for defrauding the United States Government; Democrat Joseph Starnes of Alabama, a former school-
teacher who had been decorated for gallantry in France during
the Great War; and Chairman Dies himself.

Like his father before him, who had served several terms in
Congress, Martin Dies considered himself a good man and a good
American. It was his ambition as a Congressman, he often said, to
do as well by his country as his daddy had, although he realized
that he was setting his sights pretty high. When he first appeared in
the Lower House in 1931 at the age of thirty, looking for all the
world like the all-American boy, he was immediately taken in tow
by his father's old friend, "Cactus Jack" Garner, then Speaker of
the House and soon to become Franklin Roosevelt's vice president.
Under Garner's tutelage Dies learned his lessons well, and, thanks
mainly to Cactus Jack, was given choice committee assignments
usually reserved for older and more experienced members. As a
colleague he was amiable and generally considerate. He worked
hard at his job, and it was not uncommon for him to be seen (all
six-foot-three, two hundred and five pounds of him) leaving his
office late at night, puffing serenely on one of the eight cigars he
permitted himself each day. He was not a highly educated man,
but he had a native intelligence, which, when coupled with his
determination to get to the bottom of things, usually served him
well. He also had the politician's greatest gift, a flair for communi-
cating with the people in language they understood. He goodnaturedly referred to himself as "the biggest demagogue in either
House," and few of his colleagues saw any reason to disagree with
him.

Aside from his cigars and his addiction to chewing gum, he
had what some people considered a far more serious weakness: a
limited conception of what America should be, which was essentially antiurban, antiforeign, and, despite his initial admiration for
the New Deal, antiliberal. As chairman of the new committee, he
would reap enormous political advantage for himself by applying
his narrow, old-fashioned standards of Americanism to the job of
ferreting out subversives, authentic or otherwise. Before long his
name would become a household word and his popularity solidly
established among millions of Americans who still cherished the
traditional, true-blue values that Congressman Dies stood for.
"Why, if an election were held tomorrow," said his fellow Texan,

Sam Rayburn, in late 1938, "Martin Dies could beat me in my own district."

All of this naturally led critics of the committee to denounce Dies as just another cheap political opportunist, but, while it is true that he exploited his role as committee chairman for all it was worth, and then some, there is no reason to question his basic sincerity. In fact, his conduct was entirely in keeping with the sort of man he was known to be. Indications are that he had no doubts whatsoever that sinister forces were gnawing away at the foundations of the American way of life, and he considered it his bounden duty to expose them and bring them to an accounting. Of them all, the worst by far was communism. "The teachings of Karl Marx are diametrically opposed to those of Jesus Christ," Dies declared at about the time his committee was set up. "Marx represents the lowest form of materialism; Christ symbolizes the highest and noblest conception of the spiritual." And on another occasion: "The irreconcilable conflict between the teachings of Christ and Marx is the issue upon which the future of western civilization is staked."

With an appropriation from Congress of only $25,000 (instead of the $100,000 requested) the Dies Committee found itself seriously hamstrung at the outset by not being able to afford an adequate investigative staff, a fact that doubtless contributed to the committee's slipshod gathering and handling of evidence. In an attempt to obtain more trained investigators, Chairman Dies went hat in hand to the Justice Department and asked for the loan of some of its agents. This was entirely proper and not without precedent. Indeed, not long before, Senator La Follette's notoriously left-wing (according to Dies) Civil Rights Committee had asked for similar assistance, and received it. But Dies was turned down flat and returned to his office in a huff, convinced that his committee was being discriminated against by the Administration. "Ho hum," remarked the President when the news of Dies' unhappiness reached him.

The hearings began on August 12, 1938, in an air-cooled caucus room on the second floor of the old House Office Building. After an opening statement by the chairman, in which he cautioned newsmen against jumping to conclusions and labeling someone un-American merely because of "an honest difference of opinion," the committee got down to serious business. During the first day it listened to testimony linking the Bund to the German Government, and appeared about to head off into a fullscale investigation of Bund activities. On the second day, however, the committee members unexpectedly shifted their attention from Nazis to Communists, and there, with only rare and minor exceptions, it would remain fixed for the remainder of the session.

When it became apparent (as it soon did) that the committee was much more interested in probing the left than the right, and obviously intended to steer its investigations mainly in that direction, barrages of angry protest were unleashed against Dies and his colleagues from several quarters. Foremost among the critics, or at least the loudest, were a goodly number of left-leaning publications, campus groups, and intellectual and artistic organizations (including the Communist-front John Reed Clubs). Expressions of outrage—mainly in the form of petitions, public announcements, and letters to newspapers—came also from several "concerned citizens" groups, principally in the New York City area. Among their number was the aforementioned Congressman Dickstein, who had been a prime mover in the creation of the committee and one of its strongest boosters until he discovered where it was headed. Suddenly to these people the members of the committee had become "small-town provincials," "anti-Semites," "business Babbitts," "labor-baiters," "Ku Kluxers," "hypocrites, political philanderers, and narrow-minded bigots." The popular writer Matthew Josephson lamented the "ignorance and malignity of these poll-tax Congressmen . . . , these retrograde politicians." This was the same Matthew Josephson who a few years earlier had urged his fellow Americans to join him in supporting "the frankly revolutionary Communist Party, the party of the workers."

Undaunted by the fierce outpouring of criticism and abuse, which their chairman brushed off as Communist-inspired (and, of course, he was partly right), the members of the committee continued their tracking on the left. For a while they contented themselves with investigating Communist infiltration into organized labor, the American Civil Liberties Union, and the Campfire Girls, but it was just a matter of time (and not much of it, at that) before they were bound to reach the main attraction of the session. A month before the hearings had even opened, Committeeman J. Parnell Thomas had served notice that the WPA's Federal Theatre Project was in for a bad time, when he publicly denounced it as "a hot bed of communism . . . , infested with radicals from top to bottom." The charge may or may not have been true, but one thing was certain: from the day of its inception, four years earlier, the project had been a highly vulnerable affair that had proceeded to make matters worse for itself by creating a considerable degree of public controversy and, at times, a distinctly unpleasant odor. It would be hard to imagine a more tempting target for Congressman Dies and his friends.

Although the Federal Theatre Project did not actually get underway until August of 1935, its genesis can be traced back to a day early in the Depression when Harry Hopkins, then deputy relief administrator for New York State under Governor Roosevelt, noticed a frail-looking man standing in an employment line in Manhattan. There was nothing unusual about that. Millions of frail-looking men were standing in line those days, waiting for jobs they would almost certainly never get. But this one was carrying a violin.

Later, after Roosevelt had become President and Hopkins his relief chief in Washington, the memory of the man with the violin returned. So did something that Jane Addams, the founder of Chicago's famed Hull House, once wrote. It was the story of a shipping clerk who had lost his job during the depression of 1893. Several times he came to Hull House after aid for himself and his family. "I told him," Miss Addams reported, "of the opportunity of work on the drainage canal and intimated that if any employment were obtainable he ought to exhaust that possibility before asking for help." The man replied that he was not very robust and that, being used to working indoors at a desk, he doubted he could withstand the rigors of hard physical labor outside in the Chicago winter. But Miss Addams held her ground, and the man took employment on the ditch. After two days, he came down with pneumonia and died that same week. With these thoughts in mind, Hopkins persuaded the President that something special should be done, not only for the nation's needy musicians, but also for its writers, actors, and other artists, many of whom were obviously ill-equipped for the heavy type of work that characterized most relief assignments. As a result, a number of creative arts programs were set up under the aegis of the WPA. One of these was the Federal Theatre Project.

Of all the arts, it was the theatre that was the most desperately in need of help. In fact, it is probably true that at the time the government came to its aid, theatre in the United States was dying. As the most expensive and least popular art form, it naturally felt the pangs of the Depression most severely. Besides that, now that

they had come of age, motion pictures were almost too overpower-
ing to compete with. While some 14,000 movie houses throughout
the country were attracting audiences of 70,000,000 weekly, usually at no more than twenty-five cents a head (the Roxy alone in
New York City regularly packed in 6,000 a day), legitimate theatre
had virtually disappeared in all but the largest metropolitan areas,
and even in those few remaining centers it more often than not
played to half-empty houses. By late 1933 nearly three-fifths of
the theatres in New York, the drama capital of the nation, had
closed down. The rest, by slashing prices from $6.00 to $5.00, and
finally to $2.20, managed a precarious survival. More than 50 per-
cent of all actors in the city (and 80 percent in the country as a
whole) were out of work. In February of 1934 Harry Hopkins put
in a call to Mrs. Hallie Flanagan, Professor of English and Director
of Experimental Theatre at Vassar. "We've got a lot of actors on
our hands," he told her. "Suppose you come to New York and
we'll talk it over."

Hallie Flanagan was not just a name that Hopkins had picked
out of a hat. He had known her during his New York days and was
aware of her high standing in the theatre community. A graduate
of Grinnell College in Iowa, with a master's degree from Radcliffe,
Mrs. Flanagan had been with the theatre in one capacity or another
since 1919 when the death of her husband forced her to go to
work to support her two small children. More pleasant-looking
than pretty, this tiny woman with big brown eyes and bobbed red-
dish hair had made her reputation principally as a teacher-critic
and innovator. By the mid-1930s she had acquired international
recognition for her work in experimental theatre. Although lacking in administrative experience, she knew the theatre and she
knew theatre people. She also had a seemingly inexhaustible supply of enthusiasm and energy, which, together with a tough inner
core, helps explain why Hopkins considered her an ideal choice for
what he had in mind.

During the next several months Mrs. Flanagan, working more
or less on her own, but within guidelines laid down by Hopkins,
organized the administrative machinery for setting up the country's first and only national theatre. On August 27, 1935, with the
bureaucracy finally in place but many weeks remaining before the
first curtain would be raised, the Federal Theatre Project of the
Works Progress Administration was declared officially under way.
Hopkins met with Hallie Flanagan and offered her his congratula-

tions, and a bit of advice: "Remember," he said, "whatever happens, you'll be wrong."

With eligibility open to any state with more than twenty-five unemployed actors, the Federal Theatre Project eventually came to include hundreds of local theatre groups. At its peak the project employed nearly 13,000 actors, directors, and support personnel (such as stagehands and set designers), most of whom received $22.75 a week, plus $3.00 a day for expenses while on the road. Intended primarily as a relief undertaking, the project was also supposed to make good theatre available to the largest possible number of Americans. On the whole it did both jobs remarkably well.

In the less than four years given it, the project through its member groups in thirty-one states, presented 924 different productions, which in the aggregate were performed thousands of times before more than 20,000,000 people. The average cost of admission was 50¢; the maximum, $1.10. Reaching out into the crossroads and boondocks of America, traveling companies took live theatre to places where it had never been seen before, and almost always found themselves received with great enthusiasm. For children, often unaccustomed to beauty or joy, there were puppet shows and plays about animals, and for their parents, anything from old-time vaudeville to Shakespeare. Lumbermen in flannel shirts and miners and wheat farmers stood in line to see *Macbeth* and *The Taming of the Shrew*, and then came back for more of the same the following night. Mrs. Flanagan, among others, was deeply moved by this grassroots response. Trying her hand at free verse, she wrote:

> We played Ohumpka and they came in by oxcart.
> They came in with lanterns to see *Twelfth Night*.
> An old man barefoot, helping children from an oxcart,
> Said, "They may be pretty young to understand it
> But I want they should be able to say
> They've seen Shakespeare—
> I did once when I was a kid."

Naturally the quality of production varied enormously. Some of the groups were hopelessly inept, and the best that could be said for them is that they tried and were probably better than nothing. Most, though, were at least adequate, and a few, mainly in New York where a third of the Federal Theatre's personnel were congregated, were outstanding. The project's many successes, both critical and box office, ranged from such serious pieces as *Dr. Faustus* and *Murder in the Cathedral* to entertaining musicals like *The Swing Mikado* and frothy little comedies, of which the imported French farce *Horse Eats Hat* (starring future greats Joseph Cotton, Arlene Francis, and Orson Welles) was by far the top crowd-pleaser. Also a great favorite was *The Living Newspaper*, a series of plays modeled more or less after *The March of Time*, which dealt with contemporary issues. This was said to have been mainly Mrs. Flanagan's idea. If so, she may have regretted it, for it was from *The Living Newspaper* that much of her trouble came.

Of all the productions put on by the Federal Theatre Project, however, none could begin to match *It Can't Happen Here.* Not that it was such an artistic tour de force. It wasn't. The reviews were, as they say, "mixed." But it was a box-office bonanza of the first order. A stage adaptation of Sinclair Lewis' 1935 novel about how a home-grown type of Fascist totalitarianism came to triumph right here in America, the play was a real shocker to a people who had only recently come to take Hitler and Mussolini seriously. Scheduled so as to open simultaneously in fifteen cities across the country, it became an overnight national sensation. In New York's Adelphi Theatre alone it played to 110,000 in seven weeks. A single traveling company staged 133 performances before audiences of nearly 180,000. Presented by dozens of Federal Theatre groups in over a hundred cities and towns, the play ran for a sum total of 260 weeks, or the equivalent of five years. As Mrs. Flanagan remarked: "It seemed to have an unlimited audience appeal," perhaps because a good many Americans enjoyed being scared half out of their wits and then, as one reviewer noted, "breathing in unison a sigh of thanksgiving that it was all just fantasy."

But was it really just fantasy? Congressman Dies, for one, didn't think so. There was good reason to believe that there were elements abroad in America intent upon destroying the nation's free institutions from within and replacing them with some sort of foreign-inspired slave system—maybe not exactly as depicted in *It Can't Happen Here*, but a slave system just the same, perhaps even worse than what Sinclair Lewis had conjured up. One of the most sinister of those forces working toward that end was the Federal Theatre Project.

From the first, Dies had been no friend of the project. Along with most other Americans who knew anything about it (and probably not many did until it came under congressional attack), he objected to it on several grounds. Among other things, it represented a frivolous and extravagant use of taxpayers' money. "A dole for rotten actors," Mencken called it. Or, as a disgusted, privately employed cement worker put it: "Those pansies get more from the Government for prancing around the stage in their BVD's for a couple hours a day play-acting than I get for working my ass off on this friggin' bridge." Besides that, it was a well-known fact that many of the project's plays abounded in profanity and lewd expressions. Words like "God damn," "bastard," "son of a bitch," and "rape" were common. So were risque innuendoes and double entendres, which were obviously intended to titillate and to hold up to ridicule those wholesome sexual morals that were so much a part of the national character. Just the titles alone of some of these productions were enough to offend most decent Americans: *A New Kind of Love; Up in Mabel's Room; Be Sure Your Sex Will Find You Out; Cheating Husbands; Go Easy, Mabel; Just a Love Nest; Love 'em and Leave 'em; Lend Me Your Husband;* etc., etc. "Now, if you want that kind of salacious tripe, very well," exclaimed young Illinois Congressman Everett Dirksen, "but if anyone has an interest in any real cultural values, you will not find it in this kind of junk."

What was most disturbing about the Federal Theatre Project, though, was its unveiled enthusiasm for the left. Several of its works were straight-out propaganda pieces for the New Deal, while others were pure, undisguised Marxism. This was especially true (but by no means exclusively so) of the productions put on by *The Living Newspaper*, which seemed to be constantly preying upon the American free-enterprise system. On occasion it even went so far as to sound the tocsin for class warfare, and to identify by name certain individuals, including members of Congress, as enemies of the people. "Whoever would have thought of the Federal Government getting into something like this?" asked an irate Senator after having been treated in "an opprobrious manner" by *The Living Newspaper*. "When Senators appeal to me to appropriate money in the name of the helpless and the suffering millions, it reaches my heart . . . , [but then] when I see what is being done, I raise a very serious question about it."

Although she would later deny it before the committee, Mrs. Flanagan was herself upset over what she termed the "hysterical" nature of some of the Theatre's productions. Still, she refused to interfere. That would be censorship. Even once when two of her own assistants warned her against allowing a certain play to open in New York because of its inflamatory tone, Mrs. Flanagan stuck to her hands-off policy, claiming that she had full confidence in the judgment of its director, Joseph Losey. A dozen or so years later, Losey was one of those blacklisted in Hollywood as a suspected Communist.

Picture if you will (or can) the following, and it may become clearer why a sizable number of Americans came to believe, along with Martin Dies, that the Federal Theatre Project and the people who ran it needed looking into: the setting, the Adelphi Theatre just off Broadway in New York. The time, May, 1936. A capacity crowd is on hand to see the project's opening of W. H. Auden's *The Dance of Death*. The curtain rises and the voice of an announcer is heard addressing the audience:

> We present to you this evening a picture of the decline of a class. Of how its members dream of a new life, but secretly desire the old; for there is death inside them. We show you that death as a dancer.

Soon thereafter, an imaginary audience, a chorus, and one of the characters, McLaughlin, speak these lines:

> Audience: One, two, three, four—the last war was a bosses' war. Five, six, seven, eight— rise and make a workers' state. Nine, ten, eleven, twelve—seize the factories and run them yourselves.
> McLaughlin: We will liquidate—
> Chorus: The capitalist state.
> Audience: Overthrow!
> Chorus: Overthrow!
> Audience: Attaboy!

This is how the play began. How it ended is described by the Communist *Daily Worker:*

> With Death the Dancer dead, we witness the appearance of a huge shadow on the backdrop. It is Karl Marx, who announces: "The instruments of production have been too much for him. He is liquidated."
> Exeunt, to a dead march, as capitalism is borne out on the shoulders of four pall-bearers.

Picture also:

1. The project's production of *Triple A Plowed Under*, hailed by the *Daily Worker* as "a clear call for the formation of a Farm-Labor Party," in which, not long before its opening, the roles of George Washington and Andrew Jackson were deleted to make room for Communist chief Earl Browder, whose voice is heard in the background declaiming against the Supreme Court for having recently ruled against the Agricultural Adjustment Act.

2. *Injunction Granted*, a working-class propaganda piece from beginning to end, the purpose of which was to show that labor was consistently being beaten down by the courts, and that justice could be had only through the "solidarity of the workers." This was the play that Mrs. Flanagan's assistants had advised her to cancel. During the showing, Communist pamphlets were distributed in the lobby.

3. *Power*, a real bombshell from *The Living Newspaper*. Opening in New York City in February, 1937, after an advance sale of 60,000, the play denounced private light and power companies and called for the ownership of power by "the workers." Harry Hopkins, who attended the opening, was delighted. "I want this play and plays like it done from one end of the Country to the other," he exclaimed. Later he admitted to Hallie Flanagan that he may have stuck his neck out a bit. And he was right. The play caused an immediate furor. Even such firm friends of the project as *New York Times* drama critic Brooks Atkinson seemed shocked. It was, he said, "the most indignant and militant proletarian drama of the season . . . staged with government funds."

But all this was as nothing when compared with *The Revolt of the Beavers*, a simple little fairy tale about animals (all of whom wore roller skates for some reason), presented especially for youngsters by the project's New York City Children's Theatre. Consider the plot: a small group of very greedy beavers own the "busy wheel" by which bark is made into food and clothing, etc. A crisis arises when the greedy beavers refuse the working beavers their share of the production and attempt to replace them with barkless, jobless beavers. At this point, the hero beaver, Oakleaf, returns from exile. (He had been sent away earlier for attempting to organize the beavers into a club that would make "sad beavers glad.") This time Oakleaf is successful. The greedy beavers are overthrown and driven into exile, and the working beavers take over the "busy wheel," share equally with one another, and live happily ever after in their classless beaver society.

The play made a great hit with youngsters, probably because they thought it was about beavers. It didn't make such a hit with their parents, probably because they knew it wasn't. Hallie Flanagan found it "very human and amusing and tragic and class conscious." A good many other Americans found it outrageous and, for once, agreed with the *Daily Worker*, which labeled the play "an excellent vehicle for promoting revolutionary fervor." Again the pro-project Brooks Atkinson was appalled and denounced the play as "Mother Goose Marx" in a scathing review that was widely distributed among members of both houses of Congress. The *Saturday Evening Post* thought it a superb play for teaching poor children to murder rich ones. Although the fact seems to have escaped Mrs. Flanagan's notice (or so it would seem from reading her history of the Federal Theatre Project), *The Revolt of the Beavers* was far and away her biggest single mistake as project director—except possibly taking the job in the first place. America did not take kindly to having its children brainwashed, even by beavers on roller skates.

On August 19 and 20, 1938, the Dies Committee heard testimony from a dozen or so anti-Theatre witnesses, all of whom claimed to have been associated with the Federal Theatre Project at one time or another, and all of whom had come to the same conclusion about it: from top to bottom it was a Communist-oriented operation, which had as its principal purpose the dissemination of Marxist propaganda. The first, and in many ways most effective, witness was Mrs. Hazel Huffman, who appeared as spokesman for "The Committee of Relief Status Professional Theatrical Employees of New York City," an organization about which little was known except that Mrs. Huffman was a member of it. A somewhat shadowy figure, Mrs. Huffman had formerly been employed by the New York City office of the WPA, where, she claimed, her job had been to read the mail (much of which she found to be "incendiary, revolutionary, and seditious") of certain Theatre Project administrators. She was also the wife of a project stage manager who had recently been downgraded in his job.

Among the many accusations brought forward by Mrs. Huffman, and perhaps the most damaging, was her charge that New York City's Federal Theatre Project was dominated by the Workers' Alliance, a well-known Communist-front labor organization. According to Mrs. Huffman, Mrs. Flanagan had not only permitted the Workers' Alliance to get control, but had even helped it do so. In fact, from the beginning Mrs. Flanagan had participated more or less openly in Communist activities and "has been using the Project to further Communist aims." The witness could not prove that Mrs. Flanagan was an actual member of the Communist Party, but she certainly behaved like one. With her knowledge (if not approval), Communist literature was distributed openly among the project's employees, and pressures brought upon them to join the Workers' Alliance. The Communist newspapers, the *Daily Worker* and *Red Spotlight*, were regularly seen being circulated backstage, and were the subject of spirited discussion during coffee breaks.

On the following day a parade of other witnesses confirmed Mrs. Huffman's testimony, and added some further accusations of their own. Several of the project's producers and directors were charged with dismissing employees who belonged to Actors' Equity or other non-Communist unions in order to make room for Workers' Alliance people, many of them totally unqualified. "It is a known fact," claimed one of the witnesses, himself a director, "that the way to get ahead is through the Workers' Alliance." When he had let it be known that he objected to the Alliance as a bunch of Communist troublemakers, he was sharply reprimanded by his superior. Another witness claimed that he and his fellow actors lived "in constant fear" of losing their jobs if they didn't join the Alliance. Still another charged that collections for Loyalist Spain were frequently taken up among project members, and that the theatre bulletin boards were filled with "Communist filth." A stage manager testified that his crew had knocked off to march in the May Day parade under the Red banner—on taxpayers' time. A drama coach, then working with the New York project, complained that it was common practice for actors and stagehands to sit around comparing "the bounties of Russia" with the "very bad conditions" in the United States. An actress testified that a colored man in the project had tried to date her. When she reported the incident to her superiors, they laughed in her face. This was not surprising. It was no secret that the Workers' Alliance was under orders from Moscow to try to promote "race merging."

Friends of the Federal Theatre, among others, were quick to cry "foul!" against the committee's conduct of the hearings, and not without some justification. Many of the witnesses, including "that Huffman bitch," were known to bear personal grudges against the project. Others were pathological Communist haters who saw the shadow of Moscow hovering over everything they didn't understand or approve of. A great deal of what these witnesses had to say was totally unsubstantiated; much of it was hearsay; and some of it was just plain drivel. Rumor and innuendo had been put forward as fact and duly entered into the official records, with no opportunity for challenge or cross-examination—all of which meant that the committee had obviously paid little attention to proper judicial procedure.

No matter. As Dies pointed out, his committee was not a court of law. It didn't have to concern itself with a lot of legalistic jockeying. What it was interested in was getting at the truth, and Chairman Dies was satisfied in his own mind that on balance the committee had been given a pretty accurate picture of how things really were within the Federal Theatre Project. That he was not entirely wrong was borne out by the fact that in the twelve-month period just preceding the hearings, the Appeals Board of the New York City Arts Project had found Federal Theatre directors guilty of thirty-six instances of firing employees for refusing to join a union, in all but a very few cases the Workers' Alliance. As for the dissemination of Communist propaganda, Mrs. Flanagan herself later admitted privately that there had been some problems along those lines. Once, she had felt compelled to issue a particularly stern warning to one of her New York directors against distributing Communist pamphlets, not only among project employees, but also among audiences during intermission. As a custodian of public funds, Mrs. Flanagan simply could not permit this sort of thing to go on—"whatever my personal sympathies are."

In ordinary times Mrs. Flanagan would have been knocking at the committee-room door to tell her side of the story, especially since certain segments of the press had seized upon the testimony of Mrs. Huffman and the others and sensationalized it with such damaging headlines as: "WPA Theatre a Nest of Reds," and "Secretary of N.Y. Actors' Group Says Hallie a Red." But these were not ordinary times. In a little more than two months the congressional elections would be held, and the prospects were far from bright for the Administration. It would not do to provide the opposition with the added advantage of having an agency of the New Deal appear to be in league with the Communists. Better to ignore the committee's attack altogether, at least until after the election. In that way, not so many people would notice, or if they did, they might forget about it before voting time. As a White House friend of Harry Hopkins told him: "It looks like we've got a stink on our hands, and we both know that the more you stir a stink the worse it smells." Hopkins agreed. So did the President, and the word went out that, like Brer Fox, Mrs. Flanagan and her staff were to lie low and say nothing until further notice.

Thus, it was not until early December, after the anti-Theatre pot had been simmering for three and a half months, that Mrs. Flanagan had her chance to come before the committee. As she later remembered the scene, toward the front of the large caucus room two long tables had been joined perpendicularly to form a giant T, with her seat being at the base of the stem. Side by side across the head of the T sat the seven committee members, with Chairman Dies in the center. Along the side walls were other tables for the use of stenographers and newsmen. In the rear of the room were several rows of seats, filled with spectators. Above the witness' head hung a huge chandelier that gave the impression it might drop and skewer her at any moment. Fittingly enough (but quite coincidentally) the walls of the room were decorated with blown-up photographs of scenes from Federal Theatre productions, including some of Mrs. Flanagan's favorites. Somehow the entire setting seemed unreal, almost surrealistic, like something that might be staged by the Theatre of the Absurd—especially "that cowboy with his big cigar."

From the other end of the table the view was different. To Chairman Dies there was certainly nothing surrealistic or absurd about what was going on, or if there were, he lacked the big-city sophistication to see it. He was just a simple country boy who didn't pretend to know much about such things, but he did know a Communist conspiracy when he saw one, and he saw one now in the person of this tiny, self-assured woman who sat across from him in the witness chair. "All over the United States," Dies would declare a couple of years later, after the beast had been slain, "the Federal Theatre Project produced plays which were nothing but straight Communist propaganda. This is not surprising in view of the personnel chosen by the New Deal to supervise the Project."

For Dies, there seems to have been no doubt at all that Hallie Flanagan was a Communist, or the next thing to one, and probably nothing she could have said before the committee or anywhere else would have changed his mind. There was just too much already known about her to allow for any other logical conclusion. And while it must be admitted that much of what passed as evidence against her was highly suspect, and much was circumstantial, some was neither. It was an undeniable fact, for instance, that she had been mainly responsible for preparing the stage adaptation of Whittaker Chambers' powerful "Can You Hear Their Voices?" This heavily class-oriented short story, which by Chambers' own admission had been written specifically for the Communist literary monthly, *The New Masses,* "in order to gain favor with the Party," dealt with the suffering of the farmers during the awful drought of 1931, and the attempts of the Communists to help them and give them some hope for the future. In Mrs. Flanagan's stage version, the play ends when the father, who is headed for prison, sends his sons to a Communist headquarters where they will have a chance to "make a better world." A voice then says to the audience: "These boys are symbols of thousands of our people who are turning elsewhere for leadership. Will it be to the educated minority? CAN YOU HEAR THEIR VOICES?" *The New Masses* was rhapsodic in its praise, calling it "the best revolutionary play yet produced in America."

It was also true that Mrs. Flanagan had written a book and several articles, most of them since the onset of the Depression, in which she showed a definite bias for what some people were beginning to call "class-conscious theatre." In a 1931 article, for instance, she described the rise of "workers' theatres" in various parts of the country: "The theatre being born in America today," she wrote with obvious approval, "is a theatre of the workers. Its object is to create a national culture by and for the working class of America. Admittedly a weapon in the class struggle, this theatre is being forged in the factories and the mines." Her writings also included accounts of her two trips to the Soviet Union, during the late 1920s and early 1930s, in order to study the Russian theatre, for which she had no end of praise. In contrast to the "Continental" (and presumably American) theatre, which was "tiresome and boring," the Soviet theatre was vital and exciting. "I [also] became absorbed by the drama outside the theatre; the strange and glorious drama that is Russia." But, as an earlier witness had pointed out, Mrs. Flanagan's writings were almost as remarkable for what they left out as for what they included: "Nowhere does she have a good word to say about the United States, the Government, American institutions, or the economic system which makes possible relief money for the WPA."

Mrs. Flanagan's showdown with the House Un-American Activities Committee began late in the morning of December 6, 1938, and lasted for about three hours. During that time not much new was uncovered and few minds were changed. Still, the occasion was not without its interesting moments, as committee members probed deeply, and sometimes with considerable skill, into the more controversial doings of the Federal Theatre Project and its diminutive director. For the most part Mrs. Flanagan did a good job of blunting or parrying their attack. At the same time she displayed a remarkable degree of civility and restraint. This was not always easy to do, but, as she had earlier explained to one of her co-workers, her purpose was not to antagonize the committee, but to educate it, "if such a thing is possible."

It was indeed possible, at least in one instance: that morning Congressman Joseph Starnes of Alabama learned something he was not likely to forget for the rest of his life—would that he could! Commenting on an article written by Mrs. Flanagan in which the name of Christopher Marlowe had appeared, Starnes asked: "You are quoting from this Marlowe. Is he a Communist?"

"The room rocked with laughter," Hallie Flanagan later recalled. "But I did not laugh. Several thousand people might lose their jobs."

"I am very sorry," she replied straightfaced to Starnes. "I was quoting from Christopher Marlowe."

"Well, tell us who this Marlowe is, so that we can get the proper reference, because that is all we want to do."

"Put it in the record that he was the greatest dramatist in the period immediately preceding Shakespeare."

Twenty-five years later in its obituary of Starnes the *New York Times* could not resist identifying him as the congressman who suspected a sixteenth-century English playwright of Communist subversion.

"Of course, we had what some people call Communists back in the days of the Greek theatre," remarked Starnes, now visibly embarrassed and backpedaling.

"Quite true," replied Mrs. Flanagan, anxious to help repair his vanity.

"And I believe Mr. Euripides was guilty of teaching class consciousness also, wasn't he?"

Mrs. Flanagan was quick to confirm that he was indeed.

"So we cannot really say when it began," Starnes concluded. Christopher Marlowe could have been a Communist, after all.

Of all the inquisitors it was Dies himself, with his soft Texas drawl and courtly ways, who scored the most telling points, or at least left the impression of having done so. From the first it was obvious where he was leading the witness, and it was just as obvious that he had no intention of letting go until he reached the end of the line:

> The Chairman: Now, Mrs. Flanagan, I ask you if you do not think you are treading on dangerous ground when you use an agency of the Government . . . to portray the interests or the arguments of the Workers' Alliance, or the CIO, or any other class or group, so that by subtle portrayal you paint that group, or you paint the other class in a disadvantageous role, don't you think that is more or less dangerous?
>
> Mrs. Flanagan: We are not doing plays to stir up class hatred.
>
> The Chairman: Is it not a fact that when you produce a play that gives all the breaks to one class, such as the Workers' Alliance, or such as the CIO, or such as the workers of the country generally, give them breaks over another class, over the employers or business people, would you not join me in condemning that as a dangerous policy?
>
> Mrs. Flanagan: Could you give me a specific example?
>
> The Chairman: I am asking you if that is done. I am not assuming it is done.

And it was true that Chairman Dies was not assuming; he *knew.* He made it his business to know. He may have been a big, dumb cowboy to some, and a good-natured clown to others, but he was certainly smart enough to do his homework. By any reasonable reckoning there were at least twenty-six Federal Theatre productions that dealt with so-called "sensitive social issues." Among these twenty-six there was not one in which conservatism or capitalism was presented in a favorable light, not one in which labor was not exalted over management, or the interests of the poor over those of the other classes. Earlier in her testimony the witness

had insisted that it was proper ("Absolutely"! she had said) for the
Federal Theatre to deal with current social issues. Well, maybe so,
maybe not. But, either way, Congressman Dies found it hard to
accept the fact that in all of these plays, without exception, Mrs.
Flanagan's theatre had come up with the same verdict: an indict-
ment of the very system and people who were footing the bill:

The Chairman:	What is the objective of the play, what impression is it designed to bring in the audience—the play *Power*—that public ownership is a good thing?
Mrs. Flanagan:	I think the first thing the play does is to make you understand more about power, where it comes from, and how it is evolved, and its whole historical use.
The Chairman:	All right.
Mrs. Flanagan:	I think it also does speak highly for the public owner-ship of power.
The Chairman:	Let us take that one instance. We will assume, for the sake of argument, that maybe the public ownership of power is a desirable thing. Do you think it improper that the Federal Theatre, using the taxpayers' money, should present a play to the audience which champions one side of a controversy?
Mrs. Flanagan:	No, Congressman Dies, I do not consider it improper. I have just said that I felt that in a small percentage of our plays, and pointed out that it is ten percent, that do hold a brief for a certain cause in accord with forward-looking tendencies, and I say—
The Chairman:	Who is to determine what is a forward-looking ten-dency?
Mrs. Flanagan:	Why, our play-policy board chooses these plays.
The Chairman:	They are to determine that question? As to what is a forward-looking tendency? . . . .
Mrs. Flanagan:	Yes.
The Chairman:	Then your policy board approves the public ownership of utilities. Then you think that because they approve the principle of public ownership of utilities, it is prop-er that the Federal Theatre shall exhibit a play in which it champions the right of public ownership, do you not?

Mrs. Flanagan: I do think so.

The Chairman: All right. Now, would the same thing be true with reference to the public ownership of railroads, because the policy board—

Mrs. Flanagan: I do not know. We never choose plays that way, Congressman Dies.

The Chairman: I understand that. But assume that a play is submitted to you that champions the cause of public ownership of railroads, and the majority of the policy board say, "We are in favor of public ownership of railroads," then you believe it right to exhibit that play to twenty-five million people?

Mrs. Flanagan: That is the grave responsibility, Congressman Dies, with which I am charged.

The Chairman: Do you think it would be right to show that play under those circumstances?

Mrs. Flanagan: Yes. Absolutely. . . . .

The Chairman: Now, having accepted one principle, the principle that you have the right to exhibit a play championing the public ownership of utilities, how could you draw the line?

Mrs. Flanagan: Each play draws its own line. Each play makes its own contribution and has its own question.

The Chairman: But having established that precedent of public ownership of utilities, how could you stop where plays are presented to your policy board dealing with the ownership of railroads, dealing with the ownership of land and other matters? Would it not be the same principle involved?

Mrs. Flanagan: I told you over and over again that the basic principle is: Is it a good play? . . . If someone came up with a very good play proving that the *private* ownership of railroads was the best possible thing, and the play was a good play, we would do it.

The Chairman: Then, on the other hand, if the play proved that the *public* ownership of railroads was a good thing, you would do it too, would you not?

Mrs. Flanagan: Absolutely. The test is: Is it a good play?—within the general range we have established.

The Chairman: And if somebody came with a play showing the public ownership of all the property in the United States, and it was a good play, you would also exhibit that, would you not?

Mrs. Flanagan: Well, that is a very clever move on your part to maneuver me into a certain position.

The Chairman: I do not pretend to any cleverness. I would not undertake to match my cleverness with you on this subject, because you are thoroughly acquainted with it.

Mrs. Flanagan: No, I would not, we would stop with that because that would be recommending the overthrow of the United States Government, and I do not want that, gentlemen, whatever some of the witnesses may have intimated.

The Chairman: In other words, you would favor doing it by degress, but not all at once, isn't that right?

Mrs. Flanagan: Well, we would probably not agree—

The Chairman: So, as I understand from your testimony, when a play is presented to you championing the public ownership of power, of railroads, if it is a good play, you said you would exhibit it. Now, what I want to ask you is this: Would you stop with those two forms of ownership? Or would you go further and exhibit a play that would champion the public ownership of other forms of private property?

Mrs. Flanagan: . . . You are proposing a long series of hypothetical questions.

At 1:15 the hearings recessed for lunch. Mrs. Flanagan expected to return in the afternoon and read her prepared statement, but the committee decided otherwise. "We don't want you back," Congressman Thomas laughed. "You're a tough witness and we're all worn out. At any rate, your brief will be printed," he assured her, and accepted a copy of it for inclusion in the official transcript. It never appeared.

Not that it would have made any difference. The proceedings that morning, although entertaining, had been meaningless. The truth is that the fate of the Federal Theatre Project had already been determined a few weeks earlier, and although she would refuse to believe it for years to come, Mrs. Flanagan's appearance before the committee had been nothing more than an empty charade. Harry Hopkins might put up a bold front and declare indignantly: "We are not backing down on any of these projects," but he was too much of a politician not to realize that the elections of the past month had said otherwise. Their results had come as a real shocker to the Democrats: eighty seats lost in the House, eight in the Senate, and eleven governorships. After sifting the ashes, party pundits attributed the defeat to growing voter dissatisfaction with the New Deal; and surviving Democrats in Congress, taking note, were no longer so anxious as they had once been to breakfast at the White House with "the Chief."

So it had all come down to this: if the Administration hoped to stay in control of things, it had better trim its sails, and it could start by unloading some of its more obvious liabilities. One of these was the Federal Theatre Project. By and large it had never been especially popular. The best that could be said for it was that until recently most people hadn't given it much notice one way or another. But that was before "that damned cowboy" had painted the whole thing Red, and the nation's newspapers had pounced upon the story and exploited it to the hilt. By actual column count, the House Un-American Activities Committee received more coverage than any other domestic news story of the year. It is not surprising, then, that in December of 1938, shortly after Hallie Flanagan's testimony, a Gallup poll indicated that over 60 percent of all Americans were able to identify Martin Dies. Of these, 74 percent approved of what he was doing. At the White House the President no longer said "Ho hum" when the conversation turned, as it frequently did these days, to the tall Texan and his high-flying committee.

Early the following month, January 3, 1939, when the newly elected House of Representatives opened for business, it found the committee's report on un-American activities awaiting it. Of the Federal Theatre Project the report had this to say:

> From the testimony we conclude that a rather large number of the employees on the Federal Theatre Project are either members of the Communist Party or sympathetic with the Communist Party. It is also clear that certain employees felt under compulsion to join the Workers' Alliance in order to retain their jobs.

That was all. But it was enough, because by this time everyone already knew what a cesspool of communism and immorality (which was certainly un-American) the project really was. It came as no surprise, therefore, when later in the session, amidst great applause from the gallery and a resounding silence from the Administration, the House voted overwhelmingly to kill the Federal Theatre by cutting off its appropriations.

Of the only fifty-six members who voted in the minority, one was the outspoken New Jersey Congresswoman, Mary Norton, who refused to believe that the project people had anything to do with communism. "I do not accept that. I certainly would not be here speaking for them if I had any idea that this was true." And yet, it was. The facts, however unpleasant, were there for anyone who cared to see them. A generation later, long after the heat had subsided and it was possible to take a more dispassionate view, editor-writer Walter Goodman, in his excellent and generally unsympathetic study of the House Un-American Activities Committee, concluded that while it was true that the committee was often guilty of buffoonery, colossal ignorance, high-handedness, and just about everything else, it wasn't always wrong. As for the Federal Theatre Project, in Goodman's view there could be no denying its many commendable features and contributions. Still, "the plain fact was that the Communists were exceedingly active in the WPA Theatre . . . and they did all they could to get their own people into it and to turn the whole enterprise into an agitprop machine."

Present at the roll-call vote, and savoring every minute of it, was Representative Dies of Texas, who, having used up his daily quota of cigars, worked fiercely at his spearmint chewing gum while his congressional colleagues solidly vindicated the principles that he and, he was sure, all other decent Americans stood for. Of him it would soon be written by a friend of the fallen Theatre:

> The threat of Martin Dies lies in his effort to convince a majority of his fellow-Americans that there are certain areas of human thought in which there are "right" answers to be accepted by all Americans, and that those who do not conform should be "exposed" as "subversive" and subjected to rigorous Governmental publicity at public expense.

Chairman Dies couldn't have said it better himself.

Little Boy Lost

A FUNNY THING happened on the way to World War II. In late August of 1939 there appeared in the liberal weekly publication *The Nation* a full-page letter, signed by more than four hundred of the cream of America's artistic and intellectual community, including such notables as: artist Rockwell Kent; poet Kenneth Fearing; playwrights George ("Of Thee I Sing") Kaufman and Clifford Odets; scholar-critics Max Lerner and Granville Hicks; and popular writers Dashiell ("Sam Spade") Hammett, S. J. Perelman, Louis Untermeyer, and James Thurber.

The letter, addressed to "All Active Supporters of Democracy and Peace," warned that certain reactionary elements in this country were attempting to sow seeds of discord between the Soviet Union and other peace-loving nations. They hoped to do this by promoting "the fantastic falsehood that the U.S.S.R. and the totalitarian states are basically alike . . . and equally menace American institutions and the democratic way of life." Well, they wouldn't get away with it, because it was obvious to anyone who understood the situation that "Soviet and fascist policies are diametrically opposed." For instance: "The Soviet Union as always continues to be a bulwark against war and aggression and works unceasingly for a peaceful international rule." The letter then went on to describe Communist Russia in such a way as to leave little doubt that it fell just short of paradise on earth. "It was," *The Nation* itself later commented, "an unqualified endorsement of the Soviet system."

Even before that particular issue of *The Nation* had time to hit the streets, "diametrically opposed" Germany and the Soviet Union announced that they had signed a mutual nonaggression pact. The free world was stunned. The unthinkable had happened. By a scratch of the pen the whole power equation in Europe had been drastically (perhaps disastrously) altered. Hitler had undoubtedly scored a colossal coup. At the very least this meant that Russia intended to play the role of disinterested neutral—and, of course, it could mean much more. But best not to dwell on that.

As for the fallible four hundred, most were either struck dumb or were unavailable for comment. Others insisted that what had happened was merely a ruse or a temporary expedient, undertaken by Premier Stalin in the cause of world peace. This position became somewhat untenable a few weeks later, however, when, following the outbreak of a general war in Europe, Russia joined forces with Germany in devouring their common neighbor, Poland. Shortly thereafter, Soviet forces snuffed out the independent nations of Estonia, Latvia, and Lithuania, and then in late November invaded Finland, while Germany shifted its shock troops from Poland to the Western Front. It was that kind of autumn.

Actually, before all this happened, 1939 hadn't been such a bad year, at least not for America. By late spring it was getting harder to find a place to park. The cost of hamburg was up and the unemployment rate was down. These were considered to be good signs. So was the fact that millions of Americans from Oshkosh, Tulsa, and Baton Rouge were flocking to the World's Fair in New York City to peer into the future for seventy-five cents a head. The American League was still so dominated by the Yankees that sportswriters had taken to calling it "Snow White and the Seven Dwarfs," but the prospects for stiffer competition appeared to have brightened a bit with the arrival at Boston's Fenway Park of a lanky youngster from San Diego, whose bat was as big as his mouth. "I have no weaknesses at the plate," Ted Williams announced as he proceeded to terrorize enemy pitchers. "I can hit anything they throw me."

That summer, when the British royal couple visited America for the first time ever, President Roosevelt fed them hot dogs at his manorial home on the Hudson. "Jolly good," said the king. Finally, after nearly five years, Congress got around to killing the Townsend Old-Age Pension Bill (described by Hearst columnist Westbrook Pegler as "a hand-out for itchy old loafers"), and to prove how small the world had really become, a United States Air

Corps captain flew round-trip from Washington to Moscow in just a little over five days, air time.

People sang "Three Little Fishies in an Itty Bitty Pool," fell in love with Judy Garland in *The Wizard of Oz*, and agonized over a little boy who lost his way on a mountain in northern New England.

The mountain stands aloof, like some lonely sentinel, overlooking the vast, untamed wilderness of central Maine. Huge, rugged, and defiant, it covers an area of nearly a hundred thousand acres and rises sharply to a height of more than a mile above sea level. For much of the year its summit is enshrouded in clouds and raked by fierce winds that create weird and sometimes frightening sounds among the innumerable fissures that time has carved out of the ancient granite. Long ago the Indians, who feared it as a place of evil and danger, named the mountain Katahdin, "the preeminent one." It was thought by them to be inhabited by Pamola, a powerful spirit who ruled over it as his private domain and resented all intruders. Once, in the distant past, when a band of braves had wandered above the timber line, he had called down a cloud from the heavens to engulf them, and they were never seen again.

On Monday, July 17, 1939, while all New England was sweltering in the midst of a prolonged heat wave, twelve-year-old Donn Fendler, along with his father, two brothers (one of them his twin), and a young friend, arrived by car at the Hunt Trail base camp, sixteen miles northwest of Millinocket over the old Katahdin tote road. The Fendlers were from Rye, New York, where the father owned a successful clothing firm and Donn was soon to enter the seventh grade of a Catholic parochial school. Although during the past few summers the family had spent their vacations at a lake cottage near Bangor, they were still big-city folks whose enthusiasm for the out-of-doors far exceeded their understanding of it. Back home Donn belonged to the Boy Scouts and had already earned his tenderfoot badge. He had mastered several knots and learned to identify certain trees from their pictures. He had also been introduced, through books and lectures, to the basic rules of woods safety, although he had not yet had any opportunity to apply them. That was supposed to come later, with his first-class badge. He was a shy, high-strung, affectionate boy, slight of build and rather young for his age. He was described by his parents as "somewhat delicate but in general good health."

At 1:00 in the afternoon the Fendler party began the six-mile climb from the base camp to the summit along the Hunt Trail, which ascended the west side of the mountain. For much of the distance the trail was a well-beaten path through the woods and pucker brush. After that, beginning just beyond the timber line, the way was marked by a number of large white arrows painted on the granite boulders and ledge. About halfway up the trail Donn and his friend, Henry Condon, moved out ahead of the others. Not far from the summit they entered a cloud bank, which grew progressively thicker and colder as they continued their climb. Shortly after 4:00 they spotted Baxter Peak some fifty yards ahead, and began a race to reach it. Henry, the older and stronger of the two, won easily. At the top the boys sat down to rest, but the wind and the cold drizzle soon had them on their feet again, dancing about and slapping their sides to keep warm. For a few seconds the clouds thinned and they could see a man approaching them slowly from several yards to their right. They waved to him and the man waved back.

"Let's go back down to the others now," Donn said.

"No. I don't think we'd better."

"But I'm freezing."

"So'm I, but we'd better wait for the man and go down with him."

"Well, you wait if you want to, but I'm going back right now." Donn took off his jacket and handed his sweat shirt to Henry. "Here. This will keep you warm while you're waiting. I'll tell Dad you're coming down with the man." Then he started jogging down the trail. Before he had gone more than a dozen yards he had disappeared completely into the heavy cloud cover.

Ten minutes later Henry and the Reverend Charles Austin of New York City started back down the trail together. About a mile below they met the rest of the Fendler party, making slow progress up the slope. Donn had not returned. But there was no need to worry, Austin assured the others. The boy had probably strayed a bit from the path. At Austin's suggestion the five of them spread out within sight of one another on both sides of the path and shouted Donn's name as they climbed the remaining distance to the summit. There was no answer. They retraced their steps, this time shouting in unison, but there was still no answer. Suddenly they noticed that darkness had begun to penetrate the heavy mist of the mountain top. "He's obviously farther from the path than we thought," Austin said. "I think we'd better get help up here as soon as possible."

At 7:30 young Henry Condon staggered into the ranger station at the base camp, after running almost the entire distance down the mountain. "I have never seen anyone so exhausted," reported a camper who happened to be on hand when the boy arrived. "The kid simply collapsed. It was several minutes before he could even say anything." Immediately the ranger on duty organized a search group of all experienced climbers at the camp, only six in all including himself, and within a half hour the small band had started moving quickly up the slope. Before long, just as total darkness was about to set in, they met the rest of the Fendler party heading down the trail and persuaded them to continue back to the camp and wait there. An hour later the search group reached the timber line, where they stopped to rest for a time before breaking into twos to begin their perilous all-night sweep of the dark and barren area that lay between them and the summit: "Far below in the blackness a light burned, the only sign of human habitation in the vast wilderness, and also the signal that the boy had not been found. Two lights would have called us back. One spurred us on into the dreary wasteland above."

Moving slowly now in a fanlike pattern, the searchers inched their way carefully upward through the treacherous boulders and heavy wet cloud bank that hung over the upper mountain. "In all of my life I have never been in a more desolate place," one of them later remarked. "It was dark as pitch. The wind was blowing forty miles an hour or more and the temperature was about forty, although I could swear it was less." Near the top a light sleet was falling, and a thin film of ice had glazed the naked granite, which here and there sloped sharply off into eternity. "He couldn't last through the night up here," one of the searchers declared. "If he didn't make it down to the trees, he's a goner for sure."

Meanwhile news of the boy's disappearance had reached the outside world, and by dawn of the following day several dozen men from nearby parts had already started up the west slope. Organized and led mainly by forest rangers, game wardens, and sheriff's deputies, they were all experienced woodsmen, many of

whom had spent the better part of their lives in the shadow of
the mountain. For a job such as this, no amateurs need apply,
not even the boy's father, who was forced to wait helplessly below
while others better equipped than he went about the dangerous
and exhausting business of searching for his son. Throughout the
day volunteers continued to arrive at the base camp, including
timber crews from the Great Northern Pulp and Paper Company,
mill hands from nearby Millinocket, and expert mountain climbers,
some from out of state. By the time the search was called off for
the night there were over two hundred men on the mountain—none
of whom had found the slightest trace of the boy.

Early the next morning, on order from the governor, a National Guard unit from Millinocket arrived with tents and blankets
for the searchers, and, most important of all, a field kitchen. A few
hours later a small contingent of state police brought in two bloodhounds, which were immediately taken to the summit. There they
were given a sniff of one of the boy's shoes and appeared to pick
up his trail almost at once. After dragging their handlers for several
miles back and forth among the massive boulders, they arrived late
in the afternoon at the edge of a 400-foot precipice, where they
lay down and whined. When told of this back at camp, the boy's
father was badly shaken. "I'm trying to make myself believe there's
still a shred of hope," he told reporters.

All day Thursday the operation centered about the base of
the precipice, a vast slide area strewn with acres of rocks of all
sizes, amongst which a little boy's shattered body, still breathing
life perhaps, might well lie hidden. Searching here proved both
slow and dangerous, as dozens of men threaded their way carefully
through the maze of jagged, sometimes precariously balanced
boulders, stopping here and there to crawl into a cave or be lowered by rope to the bottom of some suspicious-looking crevice.
The dogs might have helped, but during the previous day's outing
their paws had been so badly cut up by the rough granite that they
could no longer be used. Later in the search, when two other
bloodhounds were flown in from New York, they were fitted out
with special leather moccasins, which they insisted on chewing off
before budging from the camp. Once on the mountain they fared
no better than their predecessors against the sandpaper surface of
the rocks, and after a few hours had to be taken down and sent
home.

The search in the slide area yielded nothing. Mr. Fendler

greeted the news with relief. At least there was still some hope that his son was alive. And yet, another whole day had passed, which meant that Donn had now been missing for more than seventy-two hours. Just supposing he hadn't frozen that first night or fallen off a cliff or into a crevice, and supposing he had actually made his way back to the woods and not been killed by some animal or gorged himself on poison berries or got himself caught up in quicksand—how long could a twelve-year-old boy last without anything to eat? "I'm afraid the chances of finding him alive are getting pretty slim," the game warden in charge admitted that evening to the press.

"What do you plan to do now?" a reporter from the Bangor *Commercial* asked.

"Keep trying. That's all we can do."

"For how long?"

"Why, until we find him. We're here for as long as it takes."

On the following morning, Friday, a plane was sent up. Nobody believed that any good would come of it, because the wind currents that played about the mountain made it impossible to fly at a low enough altitude to see much of anything except trees and rocks, but at this point anything seemed worth a try. That same day nearly 350 searchers combed the west slope. "Now, look," one of the rangers told them before setting out, "we all know that little son of a whore is up there somewhere, and he's left signs. Everything leaves signs. So let's keep our friggin' eyes open and try to come up with something for a change." That day a cap and a scarf were found, neither of which belonged to the boy.

The weather continued warm, and over the weekend the number of searchers swelled to more than 500, up to then the largest group of its kind ever organized in New England. The main search effort was now shifted to the woods below the timber line, even though most of the experts advised against it. To them it seemed highly unlikely that the boy could have come that far. Most of them were of the opinion that he had slipped off a cliff or into a crevice during the darkness of that first stormy night. Probably he had died in the fall, although there was always the chance that he had escaped with no more than a broken leg (or maybe not even that) and was still alive up there somewhere, trapped among the rocks—provided, of course, he hadn't frozen to death. As for the woods, even if the boy had managed to reach them, the odds were a thousand to one against finding him in that endless stretch of trees and brush. Still, anything was possible, and since more than four days of intense coverage of the upper mountain had turned up absolutely nothing, it probably made sense to center the operation elsewhere. Besides, the boy's father wanted it that way.

Throughout the weekend the wooded area down as far as the base was swept and reswept by a small army of men, moving abreast of one another no more than ten yards apart. In places, especially where the woods had been cut over and had filled back in with scrub growth, the going was sometimes so difficult that rest stops had to be taken every few minutes. Still the line pushed forward, breaking only now and then to skirt a cedar swamp or beaver pond. Mosquitoes hovered relentlessly over the searchers, most of whom had doused themselves with citronella before setting out, and the tiny black flies the Indians call "noseeums" were often so thick as to resemble small grey clouds about the men's heads. The procession moved slowly, while its members combed through the underbrush and checked out the myriad windfalls and hollow tree trunks and other protected places where a small boy might have crawled in for shelter, or a place to die. But out of all this came nothing, except the passing of two more precious days. On Sunday evening back at the base camp spirits were low. Even the boy's father seemed to have lost hope. "I am ready now to accept whatever has happened," he said.

Monday. The boy had now been missing for a week. "There's virtually no chance at all he's still alive," a ranger told the press. "If it was my boy I'd have bid him a sorrowful goodbye by now." But the search went on, centering once again near the summit. During the morning most of the volunteers packed up their gear and left, some of them after having spent several days away from their jobs at their own expense. Mr. Fendler, close to tears, shook hands with as many of them as he could and thanked them. "It was a pretty sad moment for me," one of them recalled years later. "I guess I felt it more than some of the others because, you see, I had a boy at home just Donn's age, and I couldn't help thinking all the time I was up top there or in the woods, Christ, what an awful thing to have happen to a kid." That afternoon the National Guard unit pulled out, and by nightfall no more than fifty men remained, mostly the paid professionals—the rangers, game wardens, and sheriff's deputies—who from the first had been the heart and soul of the search effort. Day after day they had assaulted the mountain and the woods, and night after night they had returned to camp so exhausted by the elevation and the rigors of the search that they could barely stay awake long enough to eat. "It was a privilege to know such men," a newsman later remarked. "They made me proud to be a human being."

On the following morning, soon after the search party had left for the summit, Mr. Fendler was taken to the hospital in Bangor to have an infected eye cared for. Upon arrival he was found to be so physically and emotionally spent that he was immediately ordered to bed for a complete rest. Early in the afternoon he was visited by his wife, who, along with the children, had been looked after by friends and relatives during the long, soul-searing ordeal and was holding up as well as might be expected. At times she had talked somewhat irrationally of going to the base camp to help look for her son, but had been dissuaded by the argument that she would only be in the way. Now, for the first time since the boy's disappearance, she and her husband were together. What they talked about can only be imagined. Perhaps nothing. Around mid-afternoon the director of the hospital entered the room:

"I have some good news for you," he said.

"Have they found his body?" the father asked.

"Mr. and Mrs. Fendler, your son is alive and well. I have him on the phone."

The two parents seemed not to comprehend.

"Mr. and Mrs. Fendler, your son is on the phone. Would you like to talk with him?"

Together the parents rushed down the hall to the phone and held the receiver between them: "Hello Donn," the father said guardedly.

"Hello Pop. Hello Pip."

"He said Hello Pip. It's him! It's really him!"

"Hello Donn. Donn, this is Mother. Are you all right?"

"Hello Mummy. I'm all right."

"I love you Donn," his father shouted into the phone and then began to cry uncontrollably, while the boy's mother slumped to her knees. "Oh God," she sobbed. "We are truly grateful."

Within minutes after leaving his friend Henry on the top of

the mountain, Donn Fendler, without knowing it, had strayed from the trail and become hopelessly lost. In the thick grey mist of the summit he was unable to spot any white arrows, but he was sure he recognized the rocks as the same ones he and Henry had climbed over on their way up. Soon, though, they seemed to get bigger and at times Donn had the feeling as he clambered among them that he was actually going up instead of down. "That seemed funny to me, but I went on just the same, because a fellow forgets easily, and I figured going down was different, anyway."

Before long he realized that he was off the trail. This didn't bother him, though. He couldn't have gone very far away from it. In a little while Henry and the man would be coming down and Donn would be bound to hear them. In the meantime he would simply sit and wait. But then it started to sleet and he decided to move on in order to keep warm. He was sure to run into his father and brothers a little farther down. When after several minutes he failed to find them, he began to shout, but the sound was muffled by the heavy cloud cover. Several times he called out. There was no answer. "Boy, did I feel funny."

By now he knew he was lost and for the first time he was afraid. For awhile he managed to keep control of himself by thinking about the bacon and eggs that would be waiting for him as soon as he got back to camp. His father would probably give him a good scolding, but that was all right. The thought of food made him realize how hungry he was getting. He was also chilled to the bone. His light dungarees were stiff with ice, and crinkled when he walked. He wondered what time it was. It was hard to tell up there in the clouds. He tried to figure out how long it had been since he had left Henry, but he really had no idea. It appeared to be getting darker. Was it possible that night was coming on already? Suddenly he panicked and began to rush aimlessly among the slippery boulders, screaming for his father and brothers. He must have fallen often, but in the blind terror that had seized him he felt no pain. And then a strange thing happened: for the first time that afternoon a break appeared in the clouds. It was almost as if some giant hand had separated them to let the sun come through. For a fleeting instant Donn could see the whole world spread out before him in a panorama of unequalled beauty. In the distance he caught sight of Moosehead Lake, sparkling like a giant jewel in the sunlight. And then the clouds closed and he was again engulfed by the heavy mist. But the panic had passed.

At this point the boy sat down to rest. He was now in full command of himself and began to take stock of the situation. Since he was still on the mountain, he reasoned, the base camp must be somewhere below. All he had to do, then, was to keep moving downhill and he would be bound to find it. He had no way of knowing, of course, that since soon after leaving Henry he hadn't been going downhill at all, but had actually been circling to his right, traveling roughly parallel to the summit and at the most only a few hundred yards below it. This is why it had seemed to him that at times he had been going uphill, and this is why, after a couple of hours when he really did begin to descend, he was no longer on the west slope, but the north. Here was a possibility that would later be pondered from time to time by some of the searchers, only to be dismissed as either too far-fetched, or too ugly—for to the north of the mountain lay some of the wildest land in the state, a seemingly endless tract of heavy forest that even the most seasoned woodsmen seldom ventured into.

Just before nightfall Donn entered the woods below the timber line. A few hundred yards farther on he came across a brook where, after drinking his fill, he sat down and soaked his feet in the cool, soothing water. It wasn't until then that he noticed that his sneakers had been slashed to shreds. The air, although still chilly, had become warmer, and, safe now from the wind and mist of the upper mountain, the boy might have been almost comfortable had it not been for a light rain that was falling, and the hungry hordes of black flies and mosquitoes that swarmed over him. After wringing out his pants and hanging them inside a hollow tree to dry, he took off his shirt and tied it around his head as protection against the insects. He then crawled under the low-hanging branches of a large evergreen and curled up as best he could inside his jacket. "I said my prayers . . . and shut my eyes. I was awfully cold and wet and hungry." He was also more than six miles from that small group of men who had already gone up the mountain to look for him—the closest he would ever be to any of his intended rescuers.

Sleep did not come easily. The insects and the damp chill were bad enough, but they were nothing when compared with the terror of being alone in the total darkness of the woods at night. Worst of all were the noises—the croaking, groaning, and screaming sounds, and the sudden snapping of a nearby twig. "I said some more prayers and felt better. I felt that God would help me

if I needed help." Even so, for the first time in a long while he
cried himself to sleep that night.

When he awoke it was morning and still raining. From where
he lay he had a clear view of the brook. On the opposite bank he
saw his friend Henry and called out to him. But Henry just stood
there and said nothing. Then Donn's father drove up in a big black
auto and waved to him. "Here I am!" Donn shouted, and got up
and raced toward the brook. By the time he had waded across,
though, both Henry and his father had gone: "I yelled until I was
hoarse, but nobody answered. Then I just sat down on the ground
and cried." After several minutes he got up and waded back into
the brook where he washed his face and splashed the cold water
over his fly bites, which seemed to have set his whole body afire.
He thought for a long time about what had just happened and
vowed it would not happen again. "That's the way people go
crazy," he said aloud. "Well, I'm not going crazy—not if I can help
it." Then, remembering that he hadn't said his morning prayers,
he knelt down beside the brook:

> I never prayed like that before. Other mornings I hurry a little or don't
> think much about what I'm saying, but this morning I meant every-
> thing, and I thought of God and how He was there in the woods, and
> how He looked after everything, and I felt warm all inside of me and
> peaceful too.

With his wet dungarees slung over his shoulder, Donn began
following the course of the brook. This was one of the first things
he had been taught in Boy Scouts: when lost, follow water downstream, because sooner or later water will lead to people. He was
barefoot now, his sneakers no longer usable, and before long his
feet started to bleed. Midway through the morning he stopped to
rest for a moment and fell asleep. When he awoke, after an hour
or so, it was no longer raining but there was still no sign of the
sun. As he sat on the bank, soaking his feet in the brook, the black
flies and mosquitoes tormented him almost beyond endurance,
but not enough to take his mind off how hungry he was. In the
brook he noticed a number of large trout swimming slowly back
and forth. Some of them even bumped his toes. For several minutes he tried to catch one with his hands, but couldn't. Then he
saw some berries on a nearby bush. He thought they were blue-

berries, but wasn't sure. Remembering the warning in his Scout
Manual about poison berries, he decided that, no matter how hungry he got, he wouldn't eat anything he wasn't sure of. That afternoon, farther down the brook, he came across something he *was*
sure of—strawberries, a large patch of them, just right for eating.
Rushing into their midst, he got down on all fours and devoured
them like a bear until he could eat no more. It was the first food
he had tasted since noon of the day before.

As night settled over the woods, Donn lay back against a
moss-covered stump and went to sleep almost immediately. Sometime later he was awakened by the sound of distant thunder and
the rattling of rain on the leaves. Feeling his way through the darkness, he managed to locate a hollow tree he recalled having seen a
few yards back. It was bigger than he thought, and he was able to
curl up inside of it in a sitting position. "It was dry and warm in
there, and I just thanked God for being so good to me."

When he awoke the following morning, the sun was shining.
Beside him a little brown bird was hunting for grubs among the
roots of the tree, and Donn later remembered thinking: "This
can't be such a bad place. That little bird seems to like it." After
saying his morning prayers he found some more berries, and then
continued following the brook, which by this time had widened
and grown more rapid. With his still damp dungarees draped over
his shoulder, he fought his way for hours through the alder bushes
that lined the bank, until they became so thick that he had to take
to the water. It was then that his pants dropped into the brook
and he watched helplessly as the current carried them downstream,
"like some fat, blue snake."

An hour or so before dark he spotted a big pine tree only a
few feet from the bank. Under it was a soft bed of moss, where he
knelt and said his goodnight prayers. For a long while he lay
awake, brushing the black flies and mosquitoes from his unpro-
tected legs, which by now were completely covered with welts and
scratches. He noticed that his feet were trickling blood. Suddenly
he heard footsteps and saw a big buck deer pass by him almost
close enough to touch. Donn watched for several minutes while it
drank from the brook. Somehow, seeing the deer cheered him up
a little, and he soon dropped off to sleep.

The next morning when he awoke hordes of ants were crawling over the open sores and cuts on his legs, and his eyes were almost swollen shut from insect bites. Was it Thursday or Friday?

He couldn't be sure. It seemed to him as if he had been in the woods forever. For the first day or so he had made himself believe that the base camp was just ahead, beyond the next bend in the brook. But now, of course, he knew this wasn't so. He felt sore and tired all over. And he was lonely—lonelier than he had ever been before in his whole life. Even talking to himself didn't seem to help much. In a clearing above the brook he found a few strawberries. While there he came face to face with a bear. Paralyzed with fear, he remained frozen in his tracks, while the bear studied him for a few seconds and then ambled nonchalantly off into the woods.

The going that morning was harder than before. The alder bushes had given way to horsebrier, which seemed intent upon imprisoning him in its thickets as it clawed at his naked legs and snagged his jacket with long, sharp barbs. His feet were especially sore. Several times he stopped and soaked them to slow the bleeding:

> Every time I stepped on a stone or a broken twig, I'd have to cry with pain. I guess I cried a lot that morning. I tried not to because I knew I had to keep my head, but I did. . . . When I was feeling worst, I got down on my knees and prayed. I had to hunt for some moss because my knees were so sore they almost made me scream when I went down on them, but I found the moss under a tree and prayed as hard as I could. I prayed out loud too, asking God to help me, because I needed help, and asking him not to let Mummy and Dad worry and asking Him for food—just something to keep me going until I found a camp.

Shortly after noon he came upon a road, which appeared out of nowhere and began paralleling the course of the brook. It was an old abandoned tote road that obviously hadn't been used for years, but there it was, nevertheless. Suddenly Donn felt fresh and happy, and, unmindful now of his tortured feet, began hurrying down the road as fast as he could. Every so often he would break into a run, hoping that he could make it out of the woods before another nightfall. When night did come, he tried to keep going, but stumbled and fell in the darkness. Finally he lay down under a tree and fell asleep before he could say his prayers.

He awoke soon after sun-up. The air was already pleasantly warm. On a limb directly above him a chipmunk chattered away, as if scolding him for being there. For several minutes Donn lay

still and watched, and even laughed at the way the little animal
kept jerking its tail up and down. He knew he should get under
way again, but he was so comfortable where he was that he hated
to budge. His feet were so sore that he could barely touch them,
and he dreaded the thought of having to walk on them for another
day—or minute. When he tried to move, his body behaved like
soft wax. Only by tugging at a low-hanging branch was he able to
get up. An hour or so down the road he discovered a deserted
camp: "Holy Christmas! That was a glad moment for me. I was so
tired I was stooped over, and I thought sure that someone would
come running out and say, 'Hello, where did you come from?' But
nobody did."

Inside the camp he found some coffee and salt, but no food.
On the bed was a half-rotten blanket, which he decided to take
with him, even though the smell of it was so bad that it almost
made him throw up. Stopping often to soothe his feet in the cool
moss along the edge of the water, which by now had become a
full-fledged stream, he kept walking down the road until he was
too exhausted to go any farther. On a little rise he found a handful
of strawberries, and then, although it was still only morning,
spread the blanket over his legs and went to sleep. By the time he
awoke the sun was low in the sky, and a light breeze had come up
to drive away the black flies and mosquitoes that had tormented
him constantly since he first entered the woods. He felt strong
enough now to go on a little farther. Just before dark, as he was
about to bed down again, he noticed what at first appeared to be
a rope strung out along the trees next to the road. It was a telephone wire. "I shouted and danced and laughed. And then I cried
some. I was saved at last."

On the following morning he started out as soon as it was daylight. He had to move slowly now. Most of the feeling had gone
from his toes, and the thorns in the soles of his feet had become so
painful that from time to time he had to hop on one leg and then
the other in order to keep going. Not far down the road he found
a few scattered strawberries, which he took a long time picking
before moving on. Sometime that afternoon, while he was lying
on his stomach drinking from the stream, he heard the hum of an
airplane circling over head. Stumbling back to the road, he shouted
and waved his hands frantically, but the plane soon went away,
and the only hum left was from the black flies and mosquitoes
that had returned to plague him. "I sat down beside a tree and

cried. . . . After I'd cried a while I knelt down and prayed. I wanted the plane to come back. I wanted to hear the sound of its motor."

Was it the next morning, or later the same day? He had been sleeping. He had no idea for how long. Somehow he managed to get up and start moving, but he was so dizzy he could hardly keep his balance. His legs felt stiff and unreal, as if they belonged to someone else. Several times he fell and was barely able to make it to his feet again. When the blanket he had found the day before slipped off his shoulder onto the ground, he decided to leave it there rather than try bending over to pick it up. It had become too heavy for him to carry anyway. His head throbbed with each step he took, and he now had difficulty focusing his eyes. Once, while he was resting, a black bear came into a nearby clearing. For several minutes Donn watched it lumber awkwardly along, pausing now and then to nip berries off a bush. After it had gone he felt so lonesome that he cried.

That afternoon he came to a place where the stream went one way and the road and telephone wire went another. For a long time he stood there confused, trying to make sense out of what had happened and figure out what to do next. It was hard for him to concentrate. His mind felt funny and kept drifting off. If he stayed with the stream he would have to contend with the alders and the horsebrier again—not a very pleasant prospect—but he could at least be sure of having enough water to drink. Besides, he knew that was what the Boy Scouts would want him to do. On the other hand, there was a lot to be said for sticking to the road. It would surely make for easier traveling, and the telephone wire could mean a cabin or ranger station beyond the very next turn. Finally he decided on the stream. Had he chosen the road he would have dead-ended at an abandoned lumber camp several miles away.

Once off the road, he found the going much harder. The brush along the bank was often so thick that he had to fight his way through it. Sometimes, when the horsebrier left him no other choice, he took to the water, where he would frequently lose his footing and, too weak to resist, would be bounced along the rocky bottom by the current. Once, some distance downstream, as he was climbing out onto a sandbar, he noticed that his legs were covered with bloodsuckers. Screaming hysterically, he jumped into the water again and slithered back and forth along the sandy bottom. Finally, with his last ounce of strength he dragged himself out of the stream and collapsed on the sandbar, where the hot sun drove the leeches to cover and burned his legs a beet red.

By now he had lost all track of time. The hours and days blurred together and no longer mattered. But he could still tell daylight from darkness, and daylight meant moving downstream as far and as fast as he could. Occasionally he would come across a few strawberries, but the farther he went, the scarcer they seemed to get. The days were hot and humid—good mosquito weather—and the nights uncomfortably chilly. Somewhere along the way he abandoned his fleece-lined jacket that had served him so well, but later found a gunny sack he was able to use as a sleeping bag. His legs had grown so weak that they trembled whenever he stood on them, and threatened to buckle with each step. They brought to mind the stilts he and his brothers played with at home, and that made him cry a little. His feet felt like lead weights. They were completely numb now. When one of his big toenails got torn off, he would probably not even have noticed had it not been for the gushing of blood. His stomach had started hurting, and his head continued to throb. Often he would stumble or lose consciousness while walking and pitch forward onto the ground. That was the worst, the falling, because falling meant having to get up again. "Every time I fell I'd say, 'Maybe I can't get up this time,' but I'd pray a little, and then I'd get up." When the time came that he could no longer get all the way to his feet, he began to crawl on his hands and knees.

Sometime later, perhaps an hour, or a day, he pushed his way out from under a clump of alders and looked up to see a strange sight. There was nothing but open water ahead. He had reached the bank of a big river.

The stream the Indians named Wassataquoik has its sources in the myriad brooks and ponds near the base of Katahdin's north slope, from where it flows southeasterly for several miles through the stark wilderness before emptying into the east branch of the Penobscot River. Here, where the Stream and River meet, some fourteen miles north of the little settlement of Grindstone, Nelson McMoarn and his wife operated a rustic lodge for fishermen and hunters. They called it Camp Lunksoos. They had heard about the little boy lost on Baxter's Peak, but that was almost directly opposite them on the west side of the mountain, some thirty-five miles away.

Shortly after noon on Tuesday, July 25, eight days after the boy had last been seen, McMoarn heard a strange noise from across the river. At first he thought it might be a screech owl, but his trained ear soon told him that this was no ordinary woods sound. In his canoe he paddled across to investigate. There on the bank was a young boy, wailing like a wounded animal as he crawled slowly along the bank on his hands and knees, headed down the river. Aside from a few remaining shreds of what had once been his underpants, he was totally naked. His skin was covered with welts and cuts and bruises. His face was puffed grotesquely and his body was little more than a skeleton. When the man reached down and touched him, the boy looked up:

"I'm Donn Fendler," he said. "I've been lost on a mountain."

Valedictory: No Sad Songs

$\mathbf{A}$T A FEW MINUTES BEFORE MIDNIGHT, December 31, 1939, electrician Thomas Ward stood at the base of the *New York Times* tower with a stopwatch in his hand, as he had on every other such occasion since 1913. Below him, with its plate-glass windows boarded up and its streets closed to all but pedestrians, the area as far north as Duffy Square was an almost solid mass of noisy, hyperthyroid humanity—well over a million people, the largest crowd to have assembled anywhere in the country since Lindbergh's triumphal return from France a dozen years before, and one of the best-natured.

While more than 1700 patrolmen and mounted police mingled with the revelers ("Be as lenient as possible," their orders read, "even with the most boisterous"), hip flasks and bottles in twisted brown paperbags passed freely among the crowd, fortifying it against the twenty-two-degree temperature—cold for Manhattan. Here and there above the din of cowbells and paper horns and the obscene blats of "Bronx cheerers," people could be heard singing "A-Tisket, A-Tasket" and "Flat-Foot Floogie with a Floy Floy," while in scattered little islands of space, couples jitterbugged to a brassy rendition of "And the Angels Sing," coming from a store loudspeaker somewhere down near 42nd Street.

As the final moment neared, the crowd grew louder and more exuberant. Young women threw their arms around the police and smothered them with kisses. Strings of firecrackers tossed out of a second-story window on 55th Street rattled like machine-gun fire over the heads of the people below, and down in front of the

Astor Hotel someone began setting off skyrockets, as a sailor looked on from his precarious perch atop a nearby lamp post.

Not far away at St. Patrick's Cathedral thousands of the faithful prayed for the return of world peace. Meanwhile in neighboring hotels, where dinner reservations (some priced as high as thirty dollars a couple) had been sold out for weeks, pretty girls in peasant costumes collected donations for Finnish war relief, while men in tuxedos dined on "poitrine de faisan frais" and toasted the future with imported champagne. "Nothing like it since 1928," exclaimed a delighted hotel manager. A hundred miles up the Hudson, by special dispensation from the warden himself, Sing Sing's 2715 prisoners were permitted to stay up past midnight and welcome in the new decade by rattling their cell doors to their hearts' content.

Back at the *Times* Building, Electrician Ward divided his attention between his watch and the huge illuminated ball on top of the flagpole. At five seconds before 12:00 he shouted, "Let 'er go!" and his two companions loosened the halyards. The ball slid slowly down the sixty-five-foot pole while the crowd counted off the remaining seconds in a crescendo of excitement. When it reached the bottom at exactly midnight, its 260 lights shut off automatically. At the same instant Thomas Ward pulled a lever that lit up two large "1940"s on opposite sides of the tower. A wild cheer went up from the crowd. Horns honked, whistles tooted, bells rang, and as millions of "snowflakes" from torn-up phone books and newspapers danced about on the light breeze, friends and strangers embraced and wished one another better days ahead.

Throughout the entire country the mood was much the same. On San Francisco's Market Street, at the Copley Plaza's Merry-Go-Round Bar in Boston, and in the front parlors of Dubuque and Santa Fe—wherever people gathered to witness the changing of the guard—the atmosphere seemed charged with a brightness of spirit that had long been missing from American life. Finally, after an eon or more the 1930s, conceived in depression and nurtured on the things that might have been, had faded thankfully into the shadows of the past, thereby closing the books on the most soul-searing decade in the nation's history. Here perhaps, in the words of the poet Browning, was "cause enough for calling forth that spot of joy."

And yet—. When one came right down to it, aside from a flip

of the calendar there was precious little to cheer about. True, during the past few months there had been a decided spurt in the
economy that had put a somewhat better face on things as the
decade ended. But this was nothing new. It had happened several
times earlier (most notably in 1935 and 1937), only to be followed
by backsliding that had left the country worse off than before.
The plain fact was that the Depression continued its cruel hold on
the nation. Eight million Americans had no jobs and little chance
of finding any in the foreseeable future, while millions of others,
who in better days might have made something of their lives, remained mired in the shallows of mediocrity and stunted aspira-
tions. It was, for all the hoop-la of that noisy New Year's Eve, not
the best of times, and the American people knew it.

Still, there was a flicker of hope, as yet no brighter than a distant candle, that this time the Depression might indeed be on its
way out: since its beginnings, four months before, the war in Europe had taken on a decidedly brighter hue for most Americans.
That feeling of awful foreboding that had dogged them since Mussolini's unanswered invasion of Ethiopia four years earlier and had
peaked that past August with the German-Soviet Pact, had not
only subsided as the war continued, but had even given way to
something approaching optimism. It was clear now that the Russians intended to stay in the East, where they belonged, fattening
themselves on their neighbors' territory. And even if they didn't, it
wouldn't make much difference, because their remarkably poor
showing in the Finnish War, now entering its second month, had
already proved that despite its size the Soviet Army was nothing
but a joke. Nor had Mussolini thus far given any indication that he
seriously intended to take Italy into the war. It looked very much,
therefore, as if it would be just Germany against France and England—and in a contest such as this there wasn't much question as
to who would win. One couldn't help but feel a little sorry (but
not very) for the Germans, faced, as they were, with the prospect
of a severe drubbing by the combined power of the world's finest
army and mightiest navy.

Now, aside from providing the satisfaction (and relief) of seeing Hitler finally put in his place, all this could conceivably mean
good news for America in a very concrete way. It's true that up to
now the war hadn't amounted to much, what with both sides content to do little more than glower at one another through the slits
in their pill boxes. In fact, newspapers had taken to calling it "the

sitz-krieg," and were predicting a negotiated settlement within a matter of weeks—either that or, come spring, a quick victory by the overwhelmingly superior French and British forces. Maybe not, though. It could turn out that the war would drag on for some time. If so, sooner or later, Europe would have to come shopping for American guns and food—just like before—and this could prove to be exactly what the nation needed to get its economy back on track.

But at this stage, as the 1930s joined that relentless caravan of the past, who could really say about such things? The war might very well end within a matter of weeks or months. On the other hand, it might go on for a couple of years. Maybe even longer.

One would simply have to wait and hope for the best.

Note on Sources

THE INFORMATION contained in this book was taken principally from a large number of daily and weekly newspapers, ranging in
size and influence from the *New York Times* to the now-defunct
Bangor Daily Commercial; a half-dozen or so national newsmaga-
zines, including those hardy perennials *Time, Newsweek, The
Nation*, and *The New Republic*, together with the not-so-durable
Literary Digest and *Life*; several autobiographies and reminiscences
of persons involved in, or witness to, the events and conditions
described; public records of various sorts, especially the *Congressional Record*, 1930-40; and a host of other published materials of
the kind that can be found in any well-appointed research library.
It seems to me that no constructive purpose would be served by
listing these sources, alphabetically or otherwise, or commenting
on their merits. The general reader would not be interested in such
an accounting, while no scholar worthy of his Phi Beta Kappa key
would be apt to discover there anything of significance that he
hasn't seen before. It would be most ungrateful of me, however,
not to give special mention to Walter Goodman's *The Committee*
(Farrar, Straus, & Giroux, 1968), and George Wolfskill and John
Hudson's *All But the People: Franklin D. Roosevelt and his Critics*
(Macmillan, 1969)—two fine monographs that proved particularly
useful for my purposes. Beyond that, suffice to say that during my
several years of intermittent labor on this book, I consulted every
reputable published work I could lay my hands on, and some not
so reputable. I also on occasion (but not often) found myself sifting through certain manuscript materials, mainly police and public

health records, in hopes of filling in a gap or removing a doubt.

But, as I indicated in the introduction, there was also the spoken word, taken from an indeterminate number of interviews and conversations with people, big and small, whose recollections were freely given and gratefully received: Shep Hurd, for instance, manager of Dakins Sporting Goods Store, and Harry Johnson, the barber across the street, with their detailed eyewitness accounts of the shoot-out in Bangor; Louis de Rochemont, the movie producer, with tales of the early days of *The March of Time* and its dramatic film footage (some of it faked) of important news events; long-time Congressman Hamilton Fish, who, through the medium of my graduate student Chuck Schneider, talked freely about Communists in government, including the Federal Theatre Project, and his not-too-high opinion, political or personal, of his Hudson River neighbor, Franklin Roosevelt; Frankie Frisch, "The Old Flash," who only a week before his fatal automobile accident regaled me for hours with his stories of Dizzy and Paul and the others; Ryan Fendler, who started up the mountain with his twin brother that day nearly forty years ago and still remembers, all too vividly, Donn's failure to return, and the awful days of waiting and waning hope that followed; a letter carrier who hated FDR, and a stockbroker who felt the same way, a policeman with fond memories of "the third degree," a retired university professor and a local historian who helped add certain personal touches to my account of the San Jose kidnaping and lynching. All of these, and a multitude of others, in a very real sense collaborated with me in the making of this book, and in so doing helped flesh out its substance, and, I believe, add considerably to its vigor and verisimilitude. I hope that they will think me faithful and judicious in my use of their memories.

CAJ

TOMATOES WERE CHEAPER

was composed in 10-point IBM Selectric Century Medium and leaded two points
by Metricomp Studios;
with display type handset in Ultra Bodoni by Dix Typesetting Co., Inc.;
printed on 55-lb. Hammermill Lock Haven by Vicks Lithograph and Printing Corp.;
Smyth-sewn and bound over boards in Columbia Tanotex by Vail-Ballou Press, Inc.;
and published by

SYRACUSE UNIVERSITY PRESS
SYRACUSE, NEW YORK